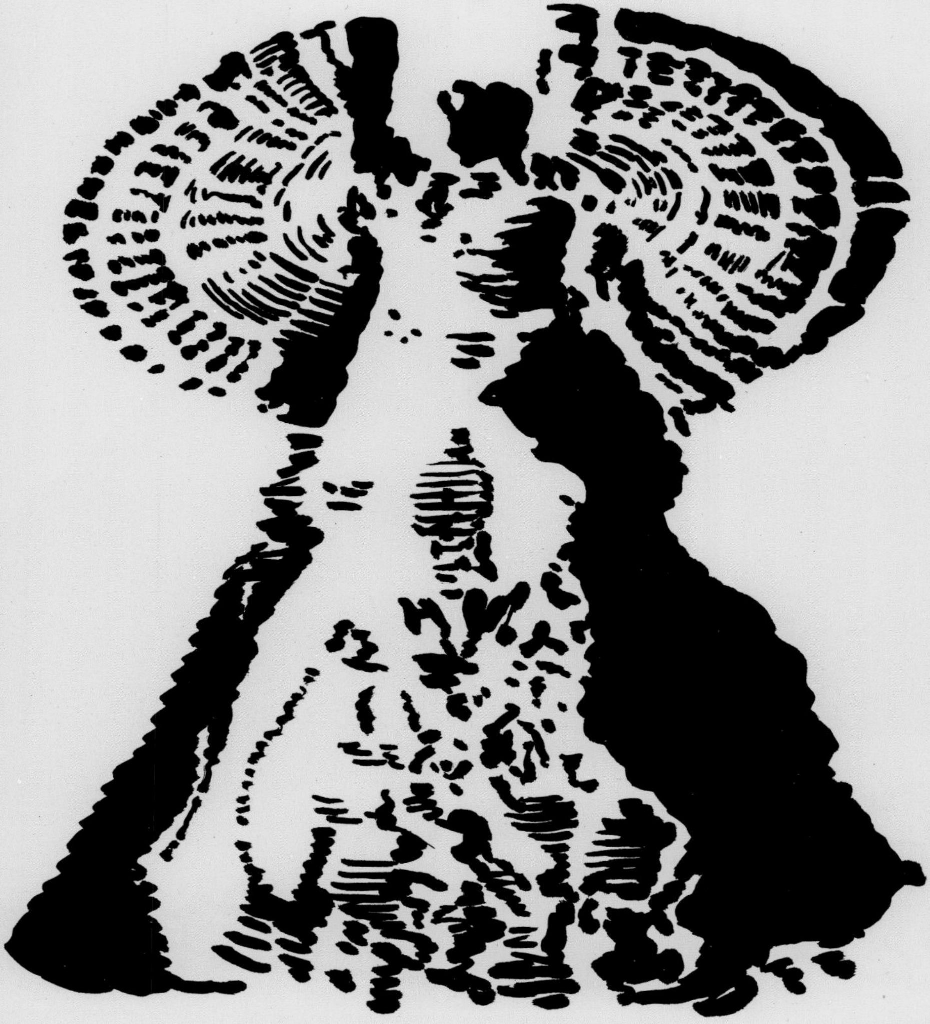

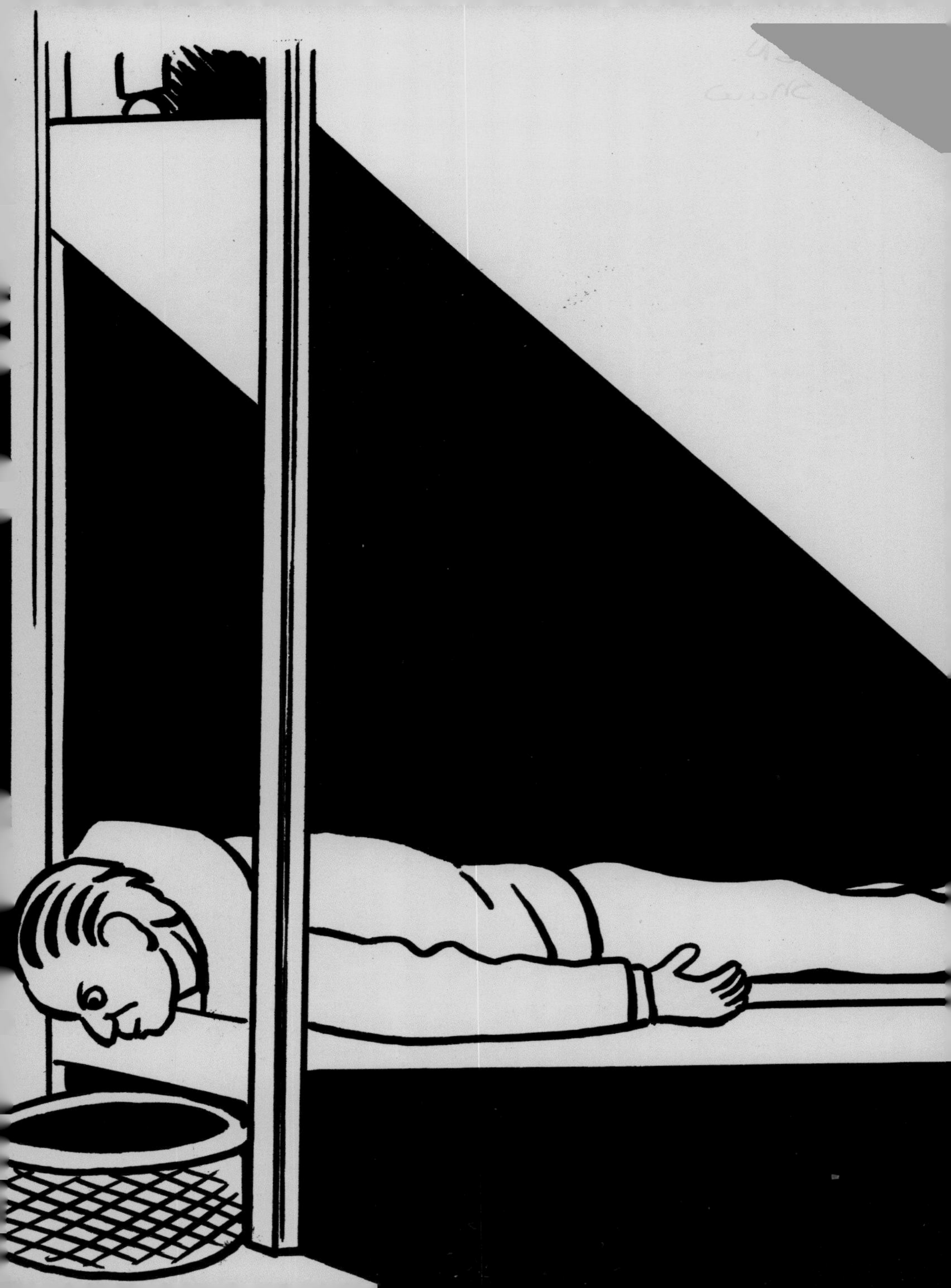

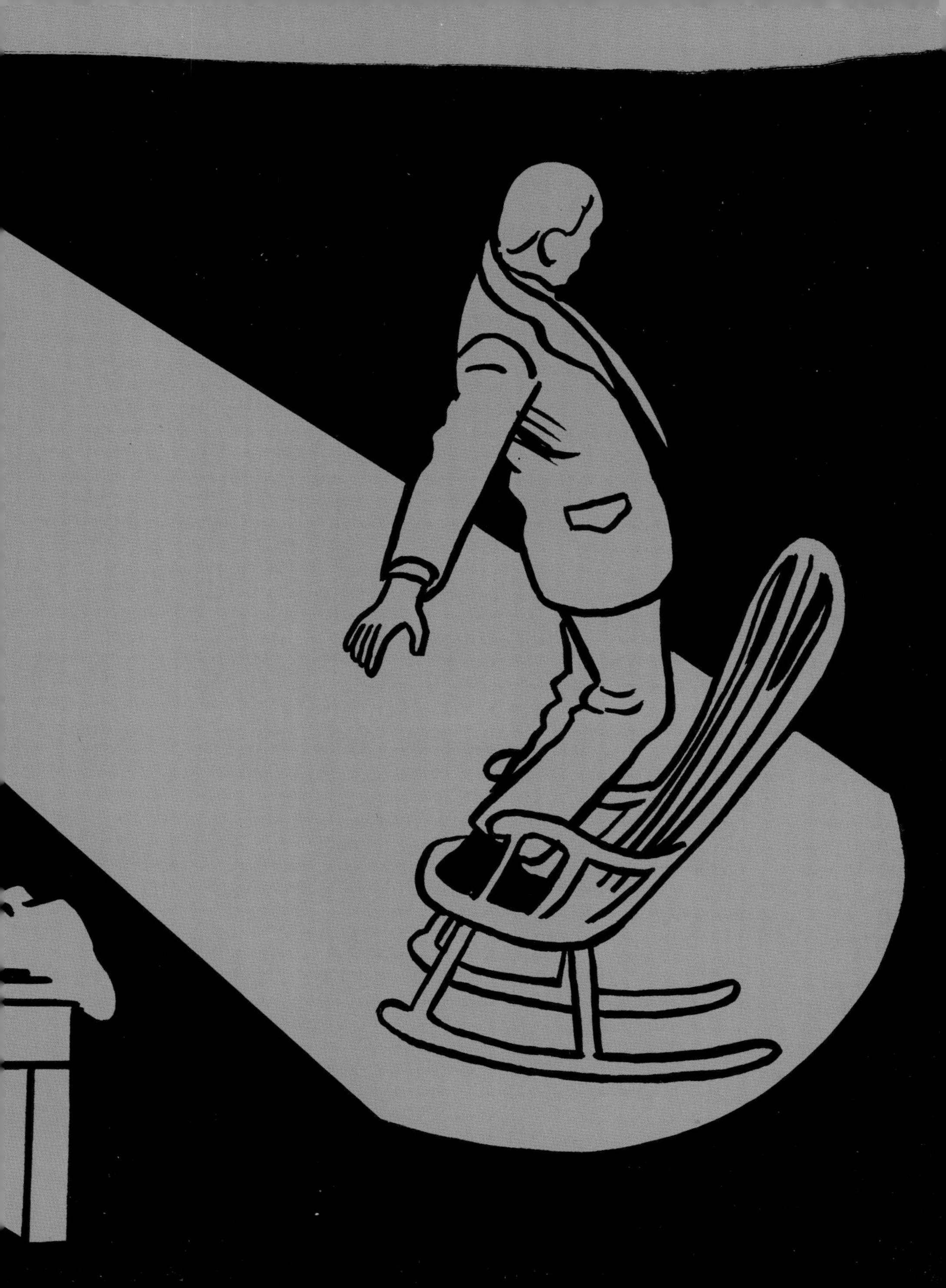

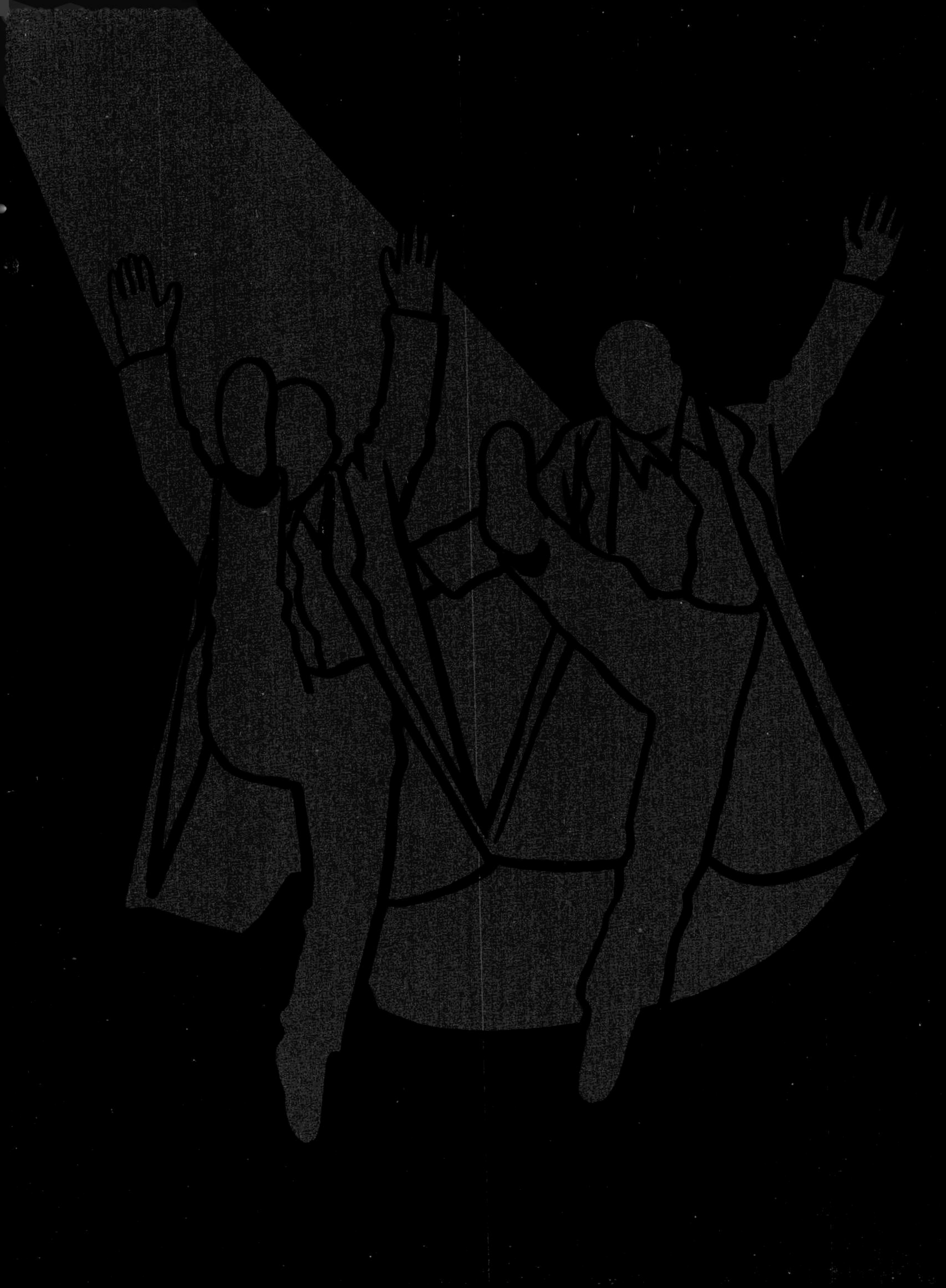

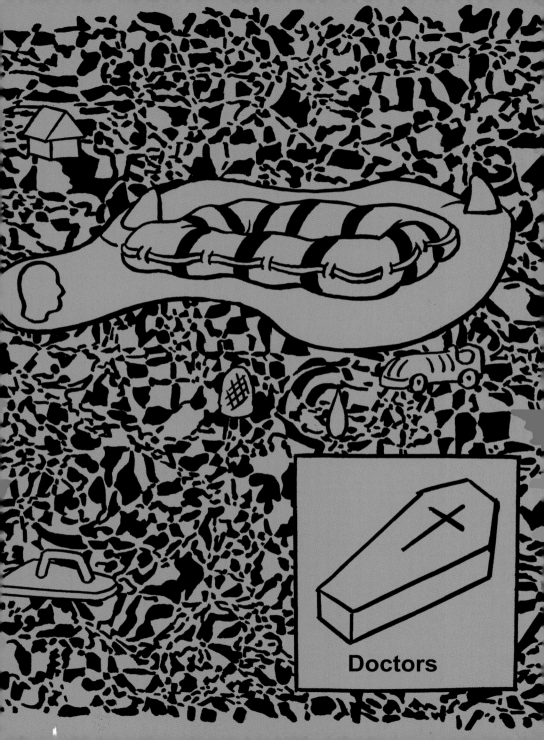

Doctors

Editor and Associate Publisher: Eric Reynolds
Book Design: Dash Shaw
Cover Design: Keeli McCarthy
Production: Paul Baresh
Proofreading: Janice Lee
Publisher: Gary Groth

FANTAGRAPHICS BOOKS, INC.
7563 Lake City Way NE • Seattle, Washington, USA

ISBN 978-1-60699-803-8

First printing: September, 2014
Printed in Hong Kong

Fantagraphics Books would like thank: Randall Bethune • Big Planet Comics • Black Hook Press, Japan • Nick Capetillo • Kevin Czapiewski • John DiBello • Juan Manuel Domínguez • Mathieu Doublet • Dan Evans III • Thomas Eykemans • Scott Fritsch-Hammes • Coco and Eddie Gorodetsky • Karen Green • Ted Haycraft • Eduardo Takeo "Lizarkeo" Igarashi • Nevdon Jamgochian • Andy Koopmans • Philip Nel • Vanessa Palacios • Kurt Sayenga • Anne Lise Rostgaard Schmidt • Christian Schremser • Secret Headquarters • Paul van Dijken • Mungo van Krimpen-Hall • Jason Aaron Wong • Thomas Zimmermann

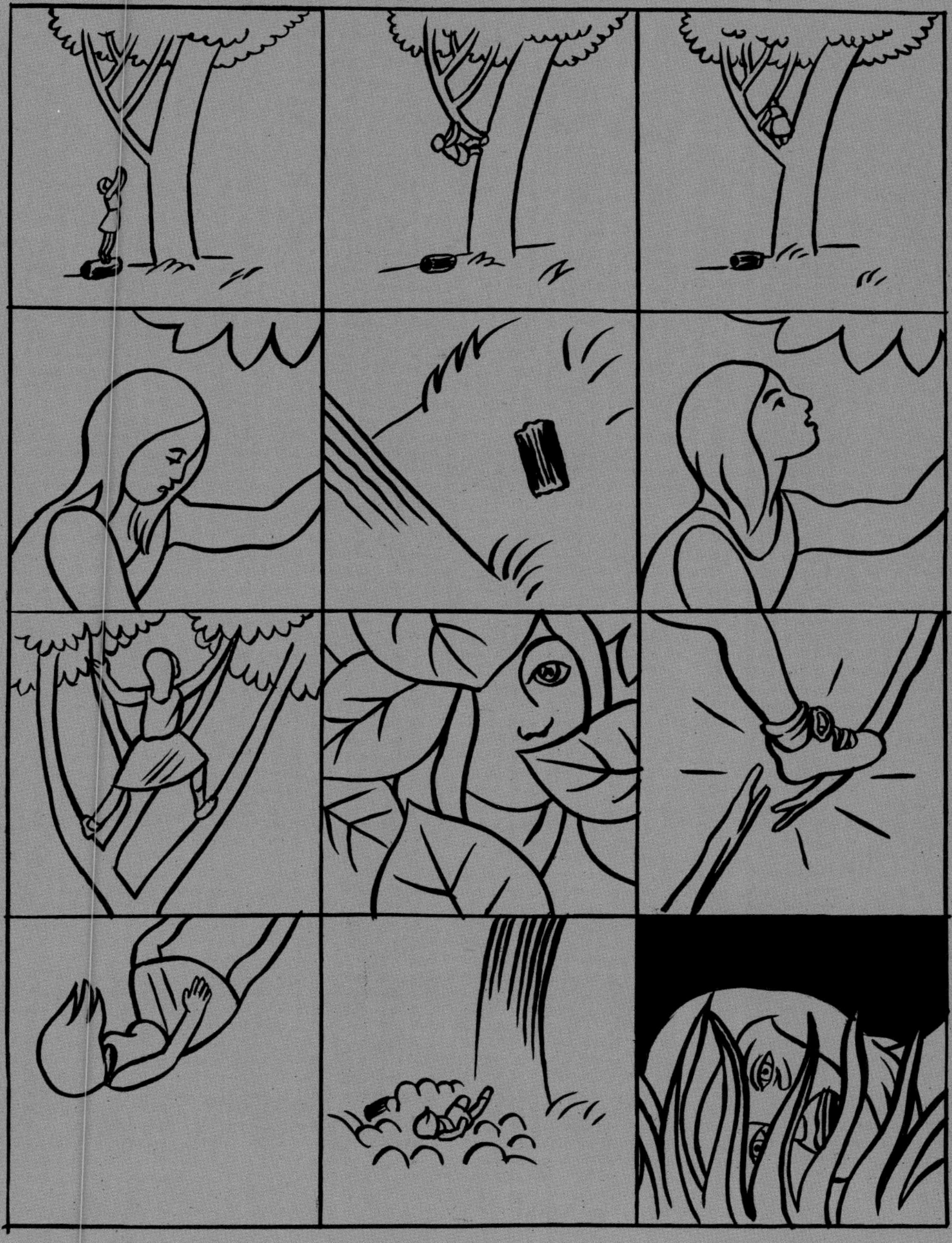

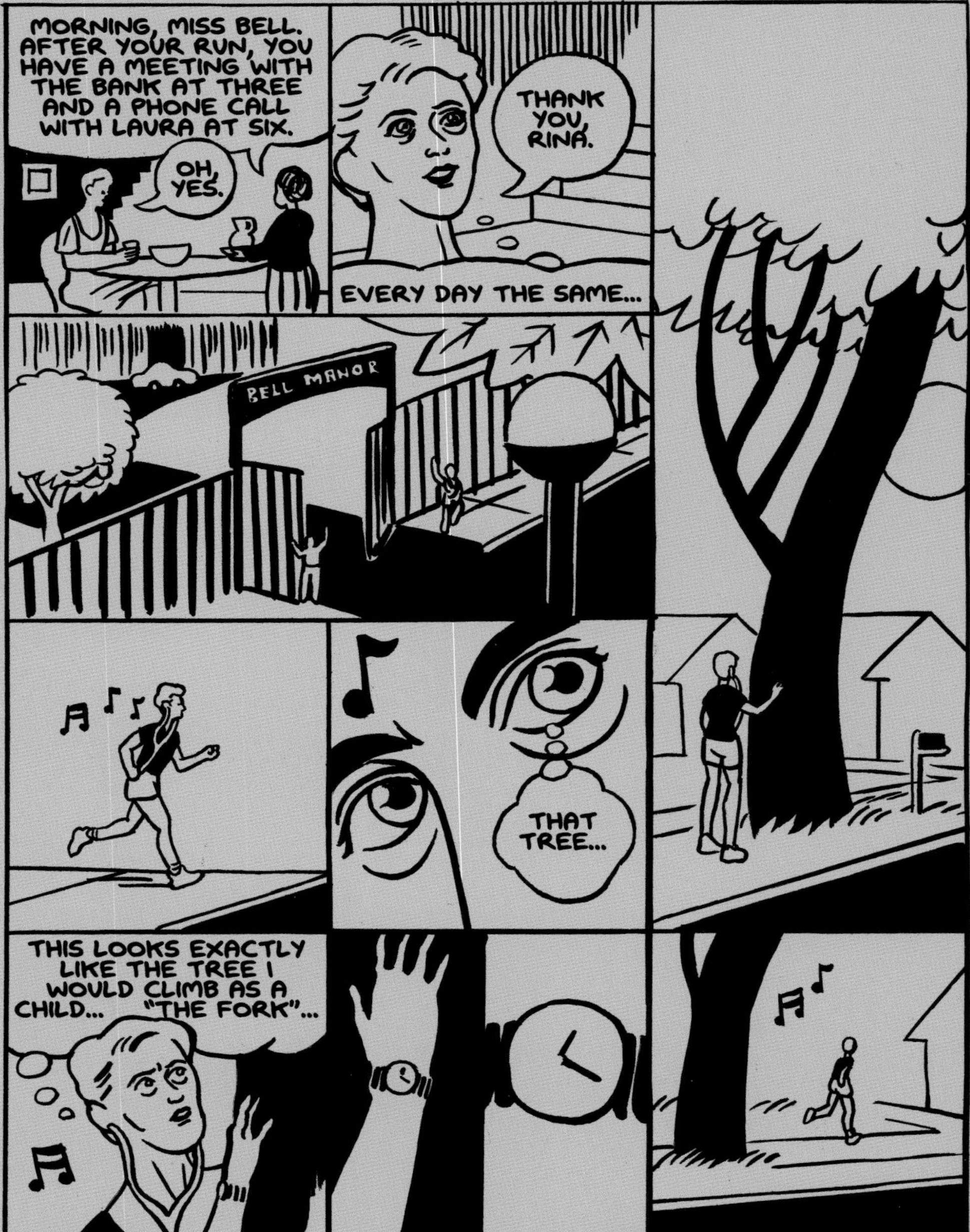
MORNING, MISS BELL. AFTER YOUR RUN, YOU HAVE A MEETING WITH THE BANK AT THREE AND A PHONE CALL WITH LAURA AT SIX.
OH, YES.
THANK YOU, RINA.
EVERY DAY THE SAME...
BELL MANOR
THAT TREE...
THIS LOOKS EXACTLY LIKE THE TREE I WOULD CLIMB AS A CHILD... "THE FORK"...

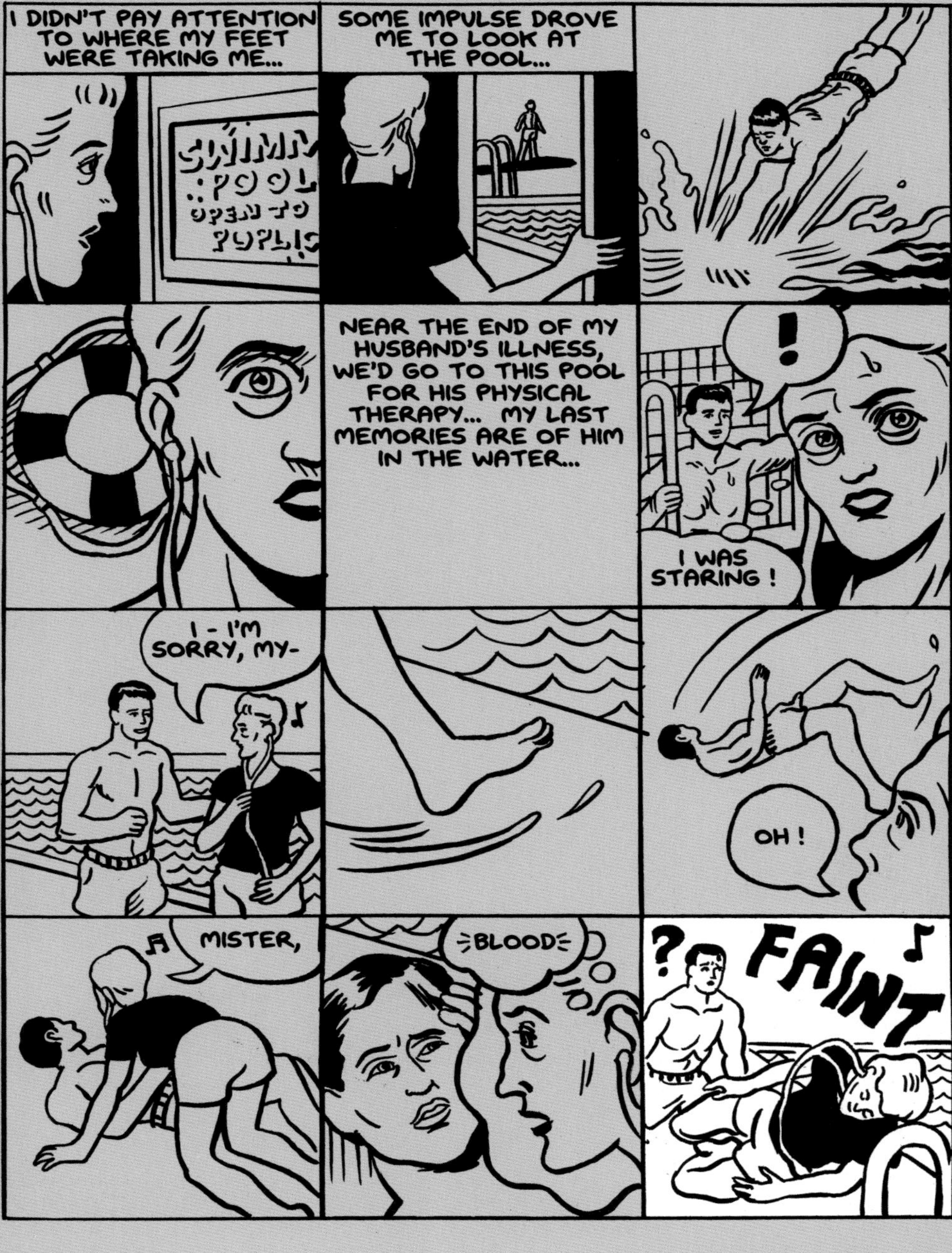

I DIDN'T PAY ATTENTION TO WHERE MY FEET WERE TAKING ME...
SOME IMPULSE DROVE ME TO LOOK AT THE POOL...
NEAR THE END OF MY HUSBAND'S ILLNESS, WE'D GO TO THIS POOL FOR HIS PHYSICAL THERAPY... MY LAST MEMORIES ARE OF HIM IN THE WATER...
!
I WAS STARING !
I - I'M SORRY, MY-
OH !
MISTER,
BLOOD
FAINT

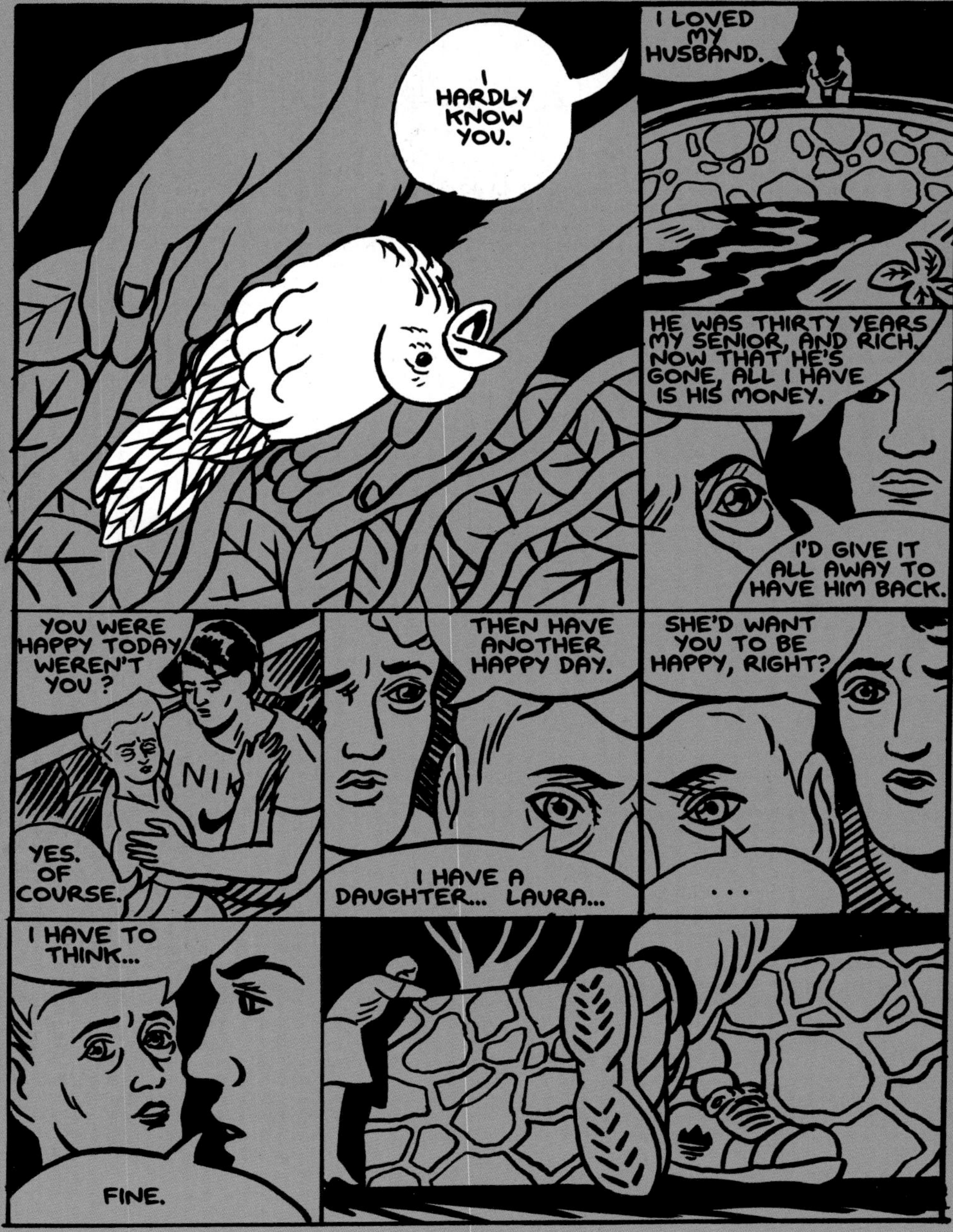
I HARDLY KNOW YOU.
I LOVED MY HUSBAND.
HE WAS THIRTY YEARS MY SENIOR, AND RICH. NOW THAT HE'S GONE, ALL I HAVE IS HIS MONEY.
I'D GIVE IT ALL AWAY TO HAVE HIM BACK.
YOU WERE HAPPY TODAY WEREN'T YOU ?
NIK
YES. OF COURSE.
THEN HAVE ANOTHER HAPPY DAY.
I HAVE A DAUGHTER... LAURA...
SHE'D WANT YOU TO BE HAPPY, RIGHT?
. . .
I HAVE TO THINK...
FINE.

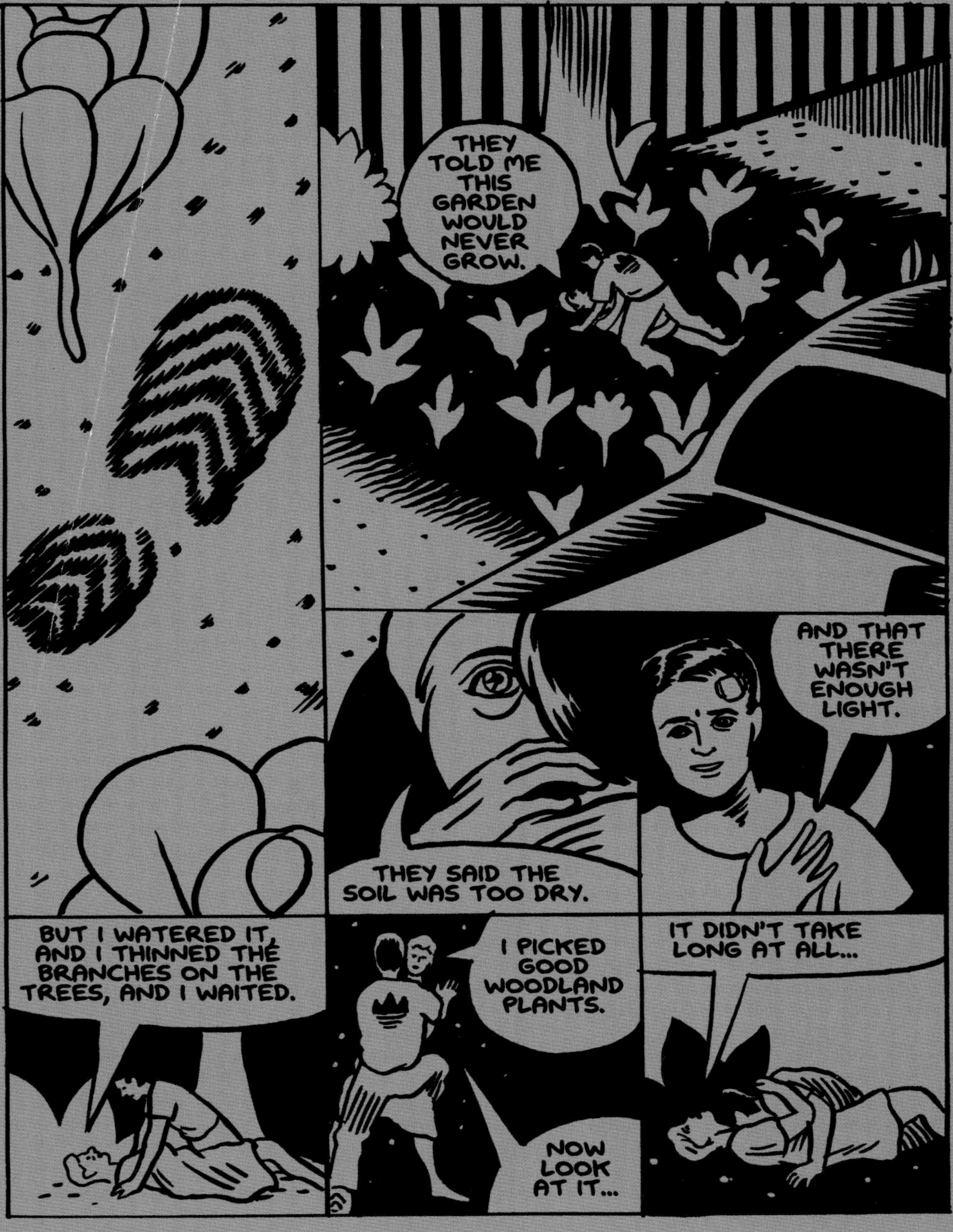
THEY TOLD ME THIS GARDEN WOULD NEVER GROW.
THEY SAID THE SOIL WAS TOO DRY.
AND THAT THERE WASN'T ENOUGH LIGHT.
BUT I WATERED IT, AND I THINNED THE BRANCHES ON THE TREES, AND I WAITED.
I PICKED GOOD WOODLAND PLANTS.
NOW LOOK AT IT...
IT DIDN'T TAKE LONG AT ALL...

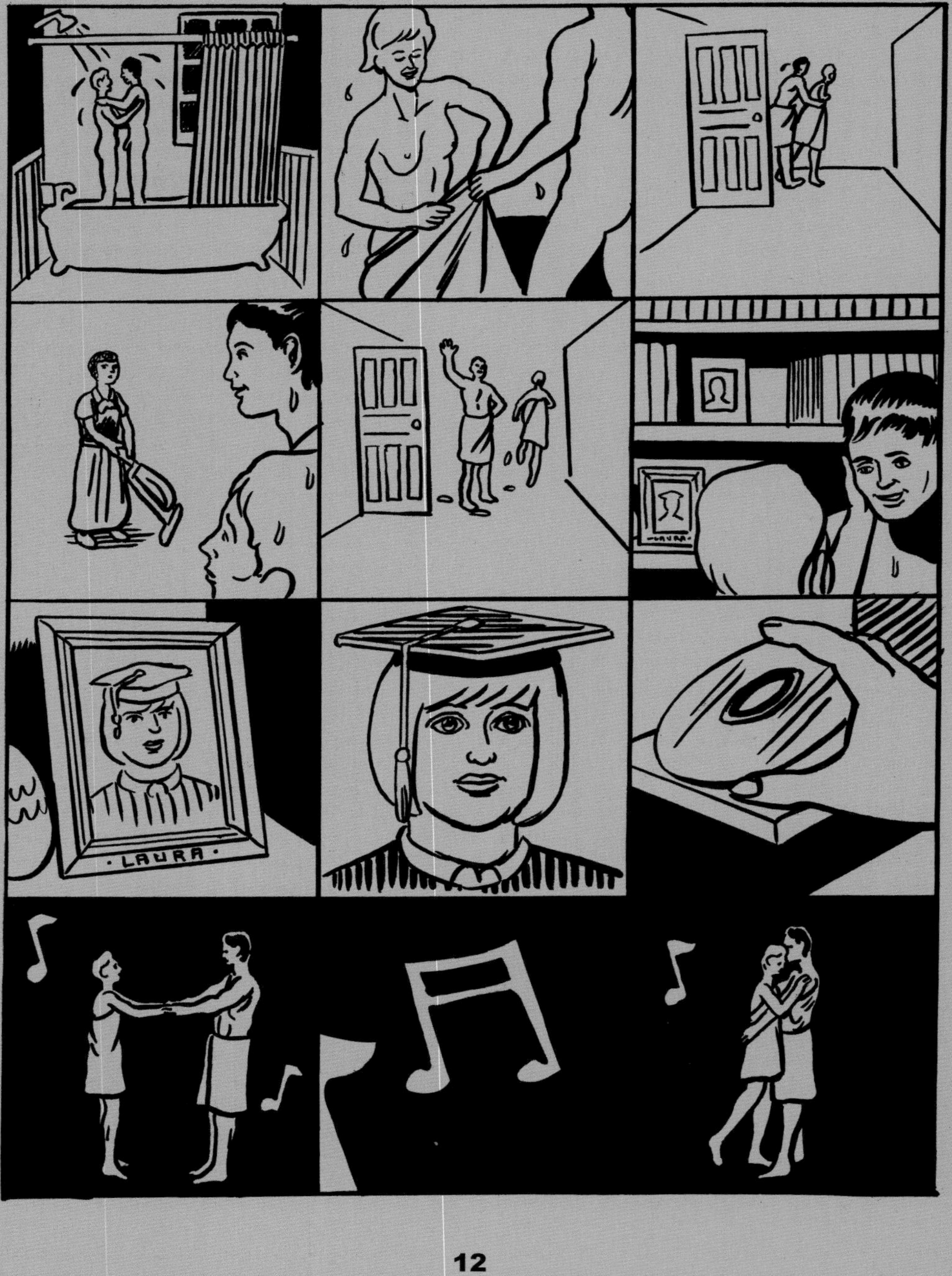
LAURA
LAURA

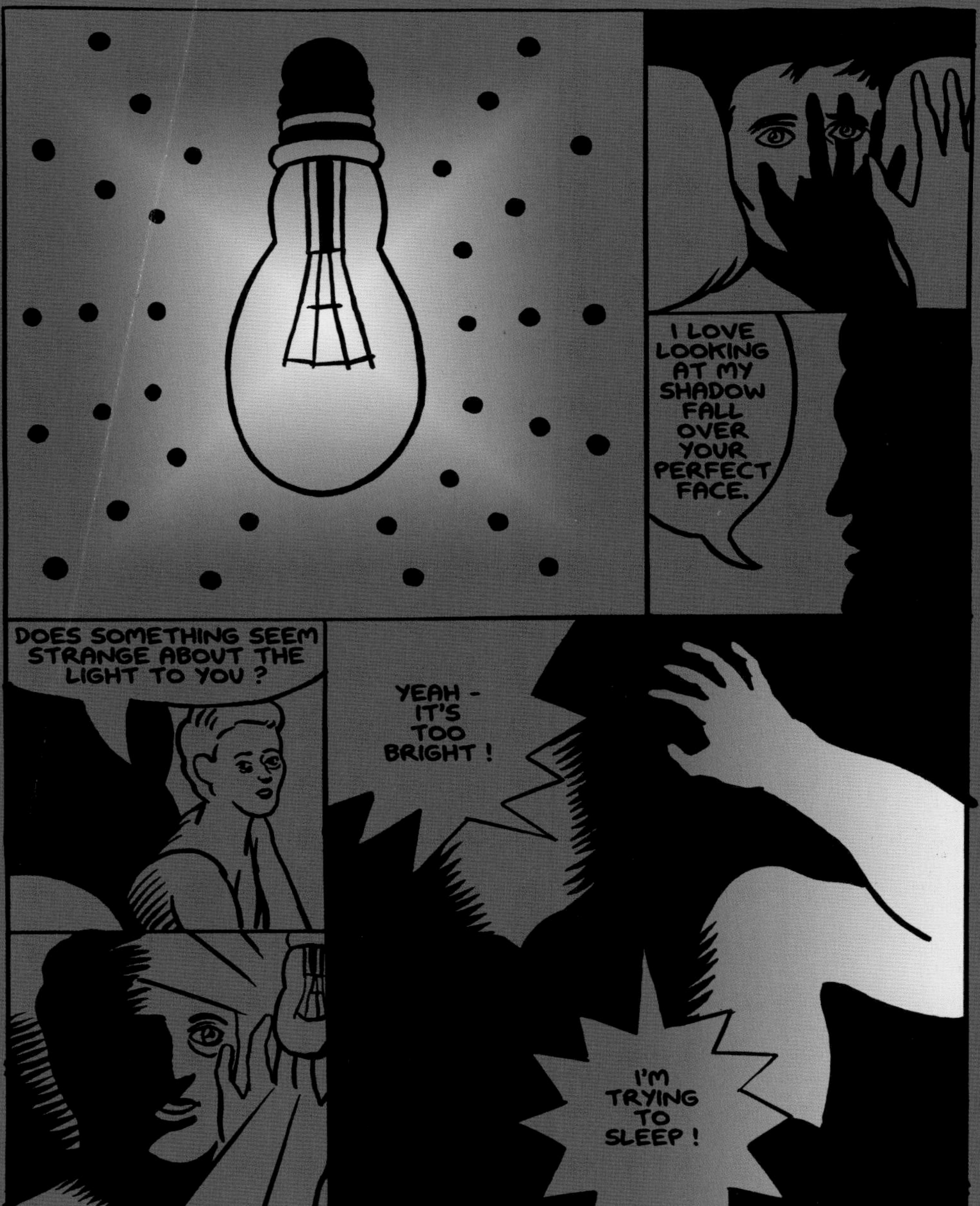
I LOVE LOOKING AT MY SHADOW FALL OVER YOUR PERFECT FACE.
DOES SOMETHING SEEM STRANGE ABOUT THE LIGHT TO YOU ?
YEAH - IT'S TOO BRIGHT !
I'M TRYING TO SLEEP !

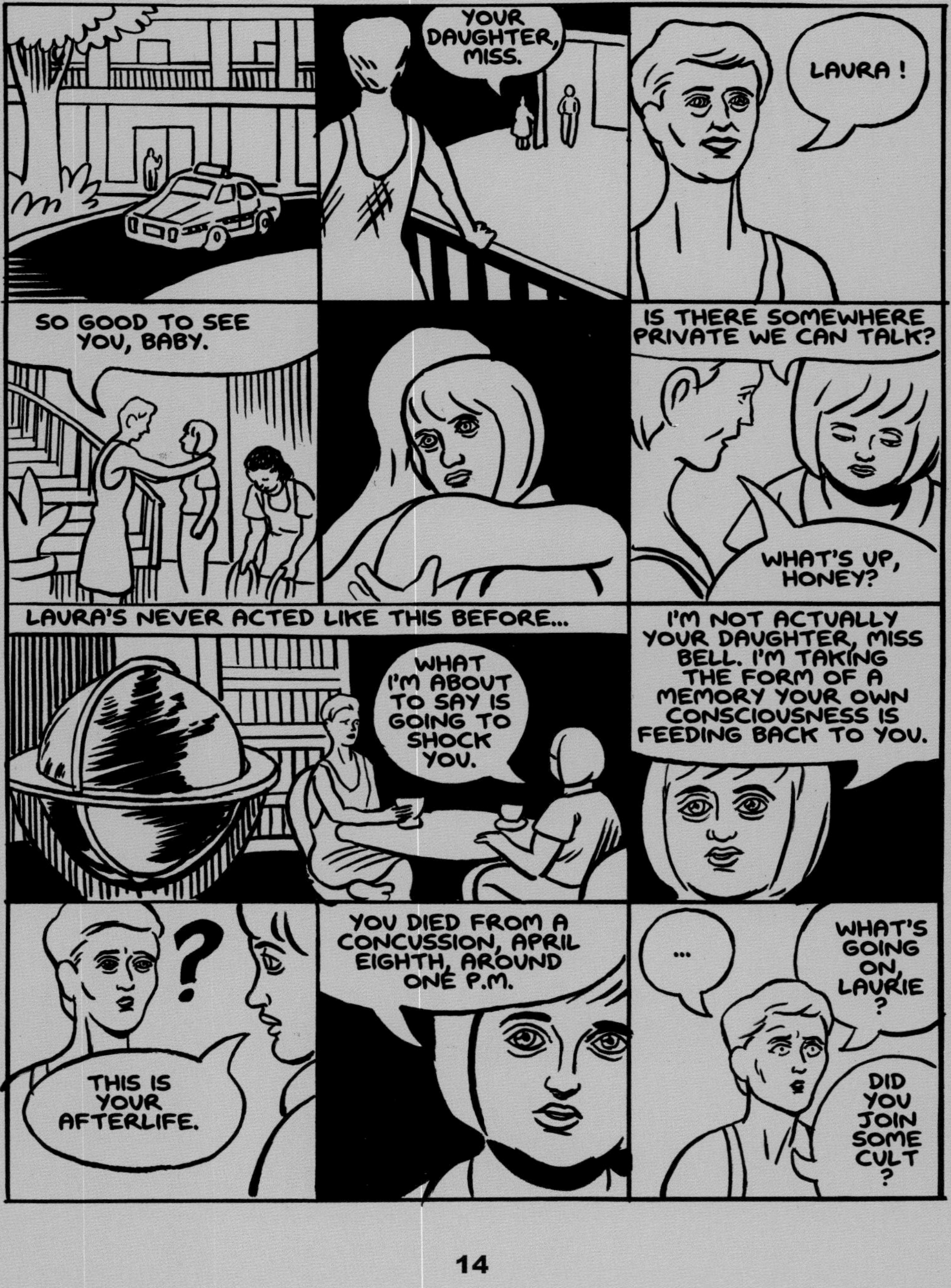
YOUR DAUGHTER, MISS.
LAURA !
SO GOOD TO SEE YOU, BABY.
IS THERE SOMEWHERE PRIVATE WE CAN TALK?
WHAT'S UP, HONEY?
LAURA'S NEVER ACTED LIKE THIS BEFORE...
WHAT I'M ABOUT TO SAY IS GOING TO SHOCK YOU.
I'M NOT ACTUALLY YOUR DAUGHTER, MISS BELL. I'M TAKING THE FORM OF A MEMORY YOUR OWN CONSCIOUSNESS IS FEEDING BACK TO YOU.
?
THIS IS YOUR AFTERLIFE.
YOU DIED FROM A CONCUSSION, APRIL EIGHTH, AROUND ONE P.M.
...
WHAT'S GOING ON, LAURIE ?
DID YOU JOIN SOME CULT ?

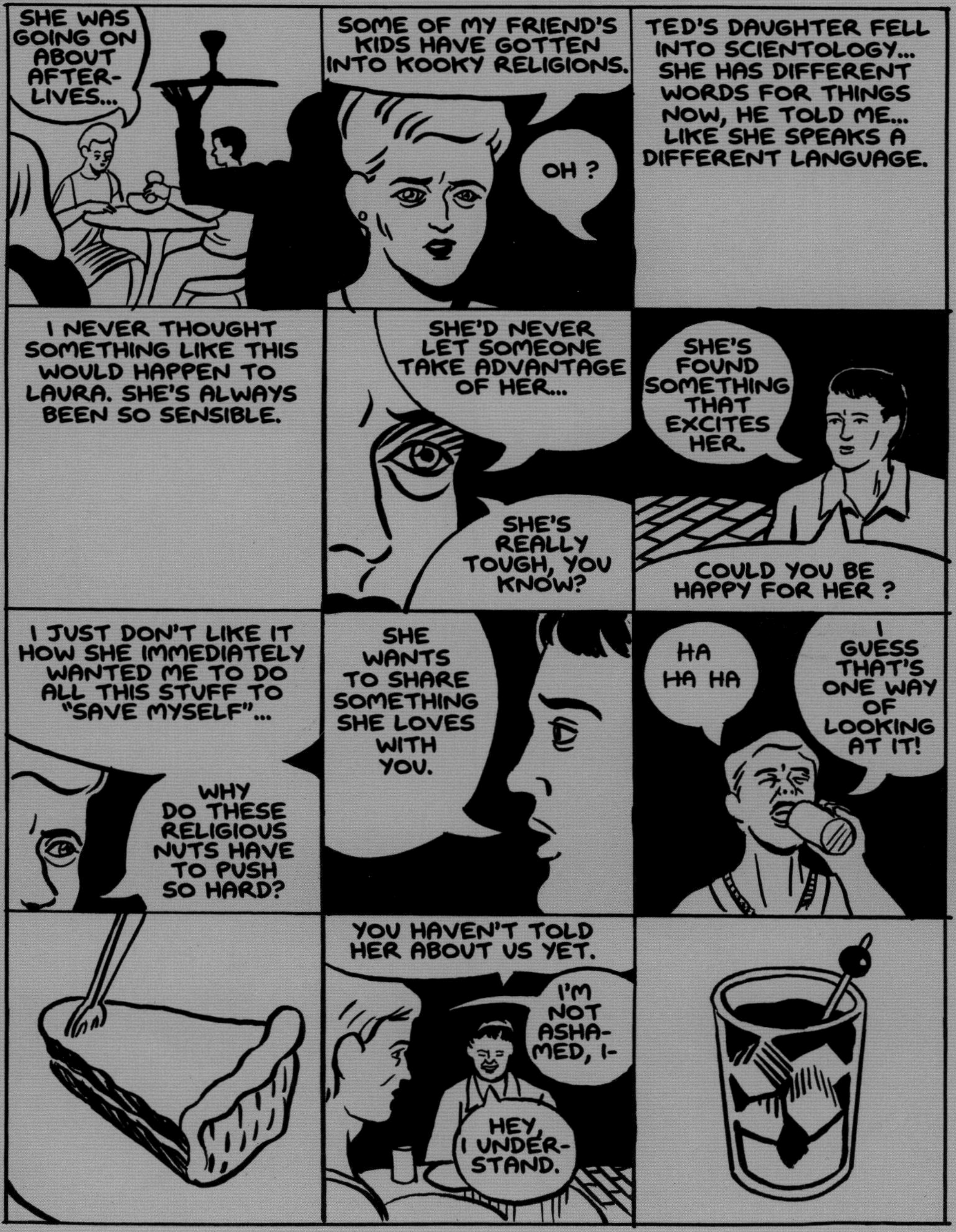

SHE WAS GOING ON ABOUT AFTER-LIVES...
SOME OF MY FRIEND'S KIDS HAVE GOTTEN INTO KOOKY RELIGIONS.
OH ?
TED'S DAUGHTER FELL INTO SCIENTOLOGY... SHE HAS DIFFERENT WORDS FOR THINGS NOW, HE TOLD ME... LIKE SHE SPEAKS A DIFFERENT LANGUAGE.
I NEVER THOUGHT SOMETHING LIKE THIS WOULD HAPPEN TO LAURA. SHE'S ALWAYS BEEN SO SENSIBLE.
SHE'D NEVER LET SOMEONE TAKE ADVANTAGE OF HER...
SHE'S REALLY TOUGH, YOU KNOW?
SHE'S FOUND SOMETHING THAT EXCITES HER.
COULD YOU BE HAPPY FOR HER ?
I JUST DON'T LIKE IT HOW SHE IMMEDIATELY WANTED ME TO DO ALL THIS STUFF TO "SAVE MYSELF"...
WHY DO THESE RELIGIOUS NUTS HAVE TO PUSH SO HARD?
SHE WANTS TO SHARE SOMETHING SHE LOVES WITH YOU.
HA HA HA
I GUESS THAT'S ONE WAY OF LOOKING AT IT!
YOU HAVEN'T TOLD HER ABOUT US YET.
I'M NOT ASHA-MED, I-
HEY, I UNDER-STAND.

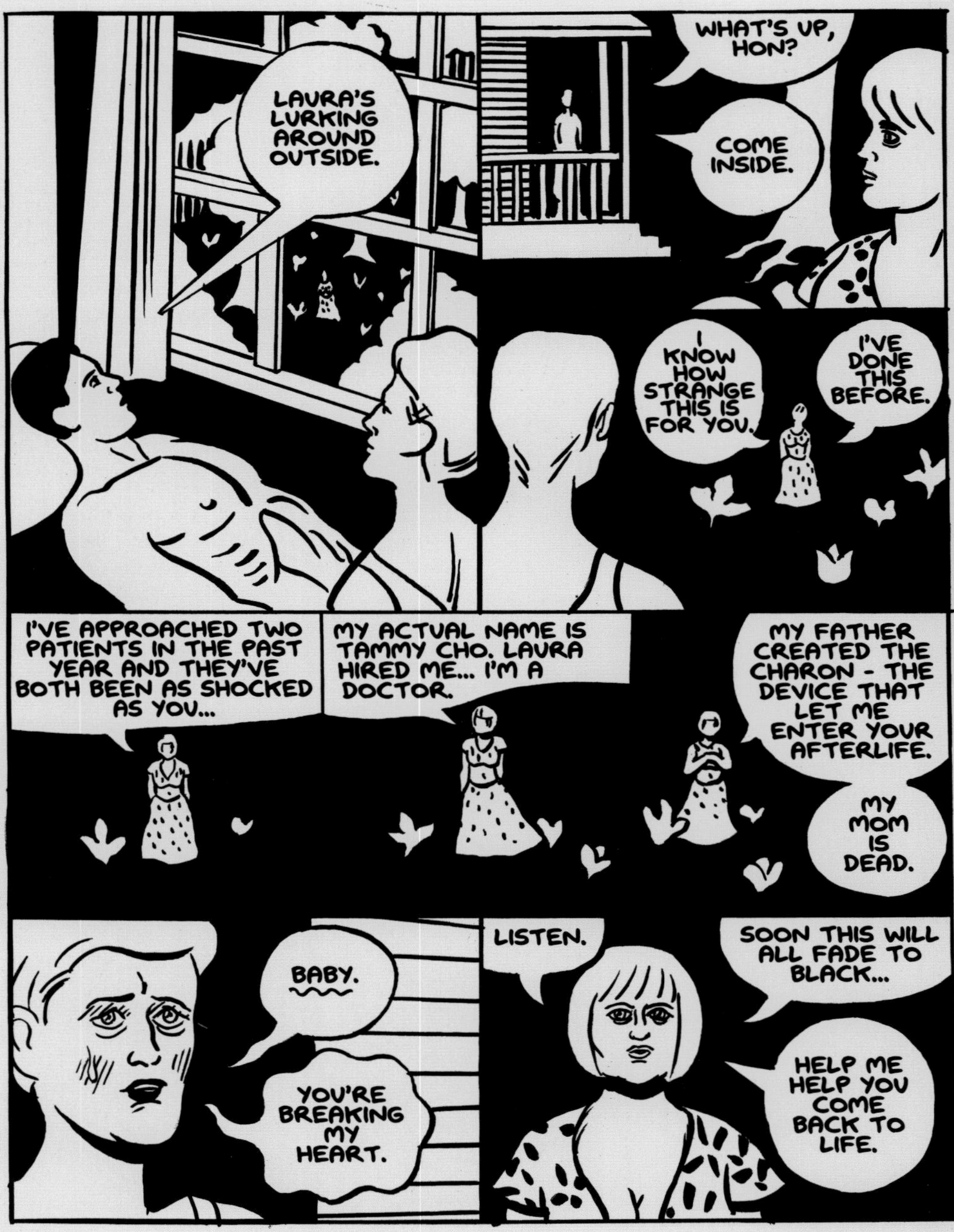
LAURA'S LURKING AROUND OUTSIDE.
WHAT'S UP, HON?
COME INSIDE.
I KNOW HOW STRANGE THIS IS FOR YOU.
I'VE DONE THIS BEFORE.
I'VE APPROACHED TWO PATIENTS IN THE PAST YEAR AND THEY'VE BOTH BEEN AS SHOCKED AS YOU...
MY ACTUAL NAME IS TAMMY CHO. LAURA HIRED ME... I'M A DOCTOR.
MY FATHER CREATED THE CHARON - THE DEVICE THAT LET ME ENTER YOUR AFTERLIFE.
MY MOM IS DEAD.
BABY.
YOU'RE BREAKING MY HEART.
LISTEN.
SOON THIS WILL ALL FADE TO BLACK...
HELP ME HELP YOU COME BACK TO LIFE.

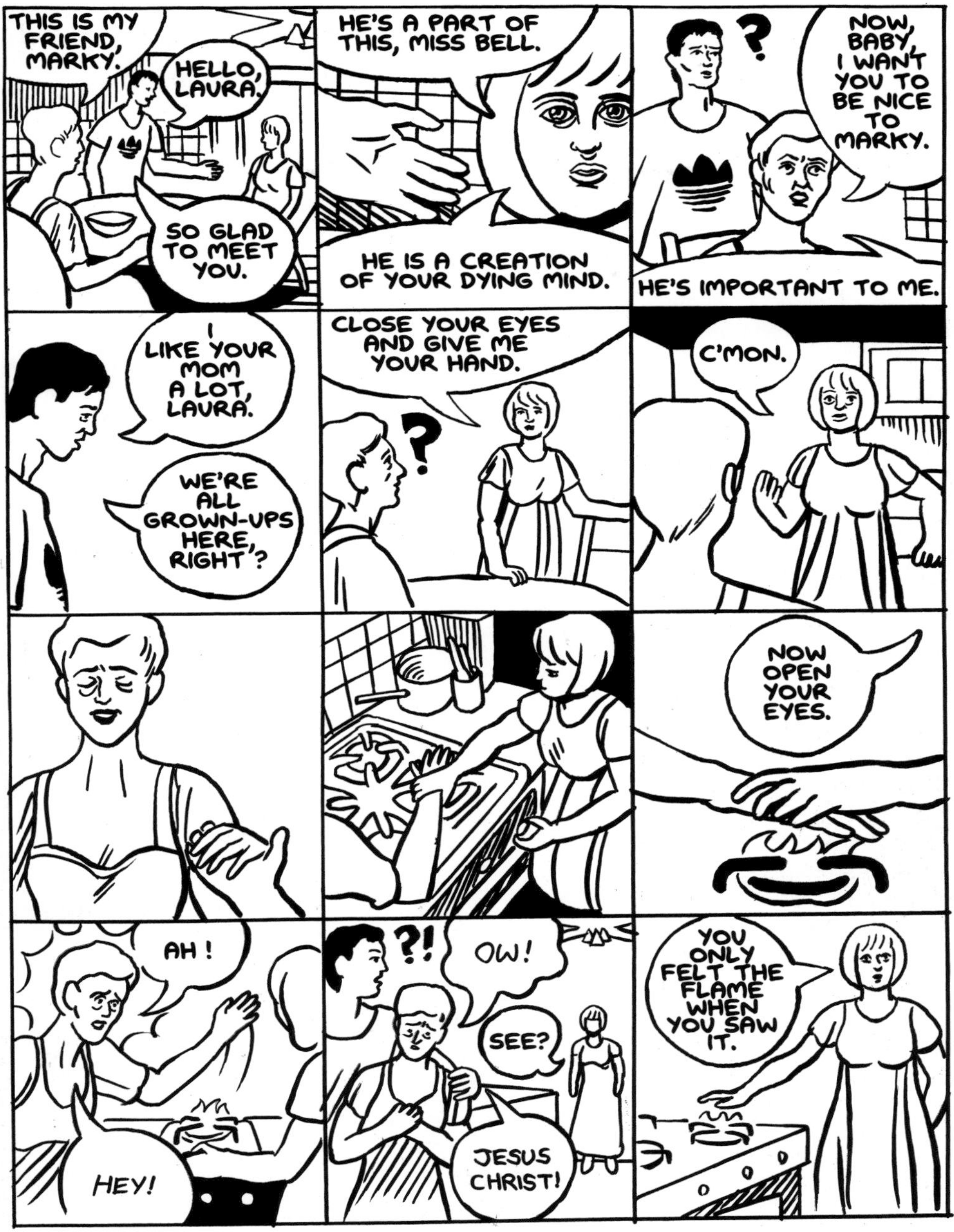
THIS IS MY FRIEND, MARKY.
HELLO, LAURA.
SO GLAD TO MEET YOU.
HE'S A PART OF THIS, MISS BELL.
HE IS A CREATION OF YOUR DYING MIND.
NOW, BABY, I WANT YOU TO BE NICE TO MARKY.
HE'S IMPORTANT TO ME.
I LIKE YOUR MOM A LOT, LAURA.
WE'RE ALL GROWN-UPS HERE, RIGHT?
CLOSE YOUR EYES AND GIVE ME YOUR HAND.
C'MON.
NOW OPEN YOUR EYES.
AH!
HEY!
OW!
SEE?
JESUS CHRIST!
YOU ONLY FELT THE FLAME WHEN YOU SAW IT.

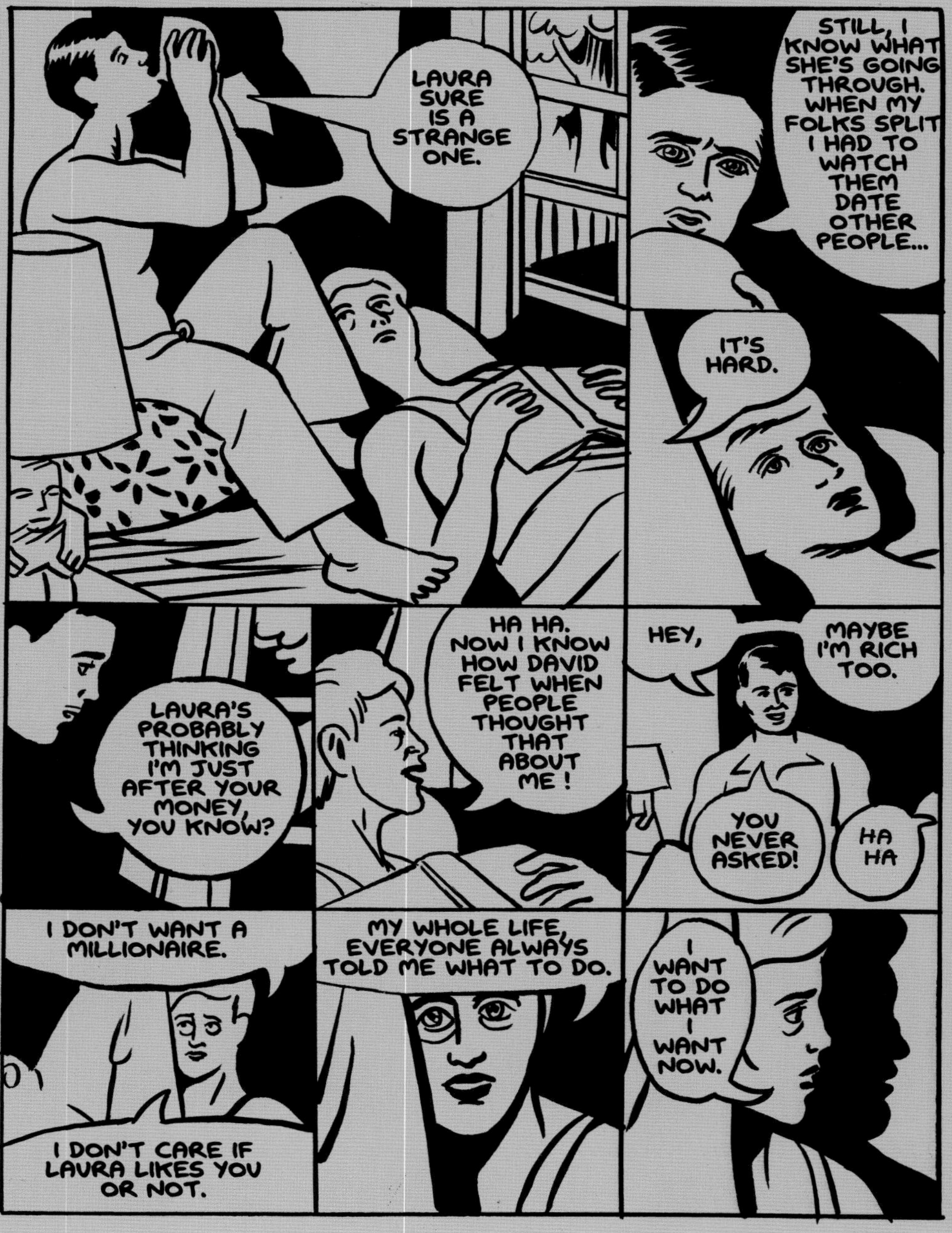
LAURA SURE IS A STRANGE ONE.
STILL, I KNOW WHAT SHE'S GOING THROUGH. WHEN MY FOLKS SPLIT I HAD TO WATCH THEM DATE OTHER PEOPLE...
IT'S HARD.
LAURA'S PROBABLY THINKING I'M JUST AFTER YOUR MONEY, YOU KNOW?
HA HA. NOW I KNOW HOW DAVID FELT WHEN PEOPLE THOUGHT THAT ABOUT ME!
HEY,
MAYBE I'M RICH TOO.
YOU NEVER ASKED!
HA HA
I DON'T WANT A MILLIONAIRE.
I DON'T CARE IF LAURA LIKES YOU OR NOT.
MY WHOLE LIFE, EVERYONE ALWAYS TOLD ME WHAT TO DO.
I WANT TO DO WHAT I WANT NOW.

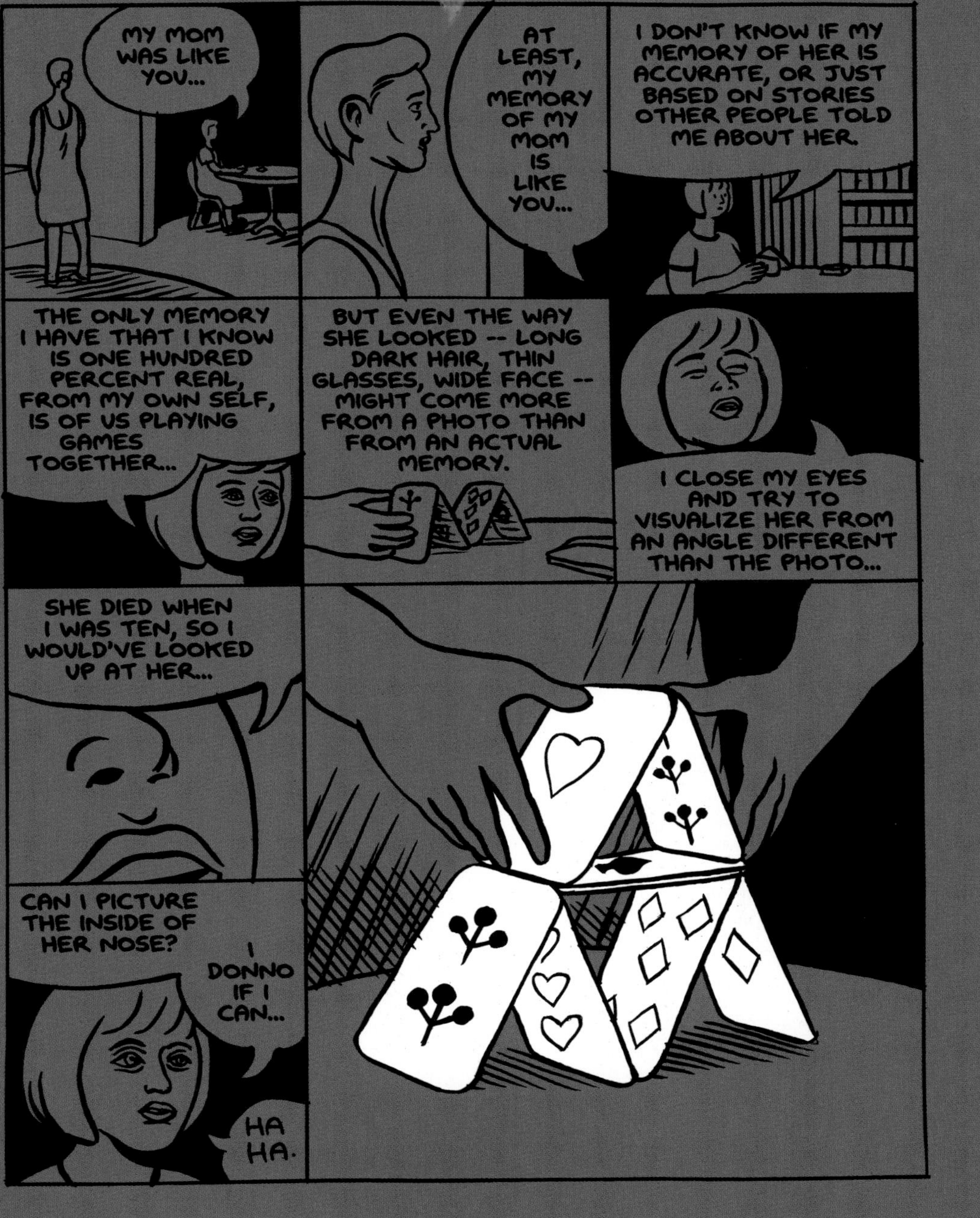

MY MOM WAS LIKE YOU...
AT LEAST, MY MEMORY OF MY MOM IS LIKE YOU...
I DON'T KNOW IF MY MEMORY OF HER IS ACCURATE, OR JUST BASED ON STORIES OTHER PEOPLE TOLD ME ABOUT HER.
THE ONLY MEMORY I HAVE THAT I KNOW IS ONE HUNDRED PERCENT REAL, FROM MY OWN SELF, IS OF US PLAYING GAMES TOGETHER...
BUT EVEN THE WAY SHE LOOKED -- LONG DARK HAIR, THIN GLASSES, WIDE FACE -- MIGHT COME MORE FROM A PHOTO THAN FROM AN ACTUAL MEMORY.
I CLOSE MY EYES AND TRY TO VISUALIZE HER FROM AN ANGLE DIFFERENT THAN THE PHOTO...
SHE DIED WHEN I WAS TEN, SO I WOULD'VE LOOKED UP AT HER...
CAN I PICTURE THE INSIDE OF HER NOSE?
I DONNO IF I CAN...
HA HA.

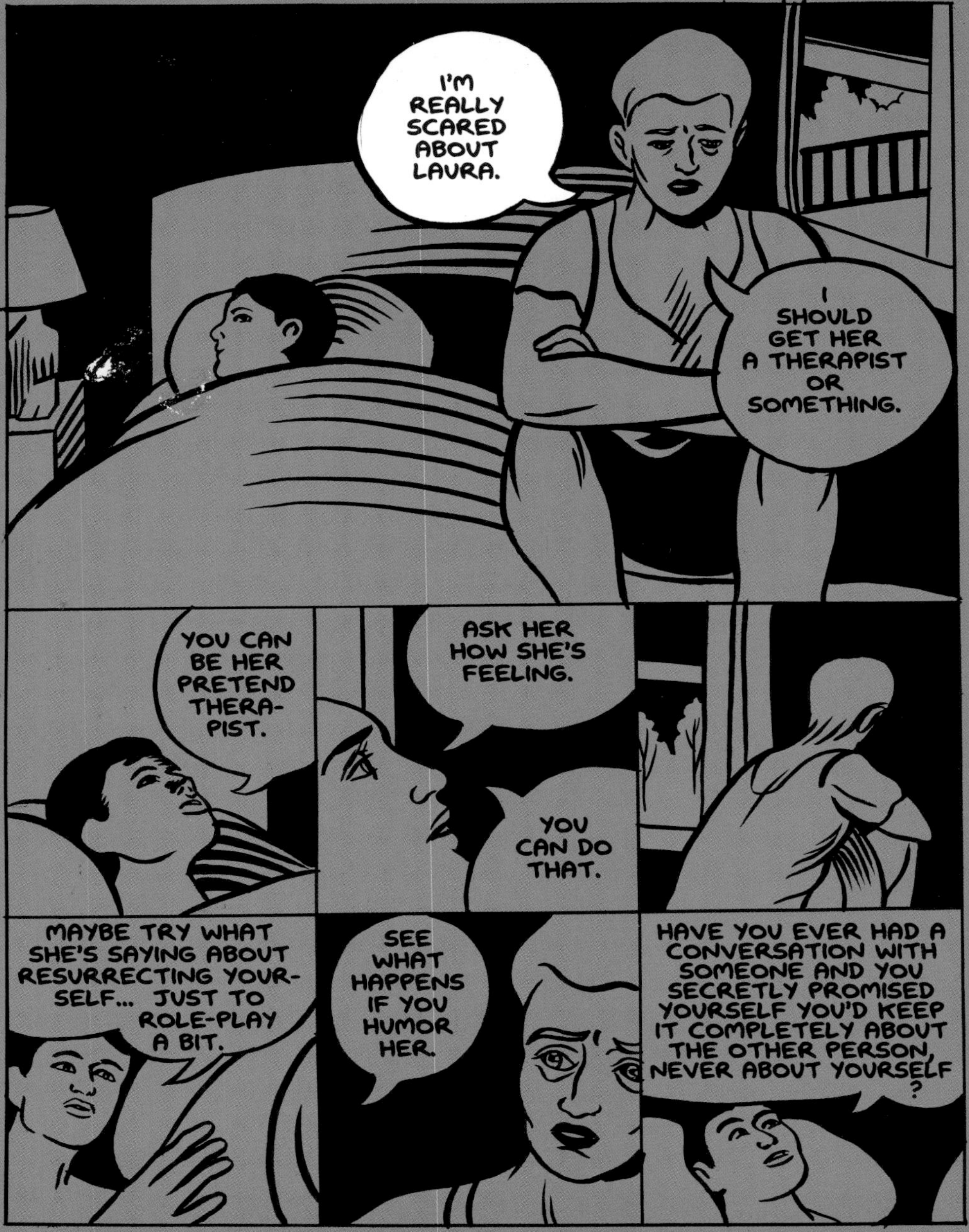

I'M REALLY SCARED ABOUT LAURA.
I SHOULD GET HER A THERAPIST OR SOMETHING.
YOU CAN BE HER PRETEND THERA-PIST.
ASK HER HOW SHE'S FEELING.
YOU CAN DO THAT.
MAYBE TRY WHAT SHE'S SAYING ABOUT RESURRECTING YOUR-SELF... JUST TO ROLE-PLAY A BIT.
SEE WHAT HAPPENS IF YOU HUMOR HER.
HAVE YOU EVER HAD A CONVERSATION WITH SOMEONE AND YOU SECRETLY PROMISED YOURSELF YOU'D KEEP IT COMPLETELY ABOUT THE OTHER PERSON, NEVER ABOUT YOURSELF?

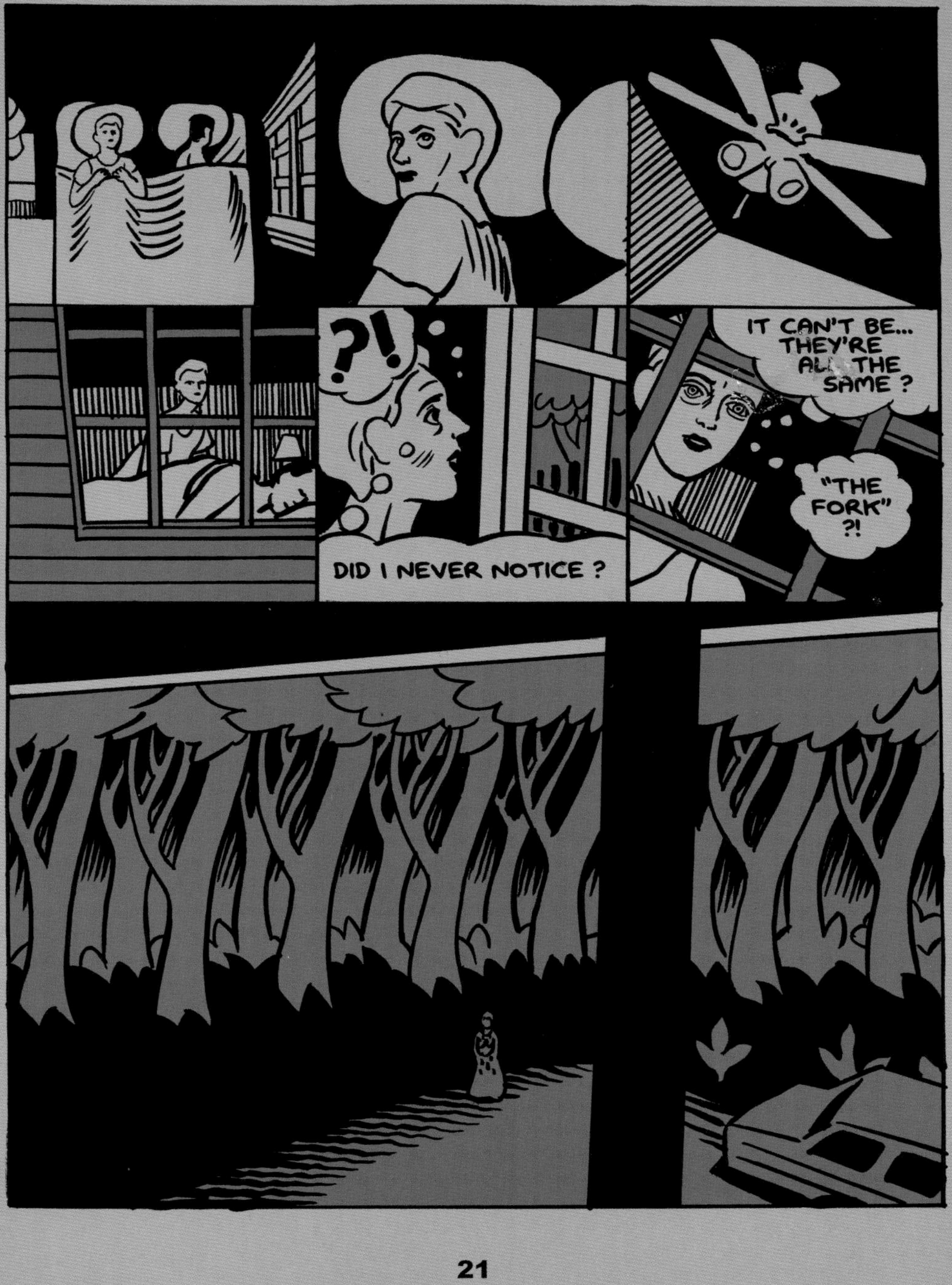
?!
DID I NEVER NOTICE ?
IT CAN'T BE... THEY'RE ALL THE SAME ?
"THE FORK" ?!

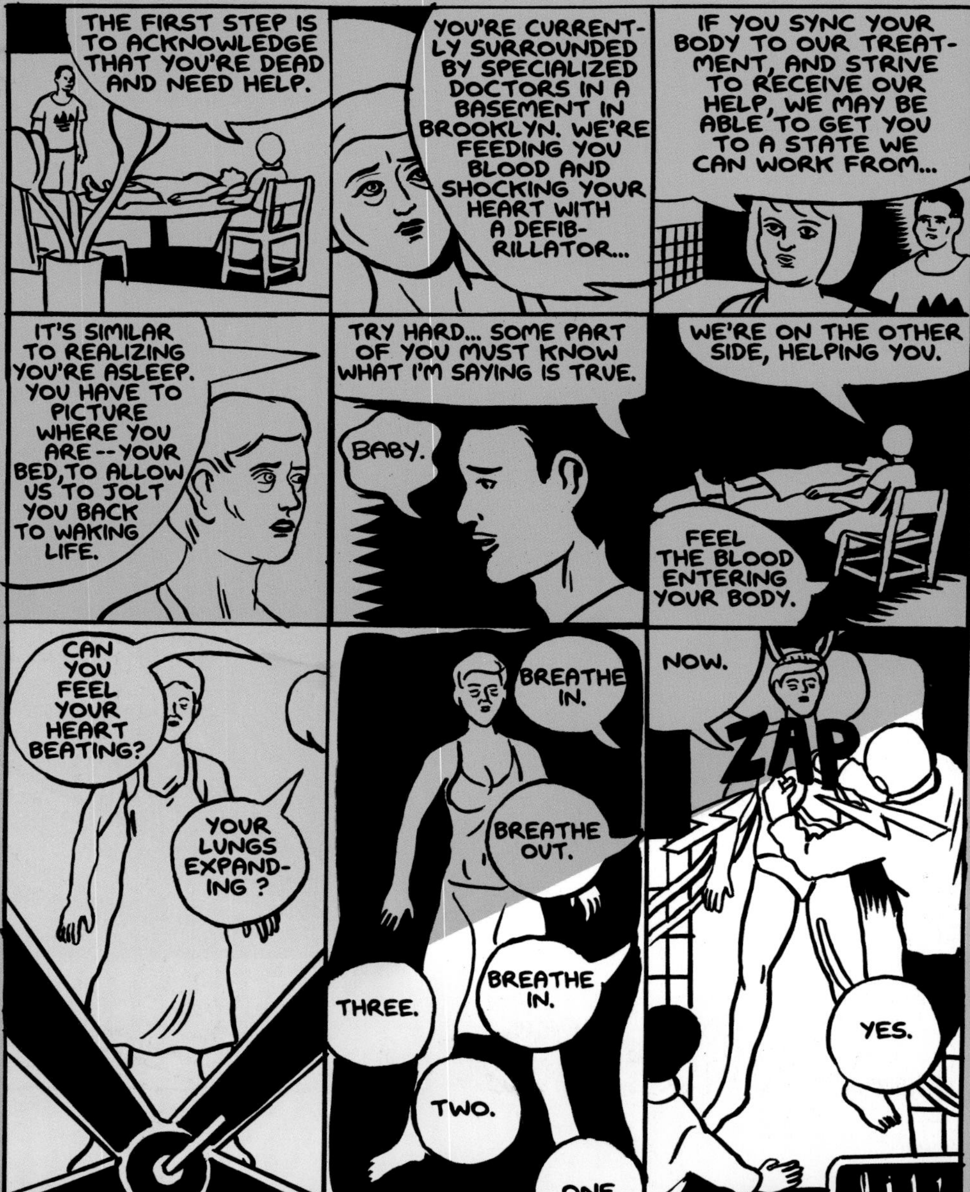
THE FIRST STEP IS TO ACKNOWLEDGE THAT YOU'RE DEAD AND NEED HELP.
YOU'RE CURRENTLY SURROUNDED BY SPECIALIZED DOCTORS IN A BASEMENT IN BROOKLYN. WE'RE FEEDING YOU BLOOD AND SHOCKING YOUR HEART WITH A DEFIBRILLATOR...
IF YOU SYNC YOUR BODY TO OUR TREATMENT, AND STRIVE TO RECEIVE OUR HELP, WE MAY BE ABLE TO GET YOU TO A STATE WE CAN WORK FROM...
IT'S SIMILAR TO REALIZING YOU'RE ASLEEP. YOU HAVE TO PICTURE WHERE YOU ARE--YOUR BED, TO ALLOW US TO JOLT YOU BACK TO WAKING LIFE.
TRY HARD... SOME PART OF YOU MUST KNOW WHAT I'M SAYING IS TRUE.
BABY.
WE'RE ON THE OTHER SIDE, HELPING YOU.
FEEL THE BLOOD ENTERING YOUR BODY.
CAN YOU FEEL YOUR HEART BEATING?
YOUR LUNGS EXPANDING?
BREATHE IN.
BREATHE OUT.
BREATHE IN.
THREE.
TWO.
ONE.
NOW.
ZAP
YES.

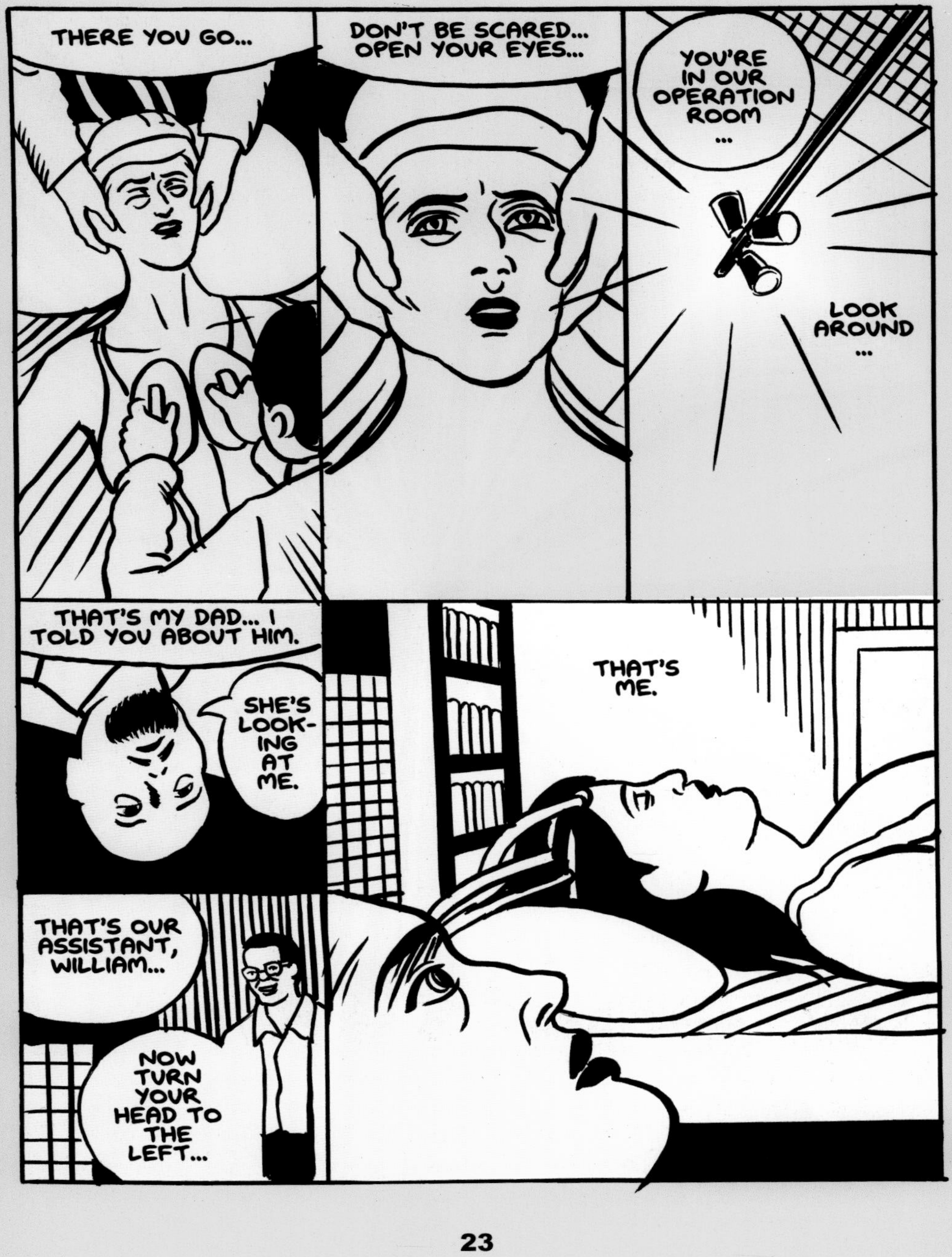
THERE YOU GO...
DON'T BE SCARED... OPEN YOUR EYES...
YOU'RE IN OUR OPERATION ROOM ...
LOOK AROUND ...
THAT'S MY DAD... I TOLD YOU ABOUT HIM.
SHE'S LOOK-ING AT ME.
THAT'S OUR ASSISTANT, WILLIAM...
NOW TURN YOUR HEAD TO THE LEFT...
THAT'S ME.

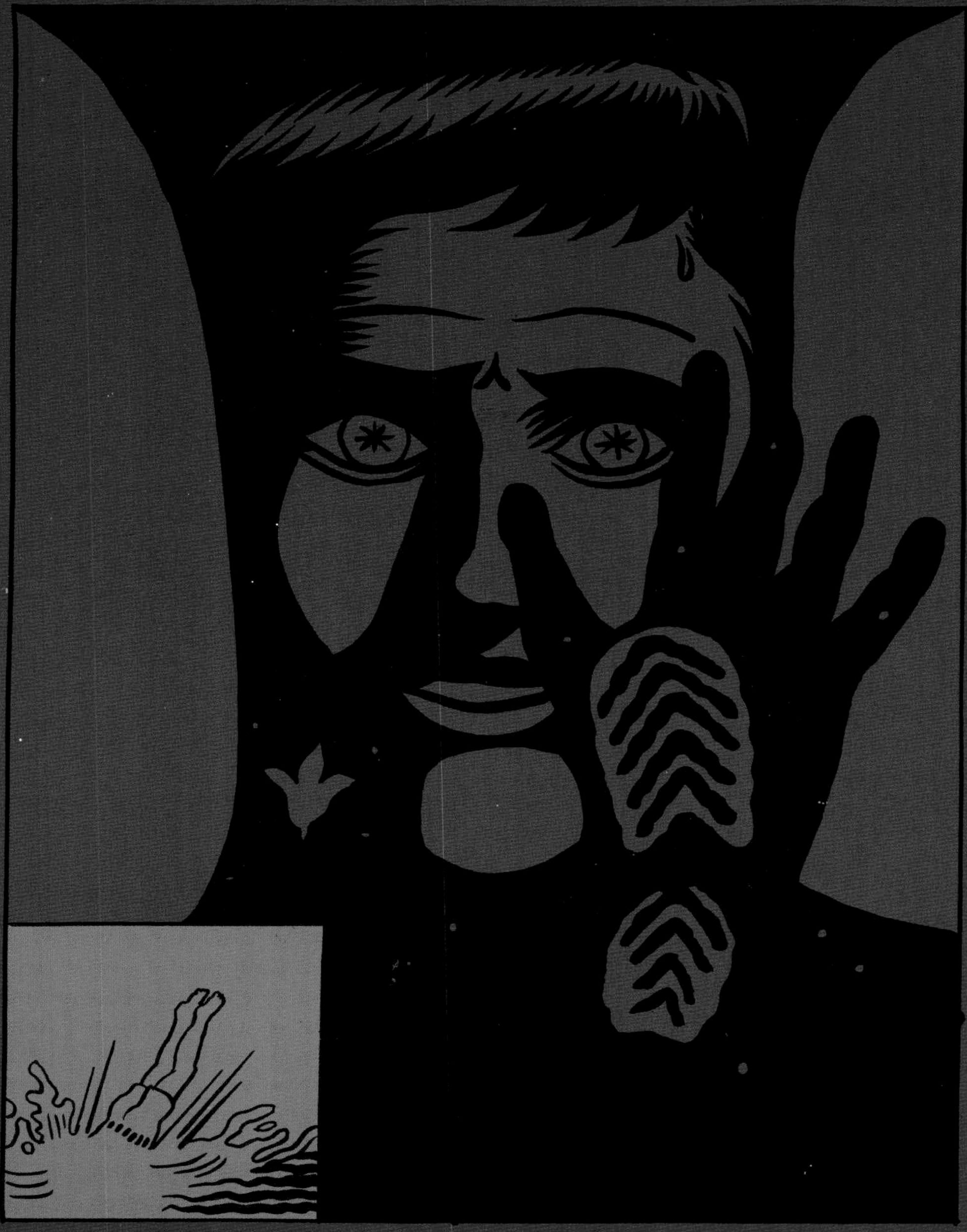

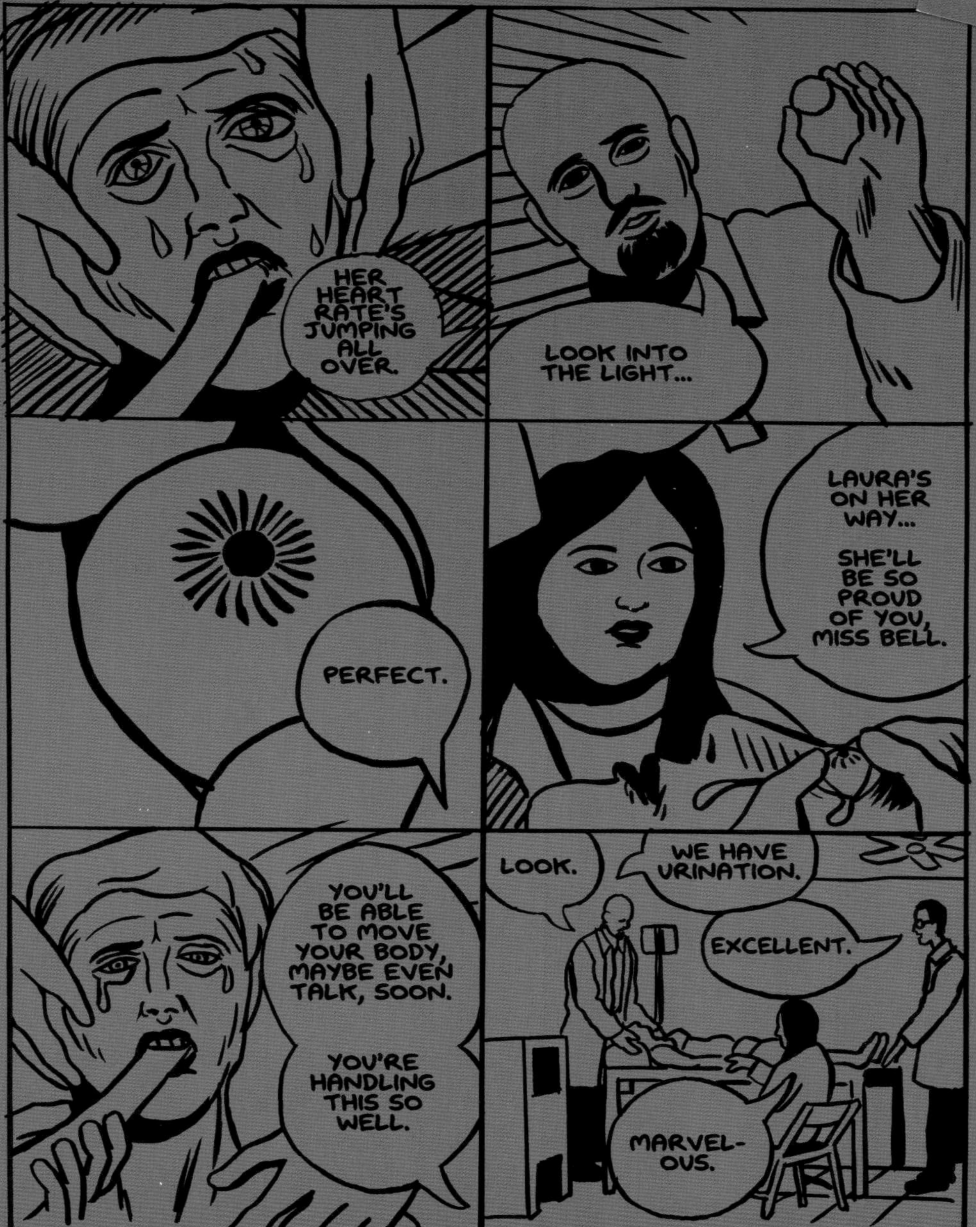
HER HEART RATE'S JUMPING ALL OVER.
LOOK INTO THE LIGHT...
PERFECT.
LAURA'S ON HER WAY...
SHE'LL BE SO PROUD OF YOU, MISS BELL.
YOU'LL BE ABLE TO MOVE YOUR BODY, MAYBE EVEN TALK, SOON.
YOU'RE HANDLING THIS SO WELL.
LOOK.
WE HAVE URINATION.
EXCELLENT.
MARVEL-OUS.

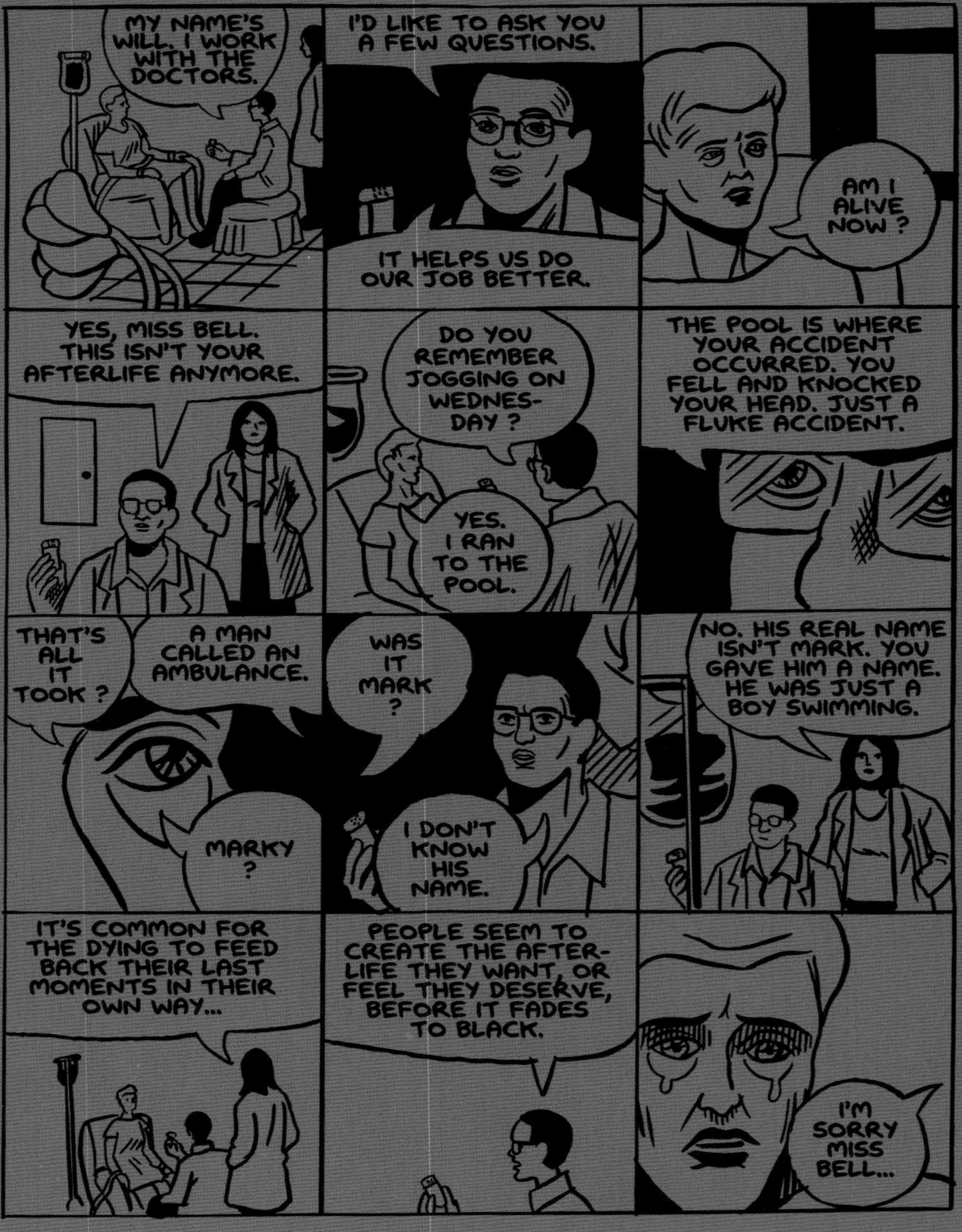
MY NAME'S WILL. I WORK WITH THE DOCTORS.
I'D LIKE TO ASK YOU A FEW QUESTIONS.
IT HELPS US DO OUR JOB BETTER.
AM I ALIVE NOW ?
YES, MISS BELL. THIS ISN'T YOUR AFTERLIFE ANYMORE.
DO YOU REMEMBER JOGGING ON WEDNES-DAY ?
YES. I RAN TO THE POOL.
THE POOL IS WHERE YOUR ACCIDENT OCCURRED. YOU FELL AND KNOCKED YOUR HEAD. JUST A FLUKE ACCIDENT.
THAT'S ALL IT TOOK ?
A MAN CALLED AN AMBULANCE.
MARKY ?
WAS IT MARK ?
I DON'T KNOW HIS NAME.
NO. HIS REAL NAME ISN'T MARK. YOU GAVE HIM A NAME. HE WAS JUST A BOY SWIMMING.
IT'S COMMON FOR THE DYING TO FEED BACK THEIR LAST MOMENTS IN THEIR OWN WAY...
PEOPLE SEEM TO CREATE THE AFTER-LIFE THEY WANT, OR FEEL THEY DESERVE, BEFORE IT FADES TO BLACK.
I'M SORRY MISS BELL...

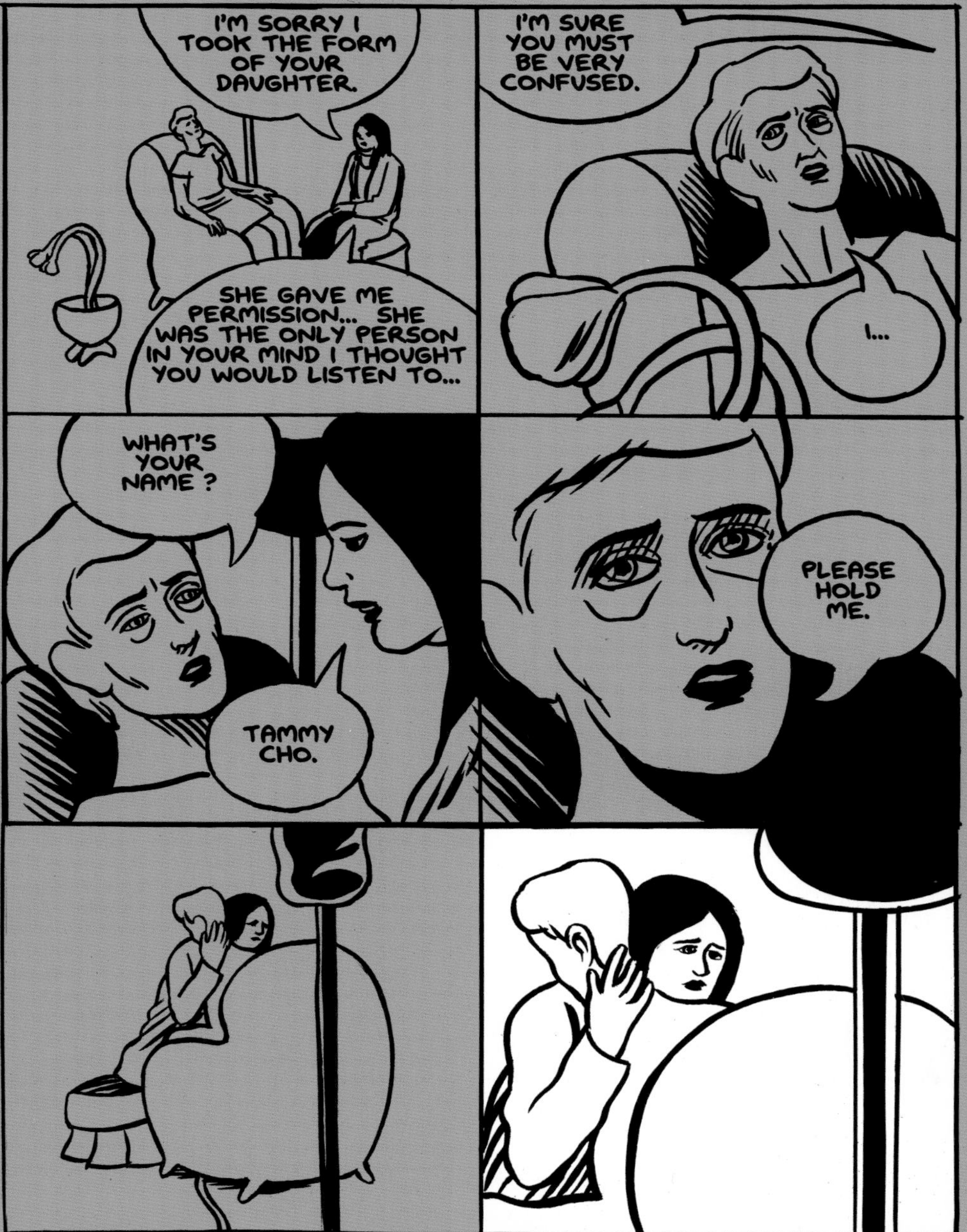
I'M SORRY I TOOK THE FORM OF YOUR DAUGHTER.
SHE GAVE ME PERMISSION... SHE WAS THE ONLY PERSON IN YOUR MIND I THOUGHT YOU WOULD LISTEN TO...
I'M SURE YOU MUST BE VERY CONFUSED.
I...
WHAT'S YOUR NAME ?
TAMMY CHO.
PLEASE HOLD ME.

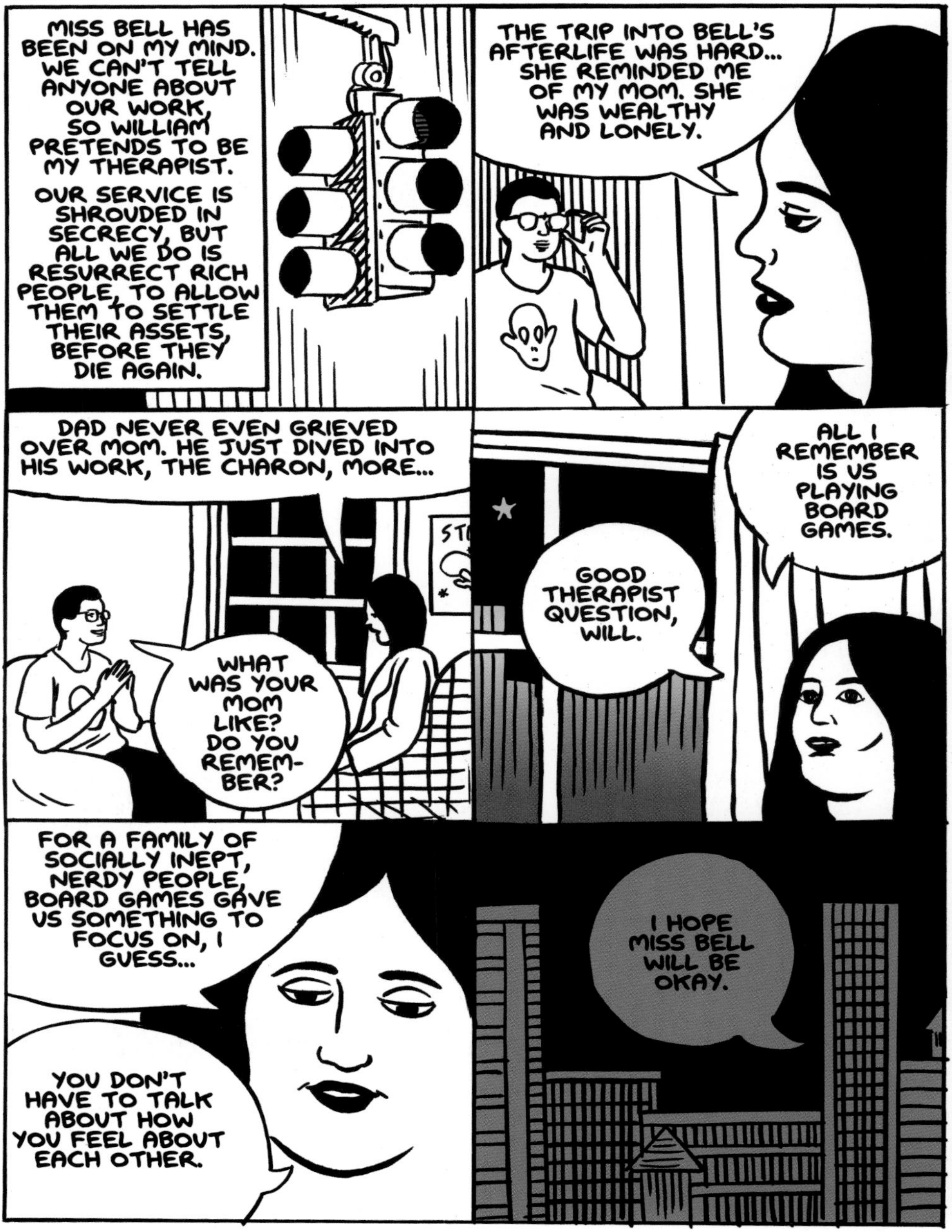

MISS BELL HAS BEEN ON MY MIND. WE CAN'T TELL ANYONE ABOUT OUR WORK, SO WILLIAM PRETENDS TO BE MY THERAPIST.
OUR SERVICE IS SHROUDED IN SECRECY, BUT ALL WE DO IS RESURRECT RICH PEOPLE, TO ALLOW THEM TO SETTLE THEIR ASSETS, BEFORE THEY DIE AGAIN.
THE TRIP INTO BELL'S AFTERLIFE WAS HARD... SHE REMINDED ME OF MY MOM. SHE WAS WEALTHY AND LONELY.
DAD NEVER EVEN GRIEVED OVER MOM. HE JUST DIVED INTO HIS WORK, THE CHARON, MORE...
WHAT WAS YOUR MOM LIKE? DO YOU REMEMBER?
GOOD THERAPIST QUESTION, WILL.
ALL I REMEMBER IS US PLAYING BOARD GAMES.
FOR A FAMILY OF SOCIALLY INEPT, NERDY PEOPLE, BOARD GAMES GAVE US SOMETHING TO FOCUS ON, I GUESS...
YOU DON'T HAVE TO TALK ABOUT HOW YOU FEEL ABOUT EACH OTHER.
I HOPE MISS BELL WILL BE OKAY.

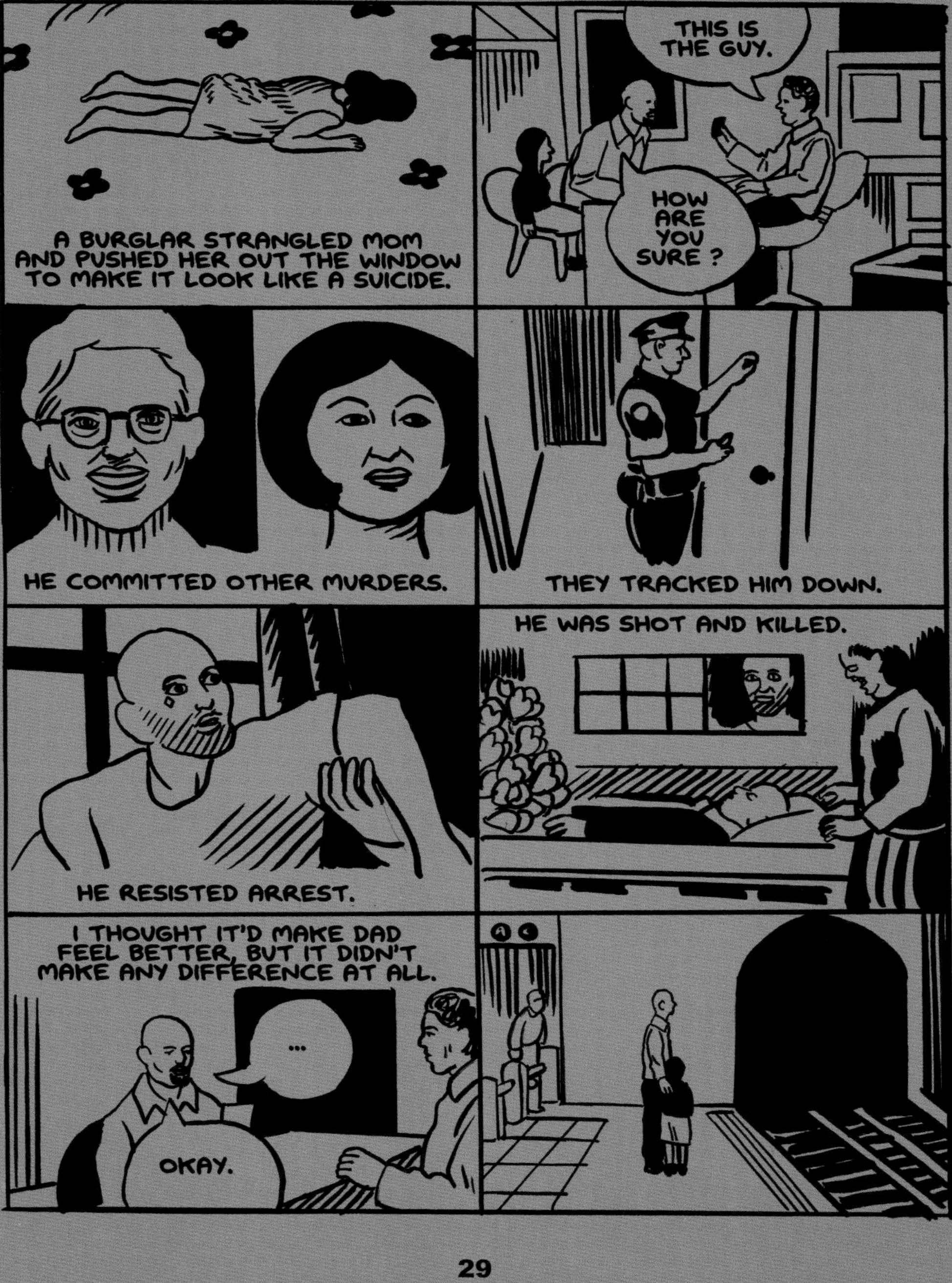
A BURGLAR STRANGLED MOM AND PUSHED HER OUT THE WINDOW TO MAKE IT LOOK LIKE A SUICIDE.
THIS IS THE GUY.
HOW ARE YOU SURE ?
HE COMMITTED OTHER MURDERS.
THEY TRACKED HIM DOWN.
HE RESISTED ARREST.
HE WAS SHOT AND KILLED.
I THOUGHT IT'D MAKE DAD FEEL BETTER, BUT IT DIDN'T MAKE ANY DIFFERENCE AT ALL.
...
OKAY.

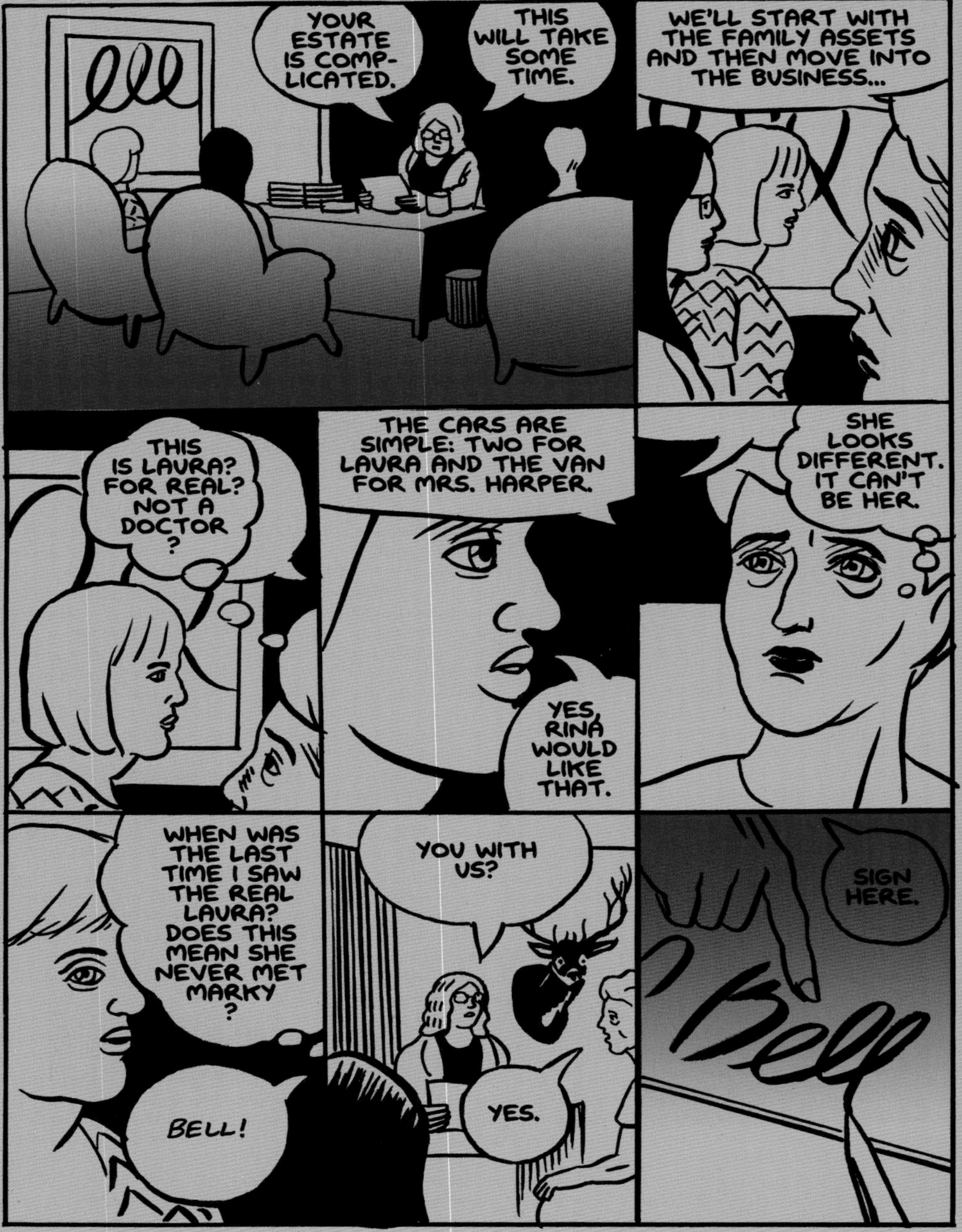
YOUR ESTATE IS COMPLICATED.
THIS WILL TAKE SOME TIME.
WE'LL START WITH THE FAMILY ASSETS AND THEN MOVE INTO THE BUSINESS...
THIS IS LAURA? FOR REAL? NOT A DOCTOR ?
THE CARS ARE SIMPLE: TWO FOR LAURA AND THE VAN FOR MRS. HARPER.
YES, RINA WOULD LIKE THAT.
SHE LOOKS DIFFERENT. IT CAN'T BE HER.
WHEN WAS THE LAST TIME I SAW THE REAL LAURA? DOES THIS MEAN SHE NEVER MET MARKY ?
BELL!
YOU WITH US?
YES.
SIGN HERE.

TAMMY HOME FROM WORK

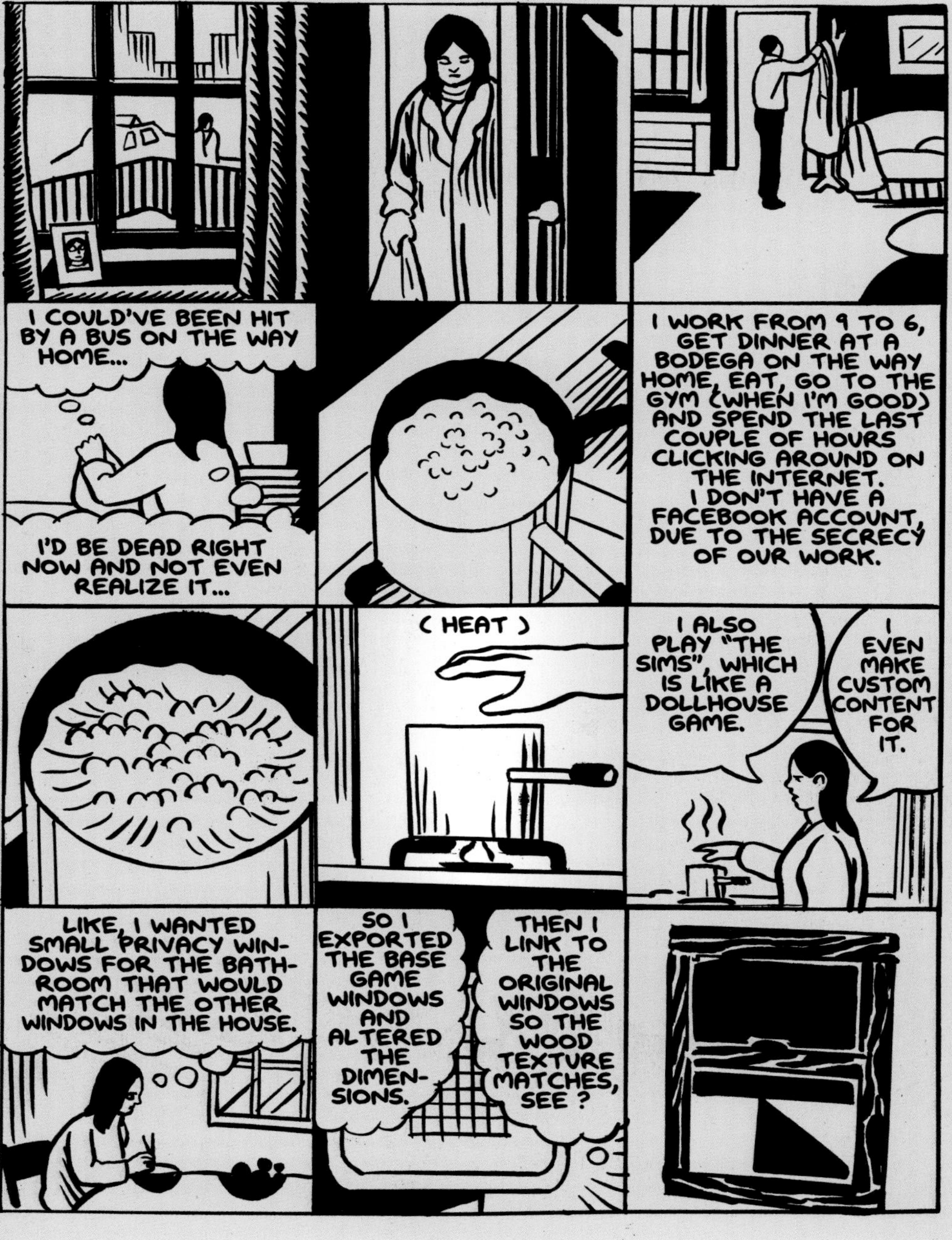
I COULD'VE BEEN HIT BY A BUS ON THE WAY HOME...
I'D BE DEAD RIGHT NOW AND NOT EVEN REALIZE IT...
I WORK FROM 9 TO 6, GET DINNER AT A BODEGA ON THE WAY HOME, EAT, GO TO THE GYM (WHEN I'M GOOD) AND SPEND THE LAST COUPLE OF HOURS CLICKING AROUND ON THE INTERNET. I DON'T HAVE A FACEBOOK ACCOUNT, DUE TO THE SECRECY OF OUR WORK.
(HEAT)
I ALSO PLAY "THE SIMS", WHICH IS LIKE A DOLLHOUSE GAME.
I EVEN MAKE CUSTOM CONTENT FOR IT.
LIKE, I WANTED SMALL PRIVACY WIN-DOWS FOR THE BATH-ROOM THAT WOULD MATCH THE OTHER WINDOWS IN THE HOUSE.
SO I EXPORTED THE BASE GAME WINDOWS AND ALTERED THE DIMEN-SIONS.
THEN I LINK TO THE ORIGINAL WINDOWS SO THE WOOD TEXTURE MATCHES, SEE ?

TAMMY'S FATHER AKA "DR. NO"

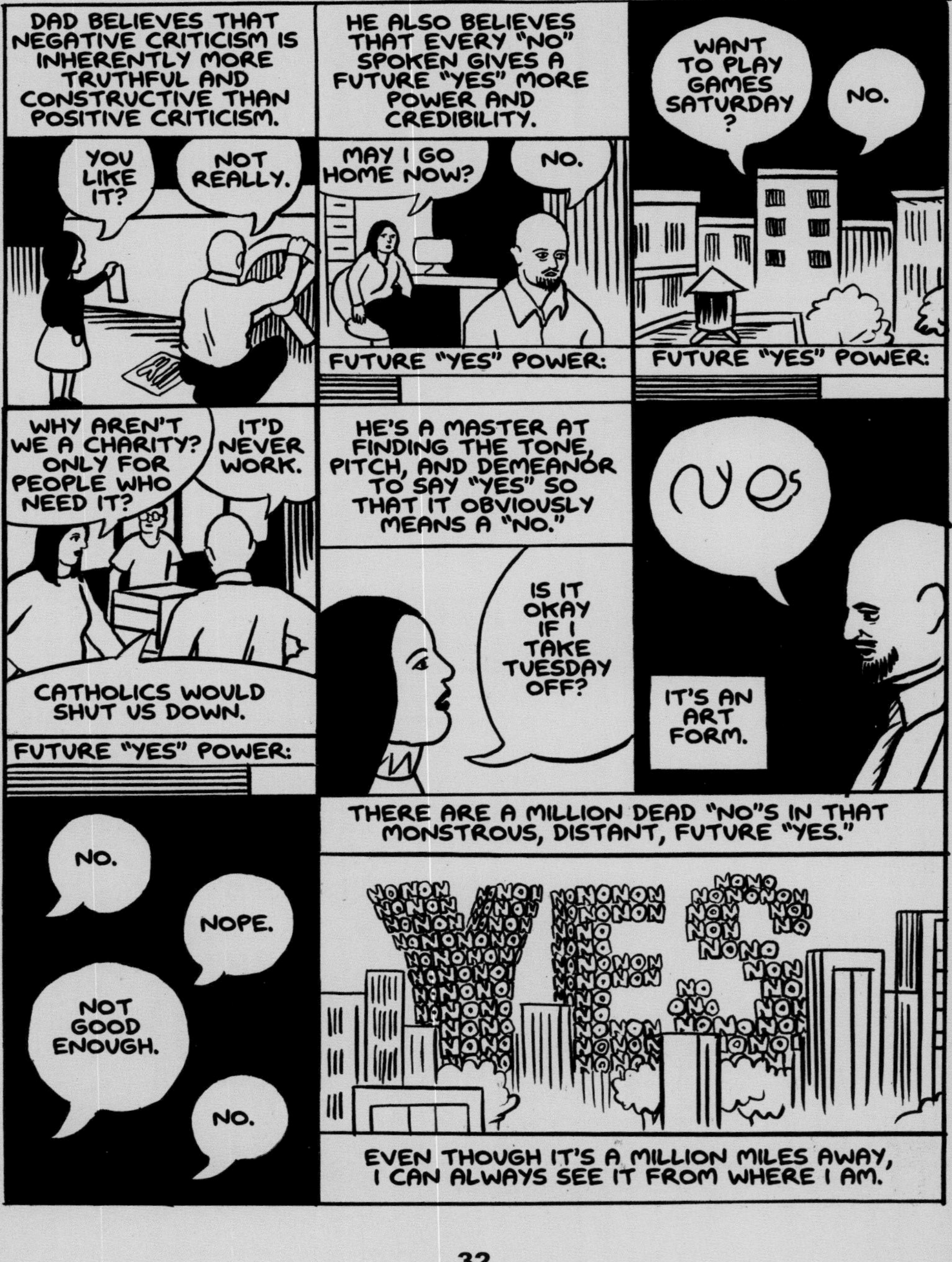
DAD BELIEVES THAT NEGATIVE CRITICISM IS INHERENTLY MORE TRUTHFUL AND CONSTRUCTIVE THAN POSITIVE CRITICISM.
YOU LIKE IT?
NOT REALLY.
HE ALSO BELIEVES THAT EVERY "NO" SPOKEN GIVES A FUTURE "YES" MORE POWER AND CREDIBILITY.
MAY I GO HOME NOW?
NO.
FUTURE "YES" POWER:
WANT TO PLAY GAMES SATURDAY ?
NO.
FUTURE "YES" POWER:
WHY AREN'T WE A CHARITY? ONLY FOR PEOPLE WHO NEED IT?
IT'D NEVER WORK.
CATHOLICS WOULD SHUT US DOWN.
FUTURE "YES" POWER:
HE'S A MASTER AT FINDING THE TONE, PITCH, AND DEMEANOR TO SAY "YES" SO THAT IT OBVIOUSLY MEANS A "NO."
IS IT OKAY IF I TAKE TUESDAY OFF?
IT'S AN ART FORM.
NO.
NOPE.
NOT GOOD ENOUGH.
NO.
THERE ARE A MILLION DEAD "NO"S IN THAT MONSTROUS, DISTANT, FUTURE "YES."
EVEN THOUGH IT'S A MILLION MILES AWAY, I CAN ALWAYS SEE IT FROM WHERE I AM.

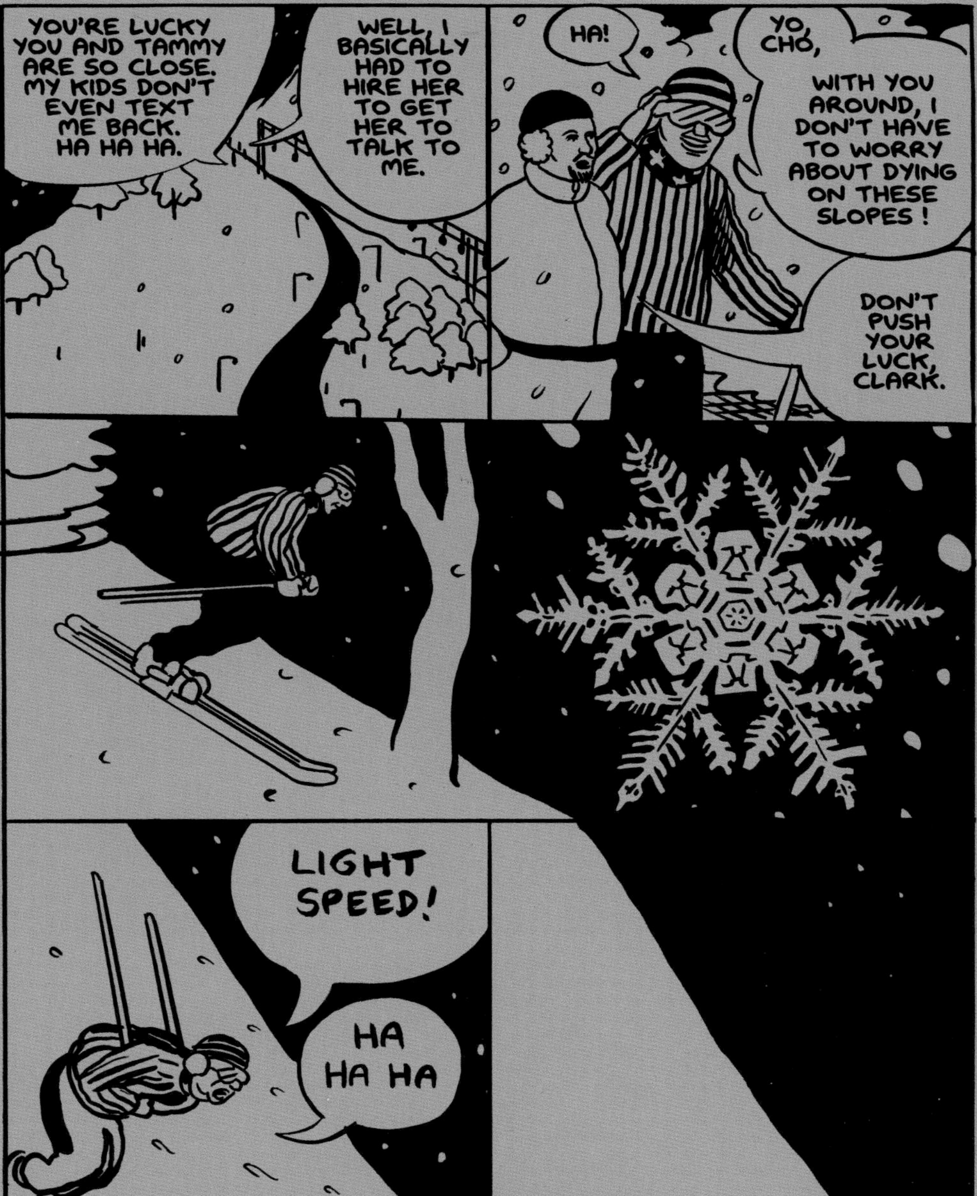
YOU'RE LUCKY YOU AND TAMMY ARE SO CLOSE. MY KIDS DON'T EVEN TEXT ME BACK. HA HA HA.
WELL, I BASICALLY HAD TO HIRE HER TO GET HER TO TALK TO ME.
HA!
YO, CHO,
WITH YOU AROUND, I DON'T HAVE TO WORRY ABOUT DYING ON THESE SLOPES!
DON'T PUSH YOUR LUCK, CLARK.
LIGHT SPEED!
HA HA HA

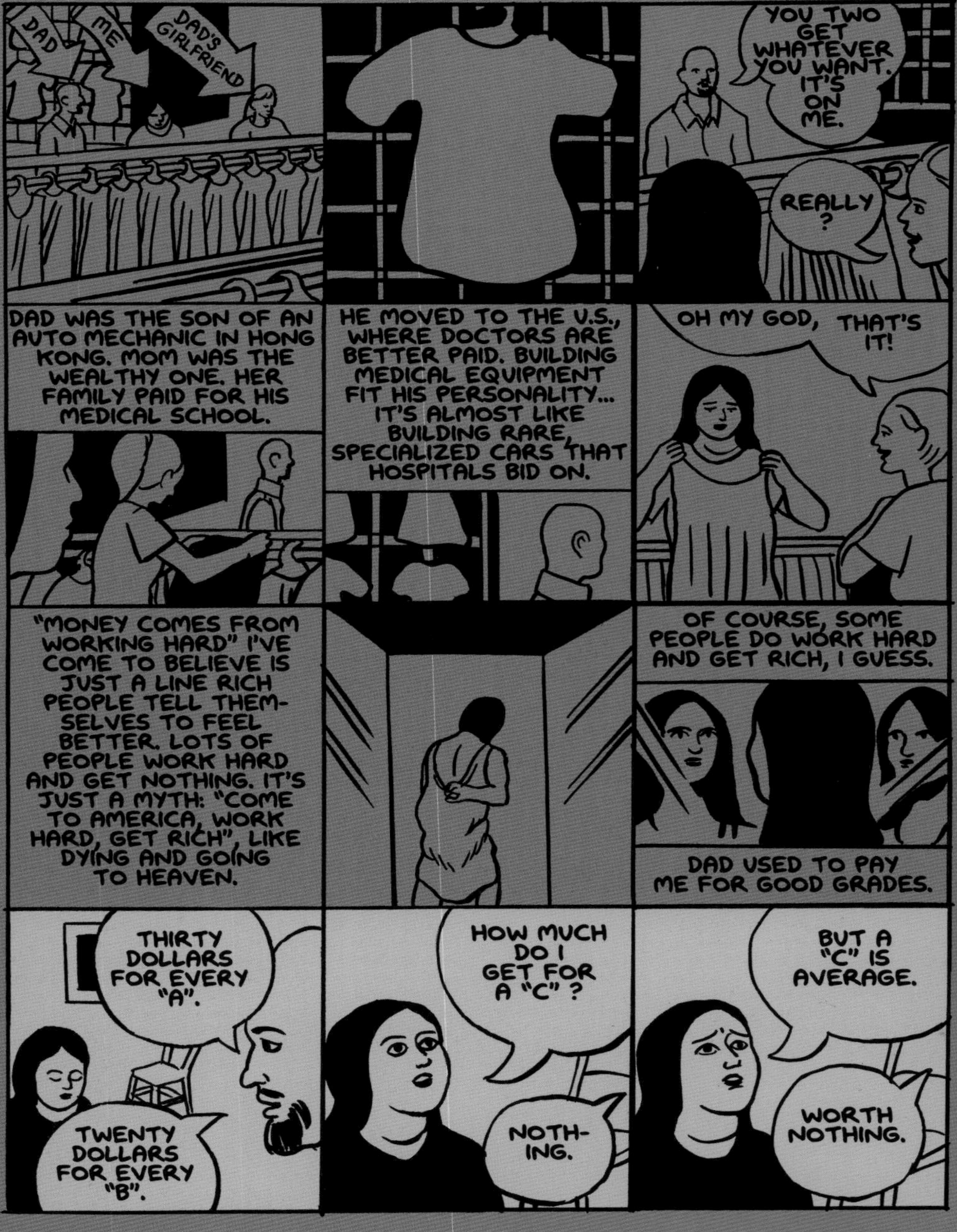
DAD
ME
DAD'S GIRLFRIEND
YOU TWO GET WHATEVER YOU WANT. IT'S ON ME.
REALLY?
DAD WAS THE SON OF AN AUTO MECHANIC IN HONG KONG. MOM WAS THE WEALTHY ONE. HER FAMILY PAID FOR HIS MEDICAL SCHOOL.
HE MOVED TO THE U.S., WHERE DOCTORS ARE BETTER PAID. BUILDING MEDICAL EQUIPMENT FIT HIS PERSONALITY... IT'S ALMOST LIKE BUILDING RARE, SPECIALIZED CARS THAT HOSPITALS BID ON.
OH MY GOD, THAT'S IT!
"MONEY COMES FROM WORKING HARD" I'VE COME TO BELIEVE IS JUST A LINE RICH PEOPLE TELL THEM-SELVES TO FEEL BETTER. LOTS OF PEOPLE WORK HARD AND GET NOTHING. IT'S JUST A MYTH: "COME TO AMERICA, WORK HARD, GET RICH", LIKE DYING AND GOING TO HEAVEN.
OF COURSE, SOME PEOPLE DO WORK HARD AND GET RICH, I GUESS.
DAD USED TO PAY ME FOR GOOD GRADES.
THIRTY DOLLARS FOR EVERY "A".
TWENTY DOLLARS FOR EVERY "B".
HOW MUCH DO I GET FOR A "C"?
NOTH-ING.
BUT A "C" IS AVERAGE.
WORTH NOTHING.

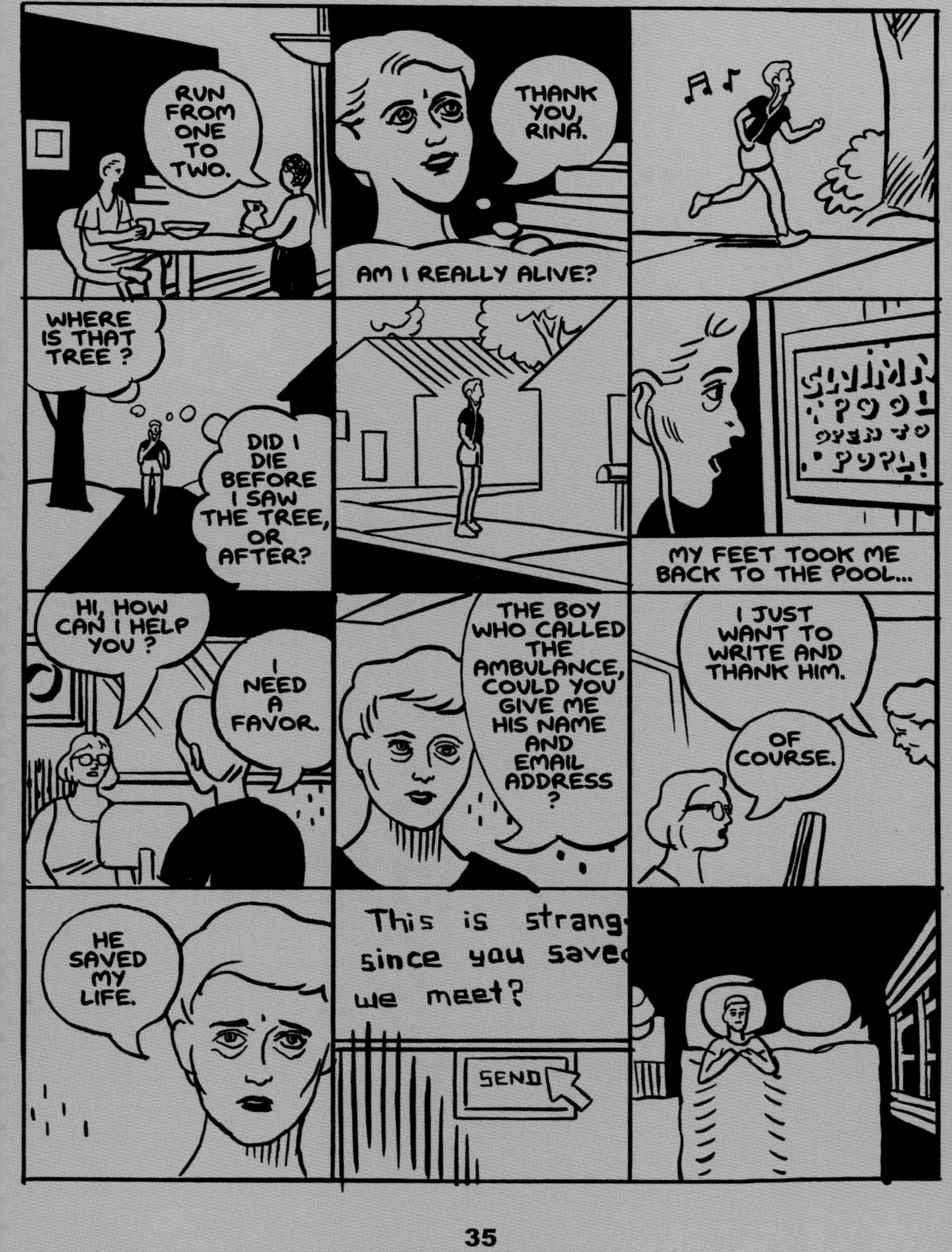
RUN FROM ONE TO TWO.
THANK YOU, RINA.
AM I REALLY ALIVE?
WHERE IS THAT TREE ?
DID I DIE BEFORE I SAW THE TREE, OR AFTER?
MY FEET TOOK ME BACK TO THE POOL...
HI, HOW CAN I HELP YOU ?
I NEED A FAVOR.
THE BOY WHO CALLED THE AMBULANCE, COULD YOU GIVE ME HIS NAME AND EMAIL ADDRESS ?
I JUST WANT TO WRITE AND THANK HIM.
OF COURSE.
HE SAVED MY LIFE.
This is strang
since you save
we meet?
SEND

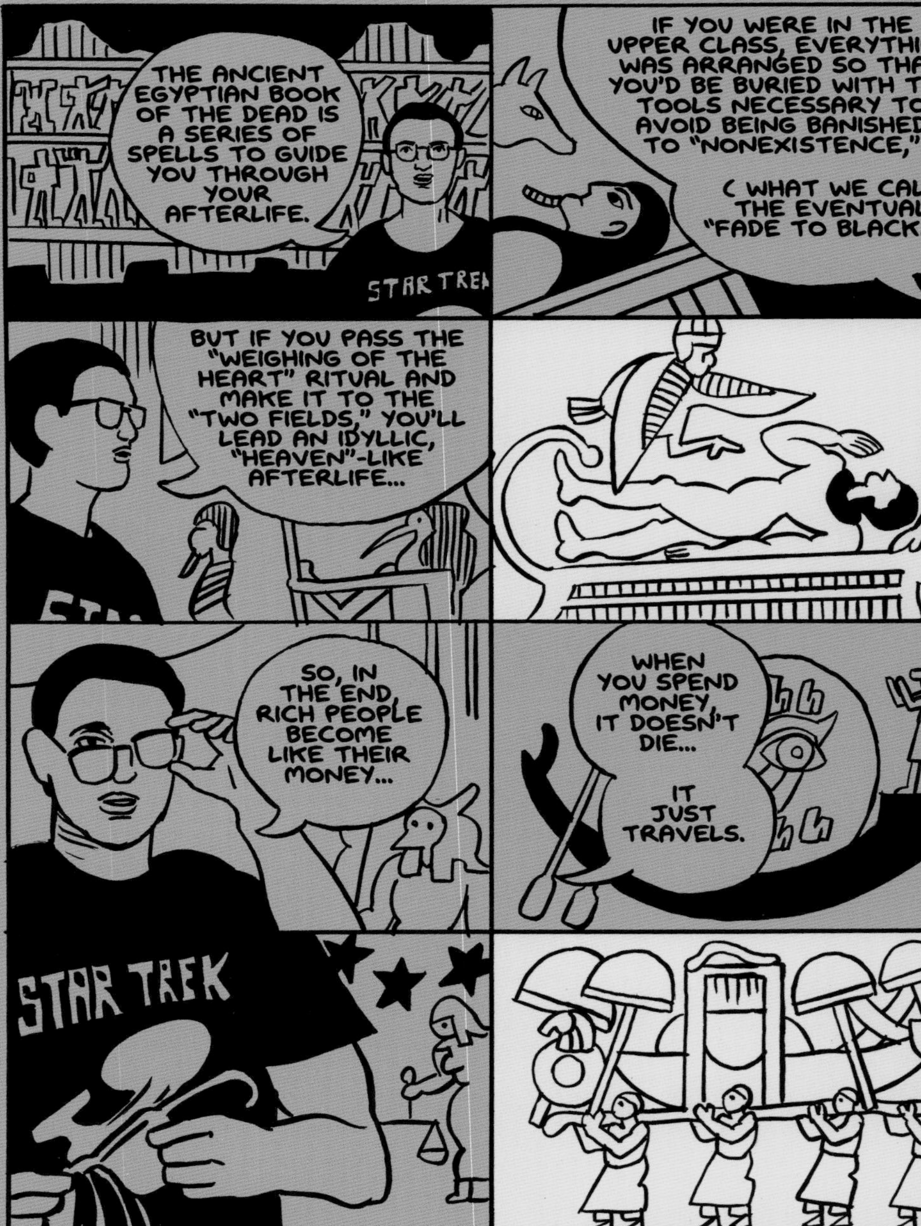
THE ANCIENT EGYPTIAN BOOK OF THE DEAD IS A SERIES OF SPELLS TO GUIDE YOU THROUGH YOUR AFTERLIFE.
STAR TREK
IF YOU WERE IN THE UPPER CLASS, EVERYTHING WAS ARRANGED SO THAT YOU'D BE BURIED WITH THE TOOLS NECESSARY TO AVOID BEING BANISHED TO "NONEXISTENCE,"
(WHAT WE CALL THE EVENTUAL "FADE TO BLACK.")
BUT IF YOU PASS THE "WEIGHING OF THE HEART" RITUAL AND MAKE IT TO THE "TWO FIELDS," YOU'LL LEAD AN IDYLLIC, "HEAVEN"-LIKE AFTERLIFE...
SO, IN THE END, RICH PEOPLE BECOME LIKE THEIR MONEY...
WHEN YOU SPEND MONEY, IT DOESN'T DIE...
IT JUST TRAVELS.
STAR TREK

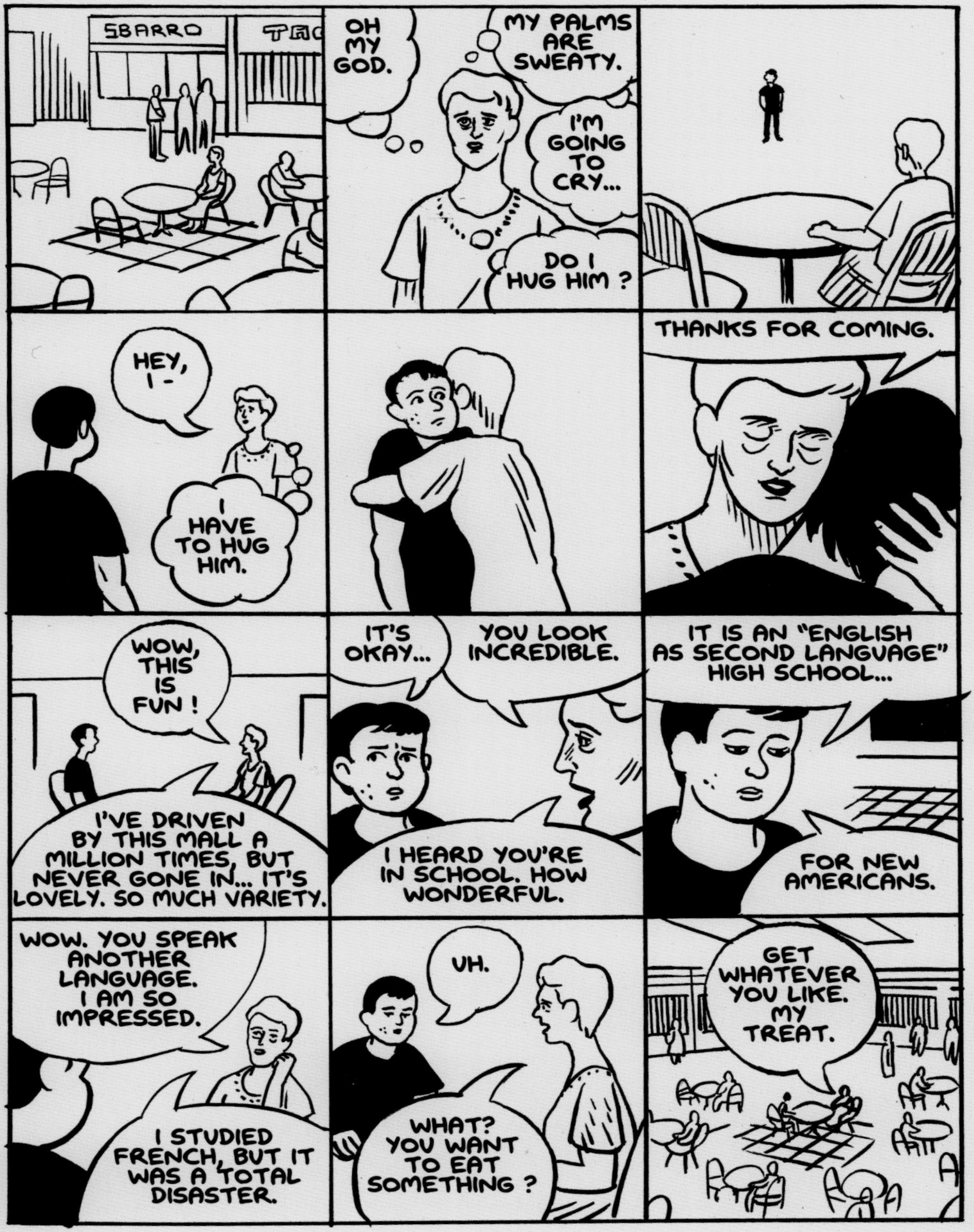
SBARRO
OH MY GOD.
MY PALMS ARE SWEATY.
I'M GOING TO CRY...
DO I HUG HIM ?
HEY, I -
I HAVE TO HUG HIM.
THANKS FOR COMING.
WOW, THIS IS FUN !
I'VE DRIVEN BY THIS MALL A MILLION TIMES, BUT NEVER GONE IN... IT'S LOVELY. SO MUCH VARIETY.
IT'S OKAY...
YOU LOOK INCREDIBLE.
I HEARD YOU'RE IN SCHOOL. HOW WONDERFUL.
IT IS AN "ENGLISH AS SECOND LANGUAGE" HIGH SCHOOL...
FOR NEW AMERICANS.
WOW. YOU SPEAK ANOTHER LANGUAGE. I AM SO IMPRESSED.
I STUDIED FRENCH, BUT IT WAS A TOTAL DISASTER.
UH.
WHAT? YOU WANT TO EAT SOMETHING ?
GET WHATEVER YOU LIKE. MY TREAT.

AM I LIKE MISS BELL? DRIFTING THROUGH LIFE, ALONE, WAITING TO DIE?

NO.

I'M LIKE A MAGICIAN.

OUR WORK IS GOING TO BE FAMOUS AND STUDIED FOR CENTURIES.

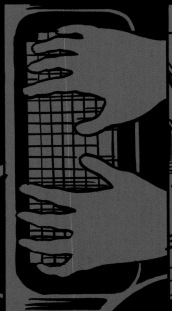

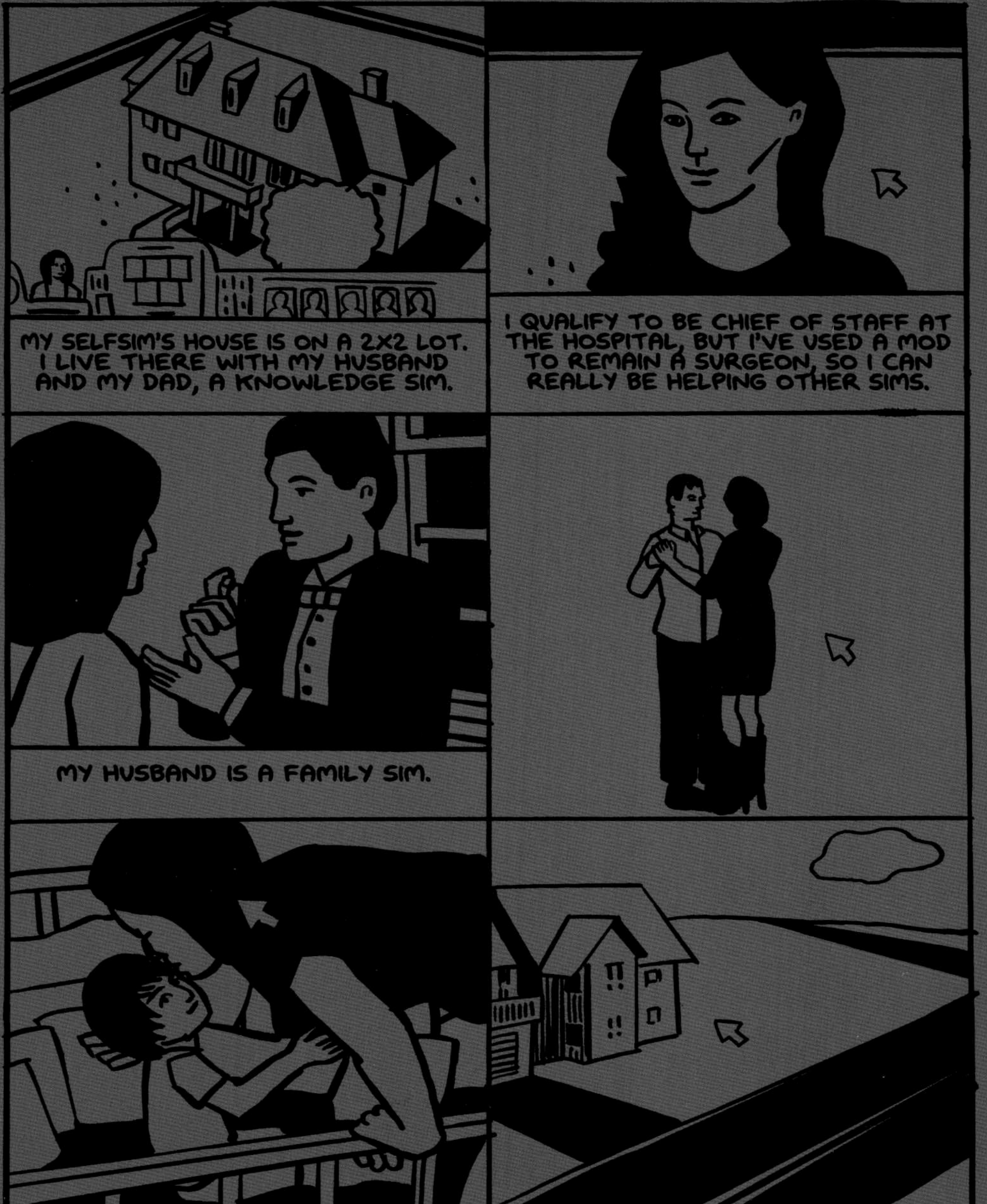
MY SELFSIM'S HOUSE IS ON A 2X2 LOT. I LIVE THERE WITH MY HUSBAND AND MY DAD, A KNOWLEDGE SIM.
I QUALIFY TO BE CHIEF OF STAFF AT THE HOSPITAL, BUT I'VE USED A MOD TO REMAIN A SURGEON, SO I CAN REALLY BE HELPING OTHER SIMS.
MY HUSBAND IS A FAMILY SIM.

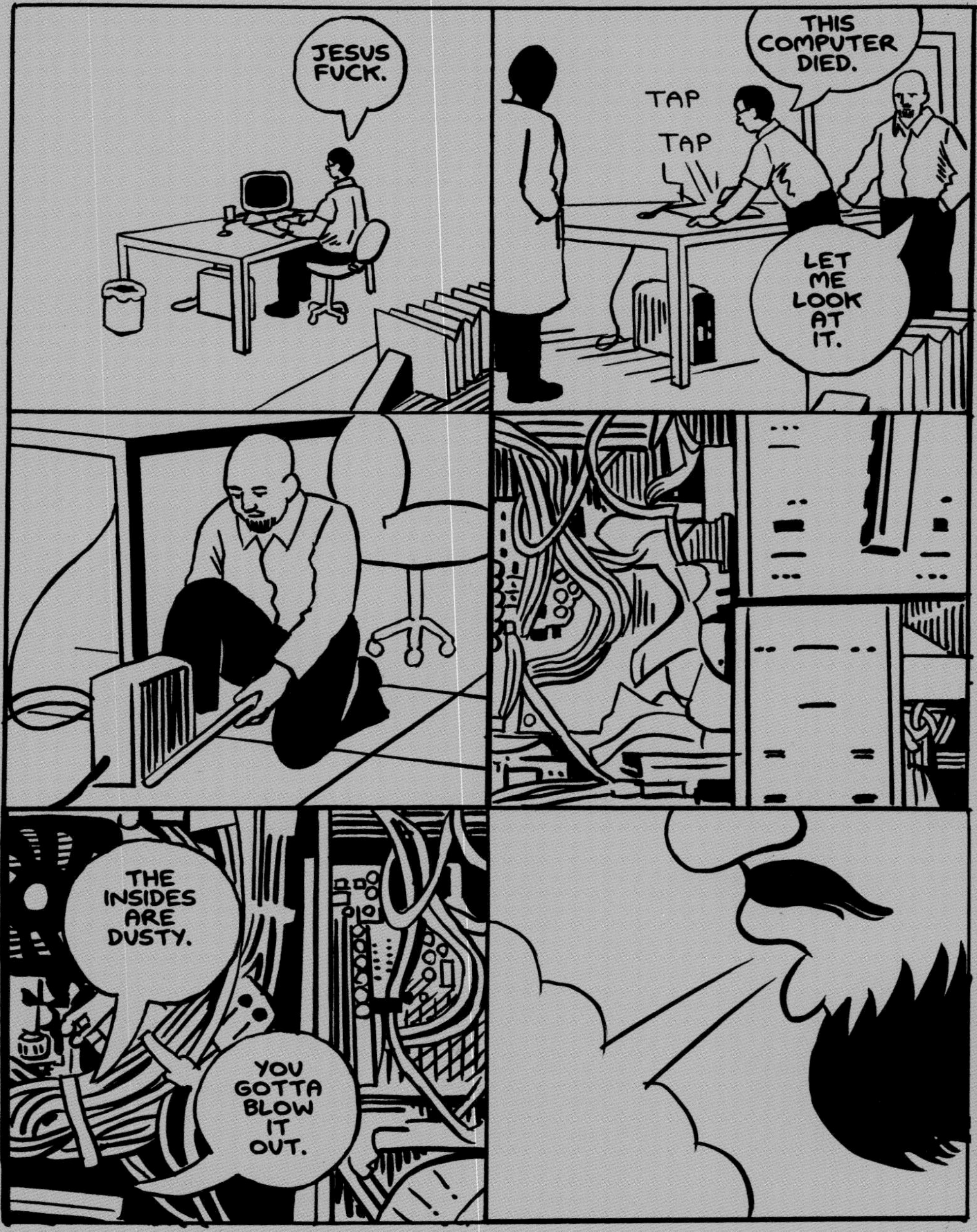
JESUS FUCK.
TAP
TAP
THIS COMPUTER DIED.
LET ME LOOK AT IT.
THE INSIDES ARE DUSTY.
YOU GOTTA BLOW IT OUT.

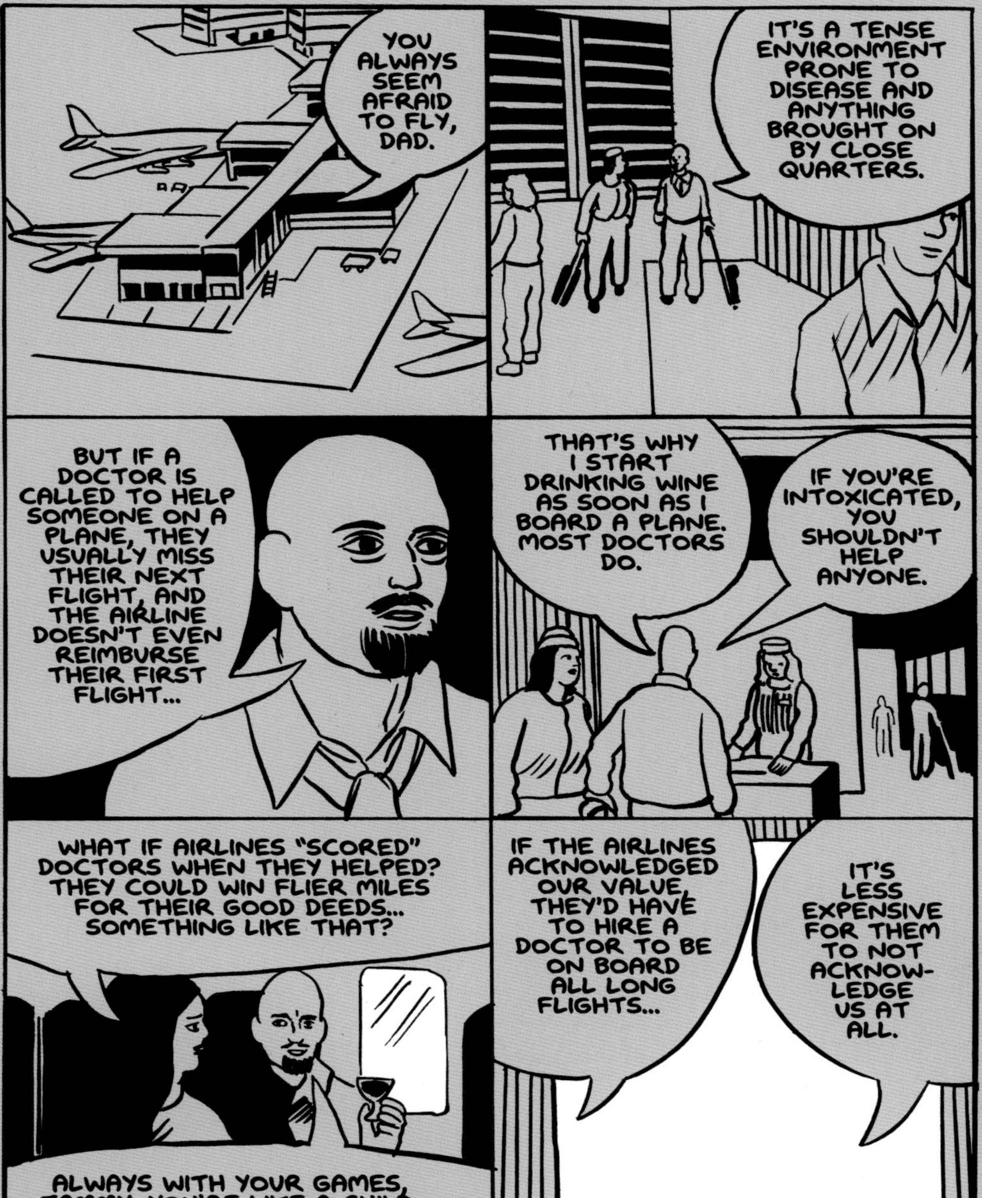
YOU ALWAYS SEEM AFRAID TO FLY, DAD.
IT'S A TENSE ENVIRONMENT PRONE TO DISEASE AND ANYTHING BROUGHT ON BY CLOSE QUARTERS.
BUT IF A DOCTOR IS CALLED TO HELP SOMEONE ON A PLANE, THEY USUALLY MISS THEIR NEXT FLIGHT, AND THE AIRLINE DOESN'T EVEN REIMBURSE THEIR FIRST FLIGHT...
THAT'S WHY I START DRINKING WINE AS SOON AS I BOARD A PLANE. MOST DOCTORS DO.
IF YOU'RE INTOXICATED, YOU SHOULDN'T HELP ANYONE.
WHAT IF AIRLINES "SCORED" DOCTORS WHEN THEY HELPED? THEY COULD WIN FLIER MILES FOR THEIR GOOD DEEDS... SOMETHING LIKE THAT?
ALWAYS WITH YOUR GAMES, TAMMY. YOU'RE LIKE A CHILD.
IF THE AIRLINES ACKNOWLEDGED OUR VALUE, THEY'D HAVE TO HIRE A DOCTOR TO BE ON BOARD ALL LONG FLIGHTS...
IT'S LESS EXPENSIVE FOR THEM TO NOT ACKNOW-LEDGE US AT ALL.

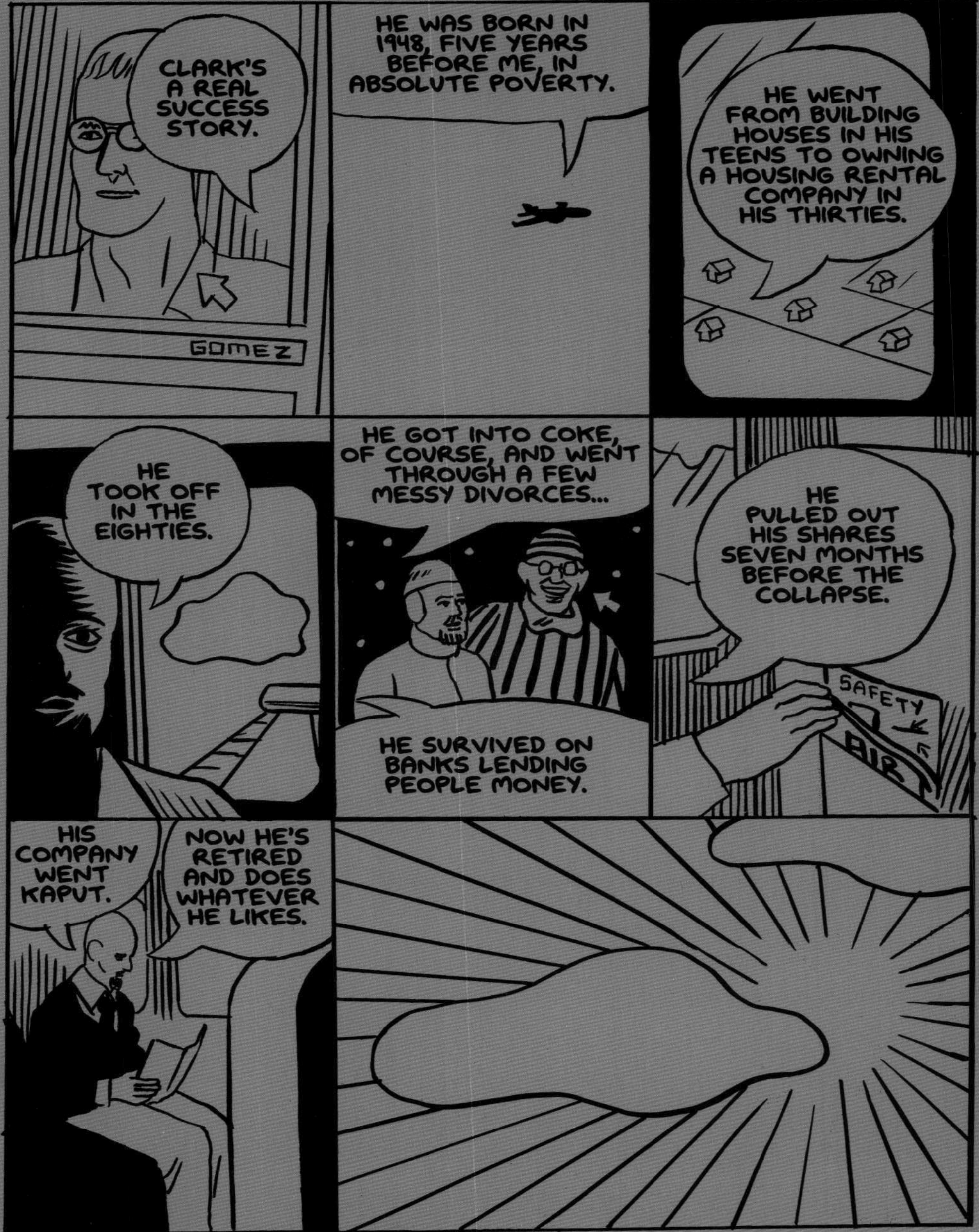
CLARK'S A REAL SUCCESS STORY.
GOMEZ
HE WAS BORN IN 1948, FIVE YEARS BEFORE ME, IN ABSOLUTE POVERTY.
HE WENT FROM BUILDING HOUSES IN HIS TEENS TO OWNING A HOUSING RENTAL COMPANY IN HIS THIRTIES.
HE TOOK OFF IN THE EIGHTIES.
HE GOT INTO COKE, OF COURSE, AND WENT THROUGH A FEW MESSY DIVORCES...
HE SURVIVED ON BANKS LENDING PEOPLE MONEY.
HE PULLED OUT HIS SHARES SEVEN MONTHS BEFORE THE COLLAPSE.
SAFETY
AIR
HIS COMPANY WENT KAPUT.
NOW HE'S RETIRED AND DOES WHATEVER HE LIKES.

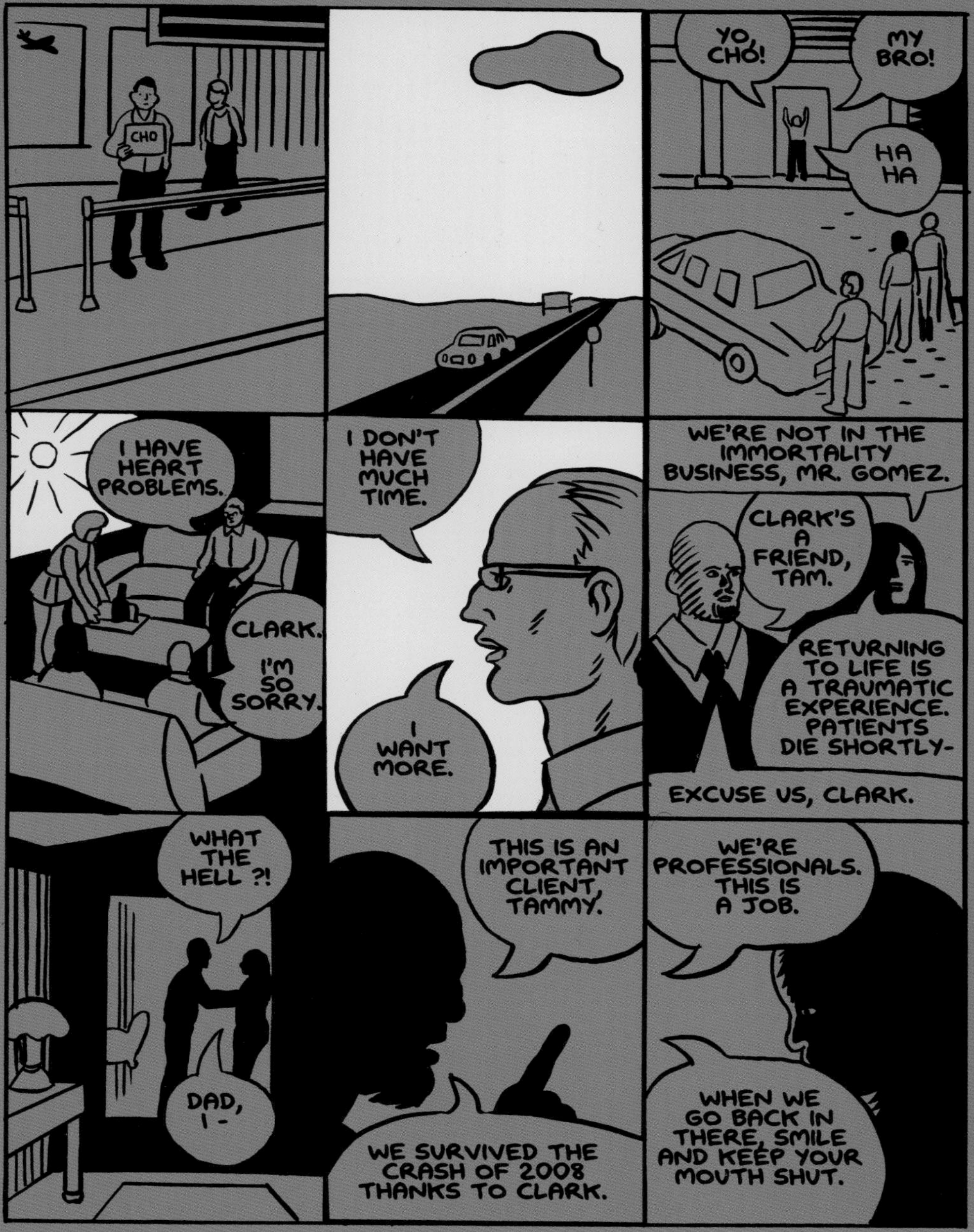
CHO
YO, CHO!
MY BRO!
HA HA
I HAVE HEART PROBLEMS.
CLARK.
I'M SO SORRY.
I DON'T HAVE MUCH TIME.
I WANT MORE.
WE'RE NOT IN THE IMMORTALITY BUSINESS, MR. GOMEZ.
CLARK'S A FRIEND, TAM.
RETURNING TO LIFE IS A TRAUMATIC EXPERIENCE. PATIENTS DIE SHORTLY-
EXCUSE US, CLARK.
WHAT THE HELL ?!
DAD, I -
THIS IS AN IMPORTANT CLIENT, TAMMY.
WE SURVIVED THE CRASH OF 2008 THANKS TO CLARK.
WE'RE PROFESSIONALS. THIS IS A JOB.
WHEN WE GO BACK IN THERE, SMILE AND KEEP YOUR MOUTH SHUT.

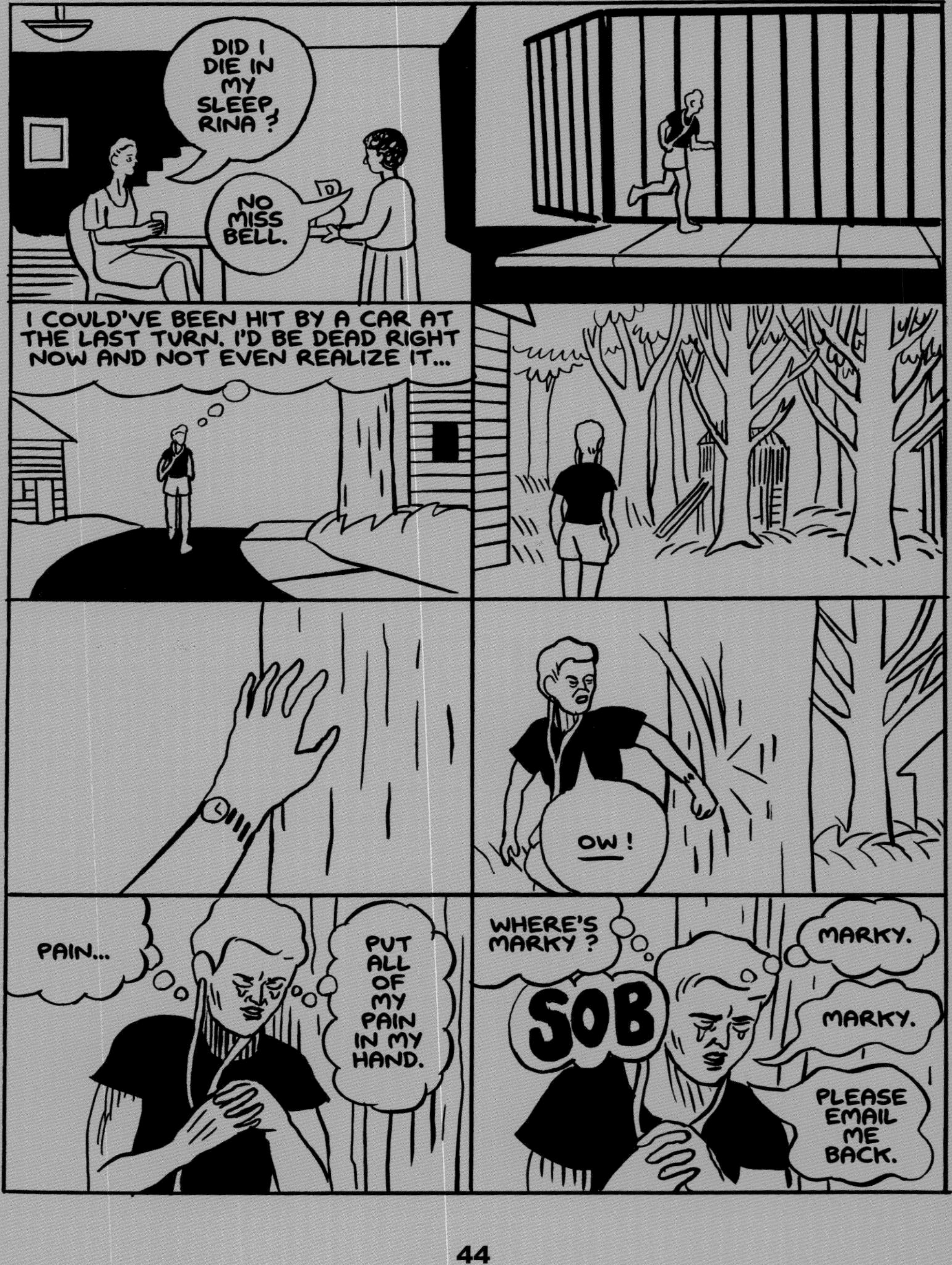
DID I DIE IN MY SLEEP, RINA ?
NO MISS BELL.
I COULD'VE BEEN HIT BY A CAR AT THE LAST TURN. I'D BE DEAD RIGHT NOW AND NOT EVEN REALIZE IT...
OW !
PAIN...
PUT ALL OF MY PAIN IN MY HAND.
WHERE'S MARKY ?
SOB
MARKY.
MARKY.
PLEASE EMAIL ME BACK.

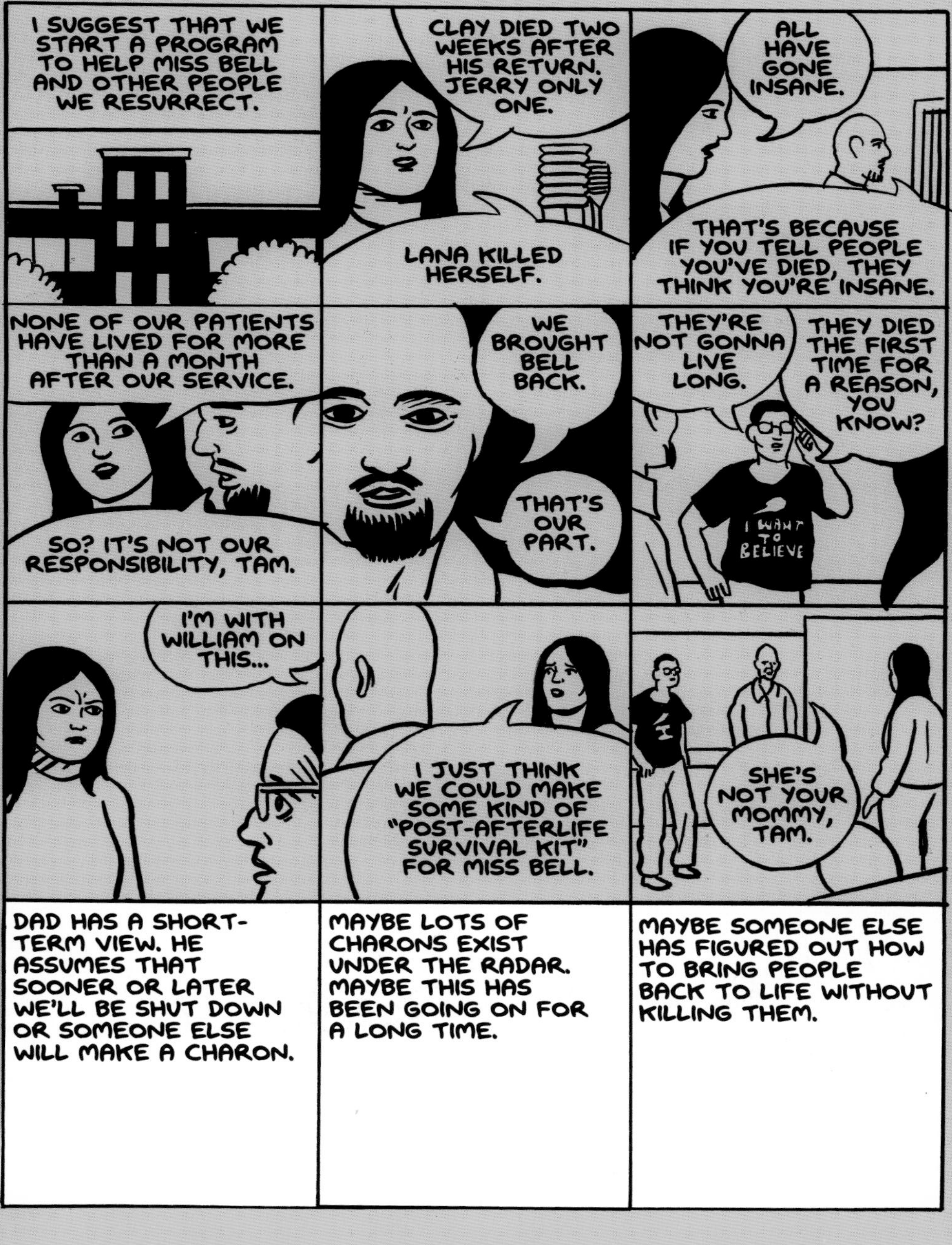
I SUGGEST THAT WE START A PROGRAM TO HELP MISS BELL AND OTHER PEOPLE WE RESURRECT.
CLAY DIED TWO WEEKS AFTER HIS RETURN. JERRY ONLY ONE.
LANA KILLED HERSELF.
ALL HAVE GONE INSANE.
THAT'S BECAUSE IF YOU TELL PEOPLE YOU'VE DIED, THEY THINK YOU'RE INSANE.
NONE OF OUR PATIENTS HAVE LIVED FOR MORE THAN A MONTH AFTER OUR SERVICE.
SO? IT'S NOT OUR RESPONSIBILITY, TAM.
WE BROUGHT BELL BACK.
THAT'S OUR PART.
THEY'RE NOT GONNA LIVE LONG.
THEY DIED THE FIRST TIME FOR A REASON, YOU KNOW?
I WANT TO BELIEVE
I'M WITH WILLIAM ON THIS...
I JUST THINK WE COULD MAKE SOME KIND OF "POST-AFTERLIFE SURVIVAL KIT" FOR MISS BELL.
SHE'S NOT YOUR MOMMY, TAM.
DAD HAS A SHORT-TERM VIEW. HE ASSUMES THAT SOONER OR LATER WE'LL BE SHUT DOWN OR SOMEONE ELSE WILL MAKE A CHARON.
MAYBE LOTS OF CHARONS EXIST UNDER THE RADAR. MAYBE THIS HAS BEEN GOING ON FOR A LONG TIME.
MAYBE SOMEONE ELSE HAS FIGURED OUT HOW TO BRING PEOPLE BACK TO LIFE WITHOUT KILLING THEM.

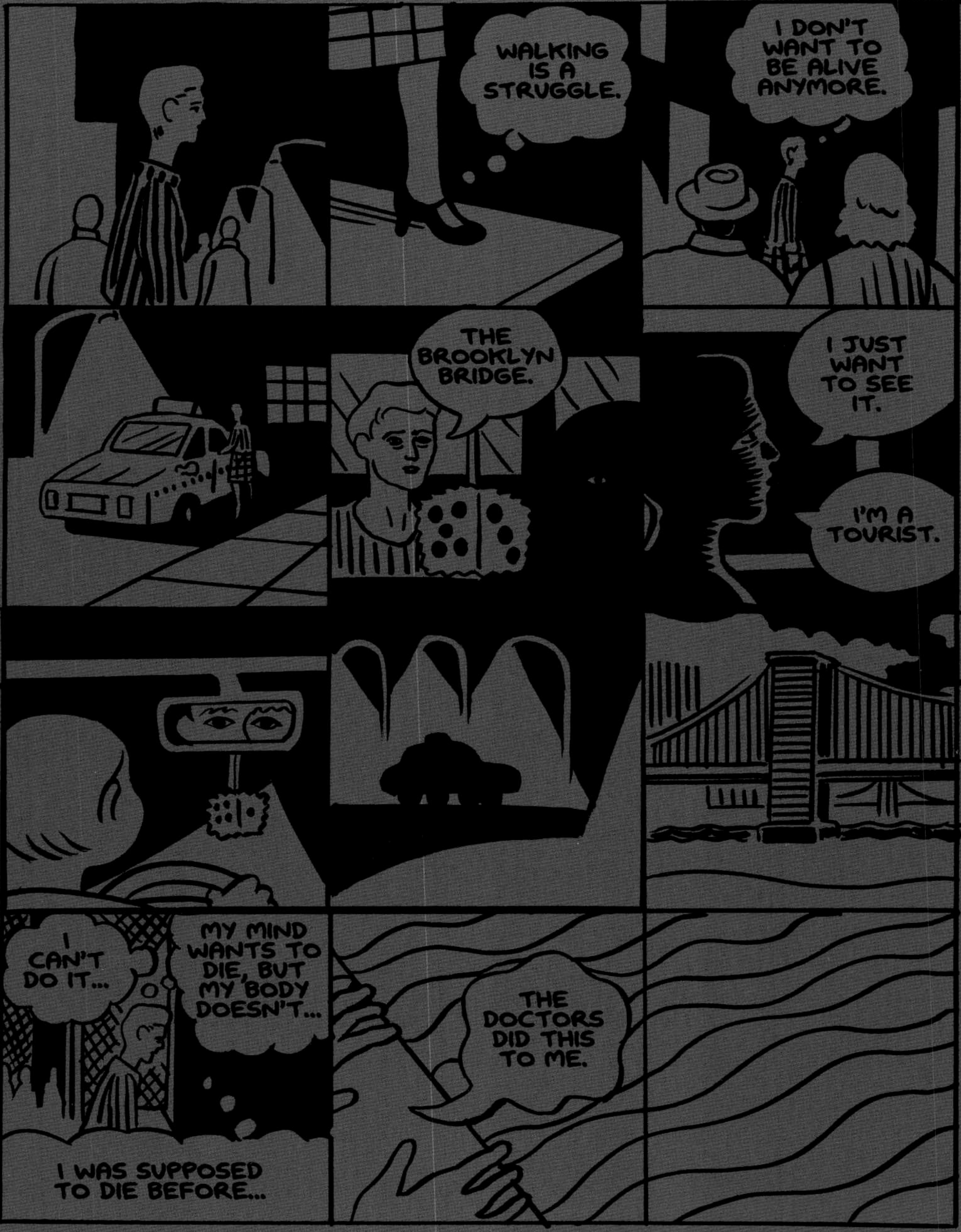
WALKING IS A STRUGGLE.
I DON'T WANT TO BE ALIVE ANYMORE.
THE BROOKLYN BRIDGE.
I JUST WANT TO SEE IT.
I'M A TOURIST.
I CAN'T DO IT...
MY MIND WANTS TO DIE, BUT MY BODY DOESN'T...
I WAS SUPPOSED TO DIE BEFORE...
THE DOCTORS DID THIS TO ME.

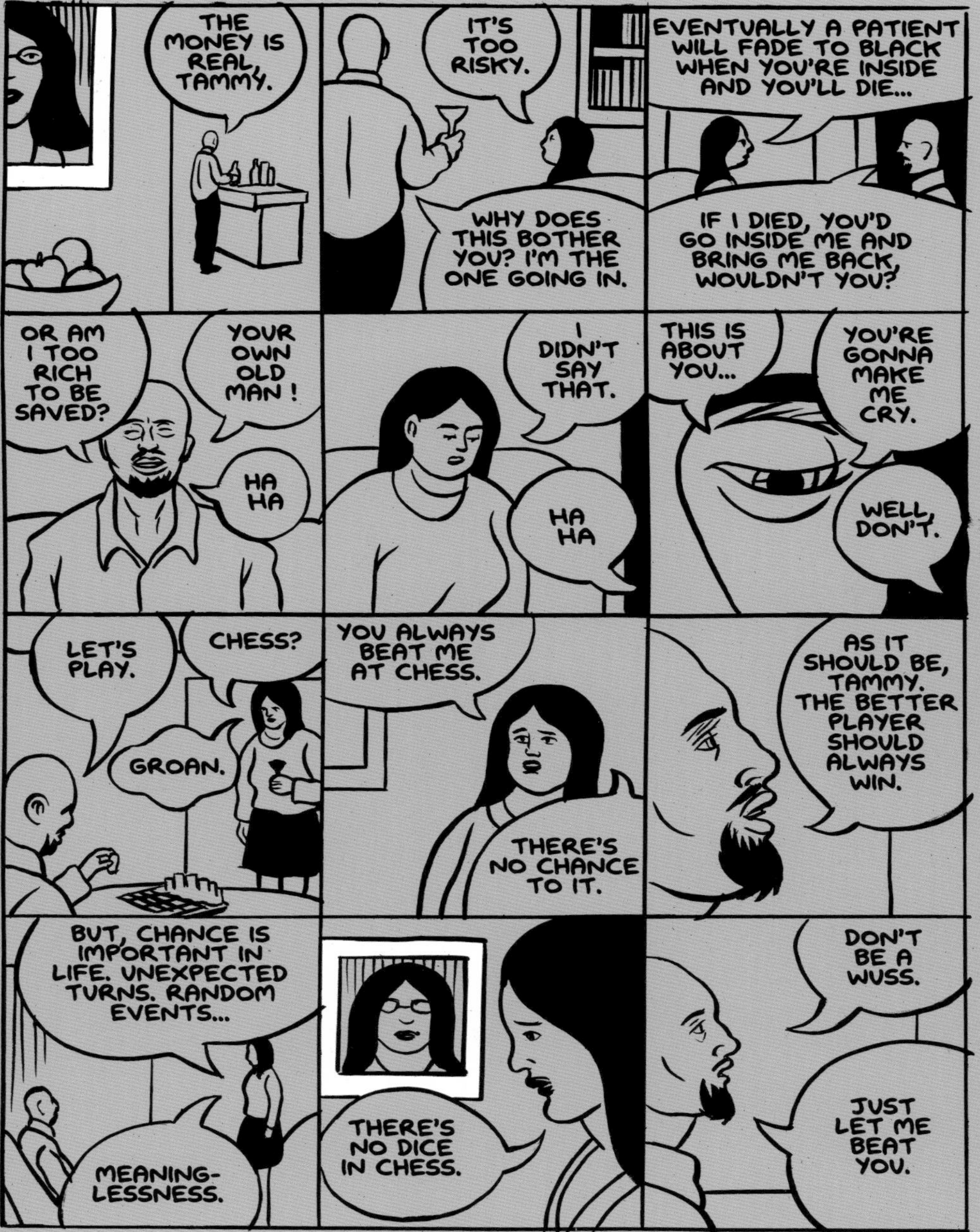
THE MONEY IS REAL, TAMMY.
IT'S TOO RISKY.
WHY DOES THIS BOTHER YOU? I'M THE ONE GOING IN.
EVENTUALLY A PATIENT WILL FADE TO BLACK WHEN YOU'RE INSIDE AND YOU'LL DIE...
IF I DIED, YOU'D GO INSIDE ME AND BRING ME BACK, WOULDN'T YOU?
OR AM I TOO RICH TO BE SAVED?
YOUR OWN OLD MAN !
HA HA
I DIDN'T SAY THAT.
HA HA
THIS IS ABOUT YOU...
YOU'RE GONNA MAKE ME CRY.
WELL, DON'T.
LET'S PLAY.
CHESS?
GROAN.
YOU ALWAYS BEAT ME AT CHESS.
THERE'S NO CHANCE TO IT.
AS IT SHOULD BE, TAMMY. THE BETTER PLAYER SHOULD ALWAYS WIN.
BUT, CHANCE IS IMPORTANT IN LIFE. UNEXPECTED TURNS. RANDOM EVENTS...
MEANING-LESSNESS.
THERE'S NO DICE IN CHESS.
DON'T BE A WUSS.
JUST LET ME BEAT YOU.

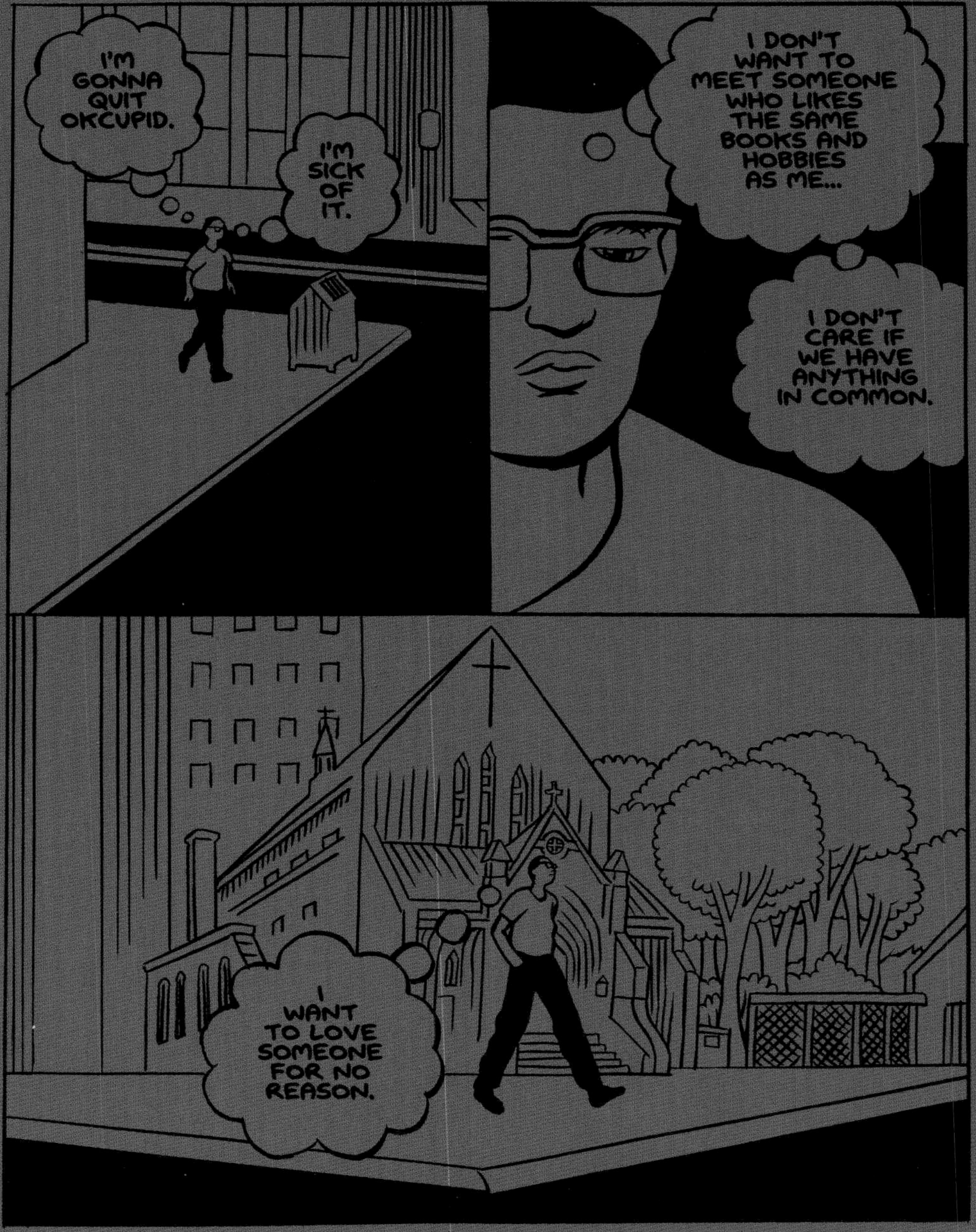
I'M GONNA QUIT OKCUPID.
I'M SICK OF IT.
I DON'T WANT TO MEET SOMEONE WHO LIKES THE SAME BOOKS AND HOBBIES AS ME...
I DON'T CARE IF WE HAVE ANYTHING IN COMMON.
I WANT TO LOVE SOMEONE FOR NO REASON.

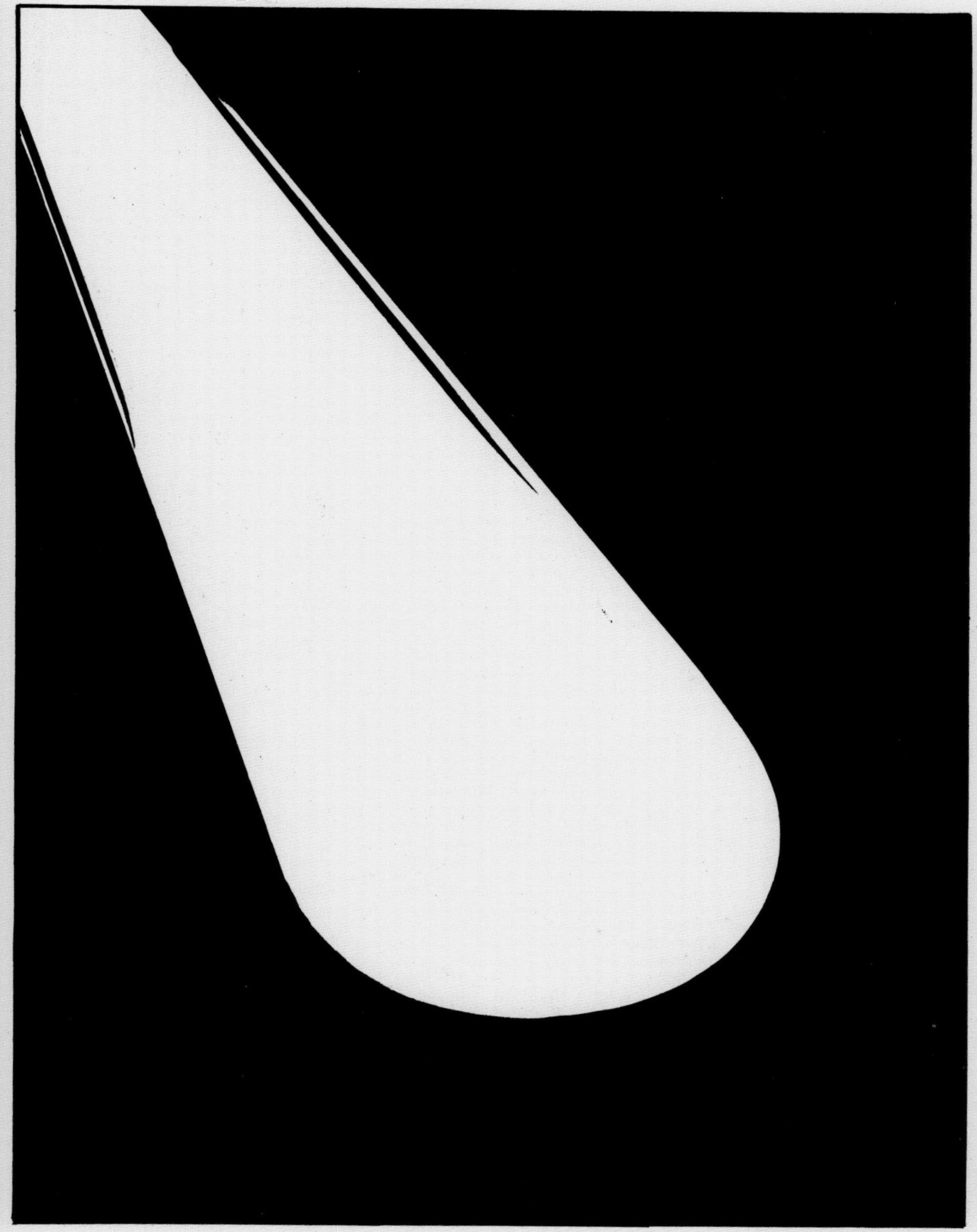

ON THE WAY TO WORK

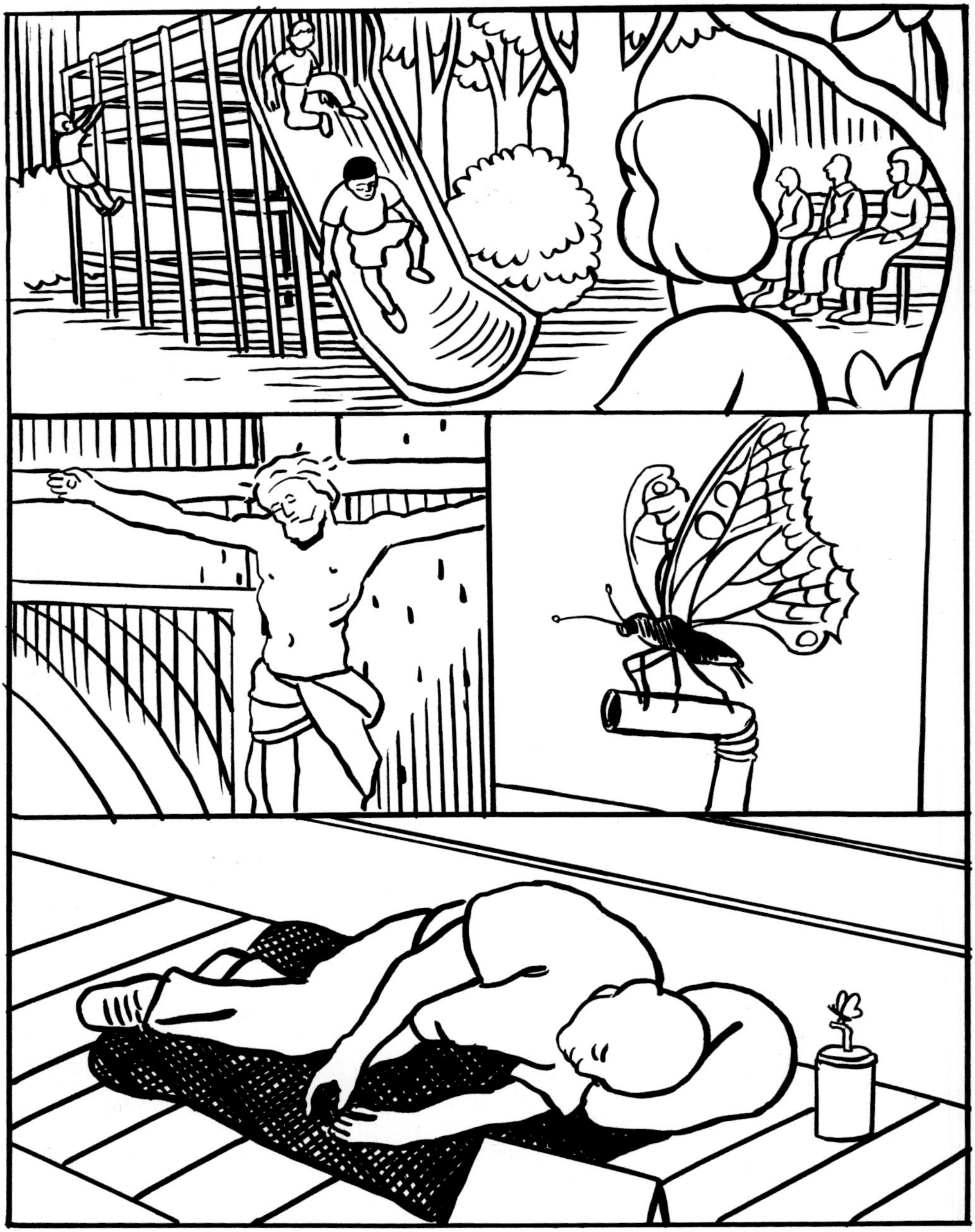

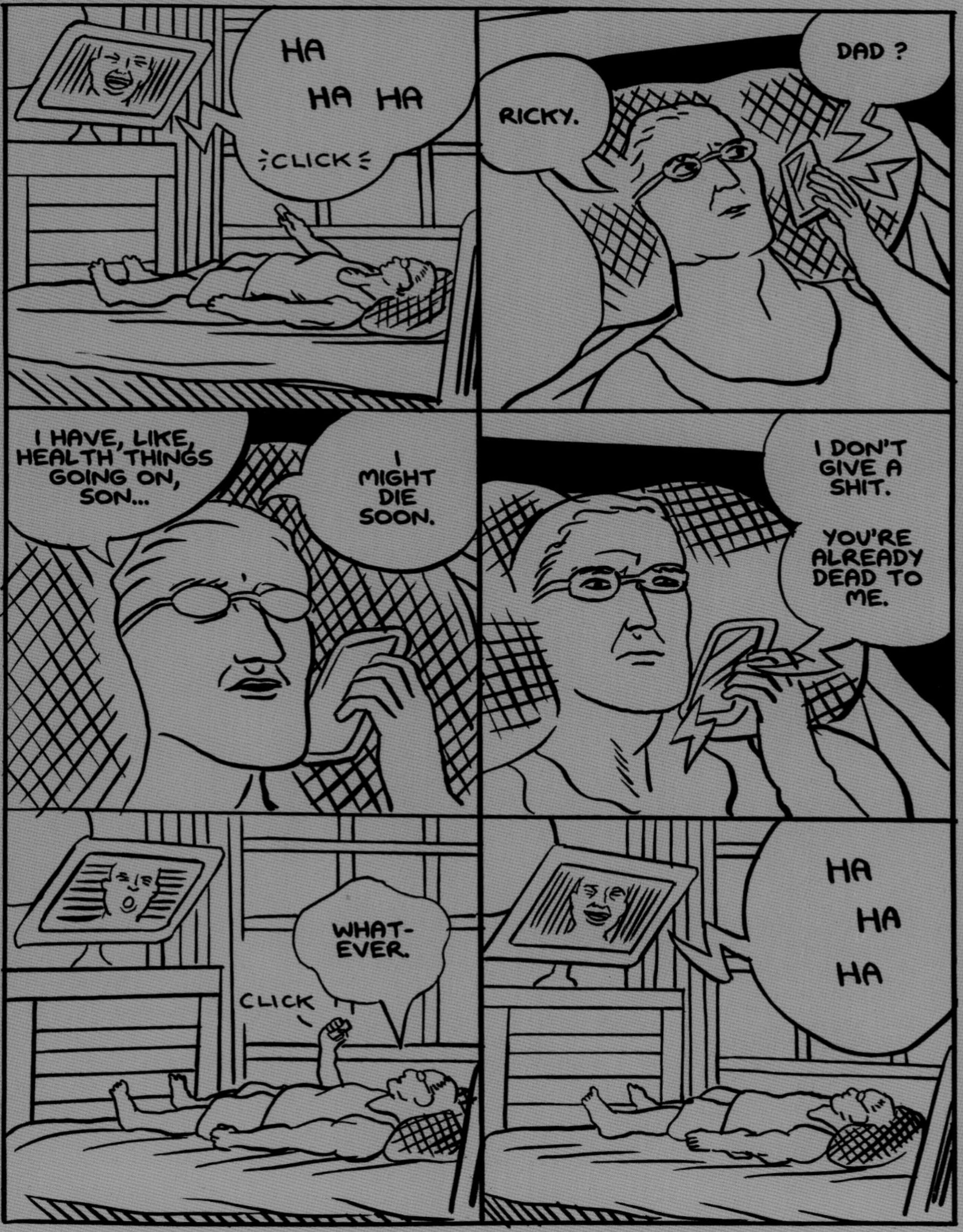
HA
HA HA
CLICK
DAD ?
RICKY.
I HAVE, LIKE, HEALTH THINGS GOING ON, SON...
I MIGHT DIE SOON.
I DON'T GIVE A SHIT.
YOU'RE ALREADY DEAD TO ME.
WHAT-EVER.
CLICK
HA
HA
HA

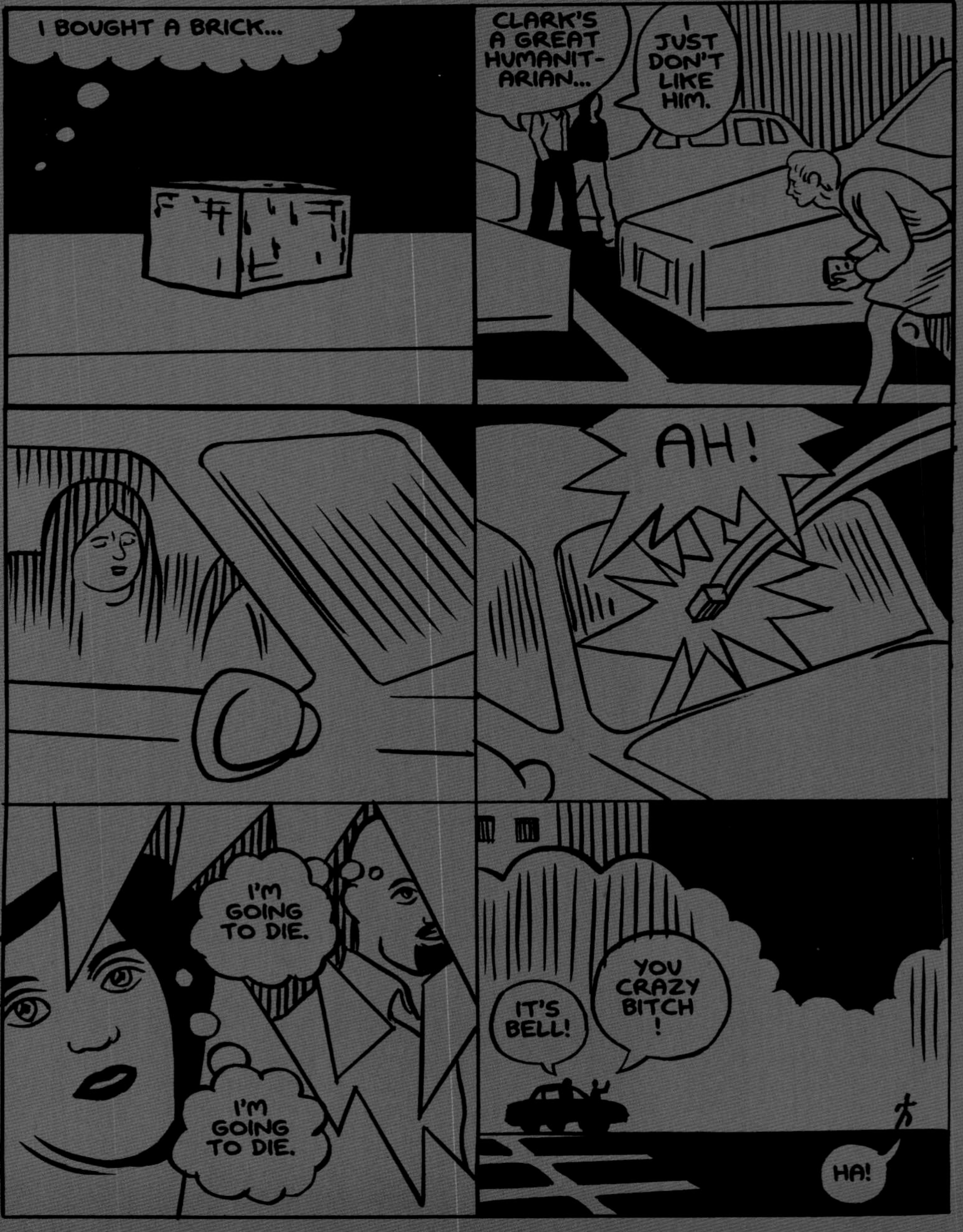
I BOUGHT A BRICK...
CLARK'S A GREAT HUMANIT-ARIAN...
I JUST DON'T LIKE HIM.
AH!
I'M GOING TO DIE.
I'M GOING TO DIE.
IT'S BELL!
YOU CRAZY BITCH!
HA!

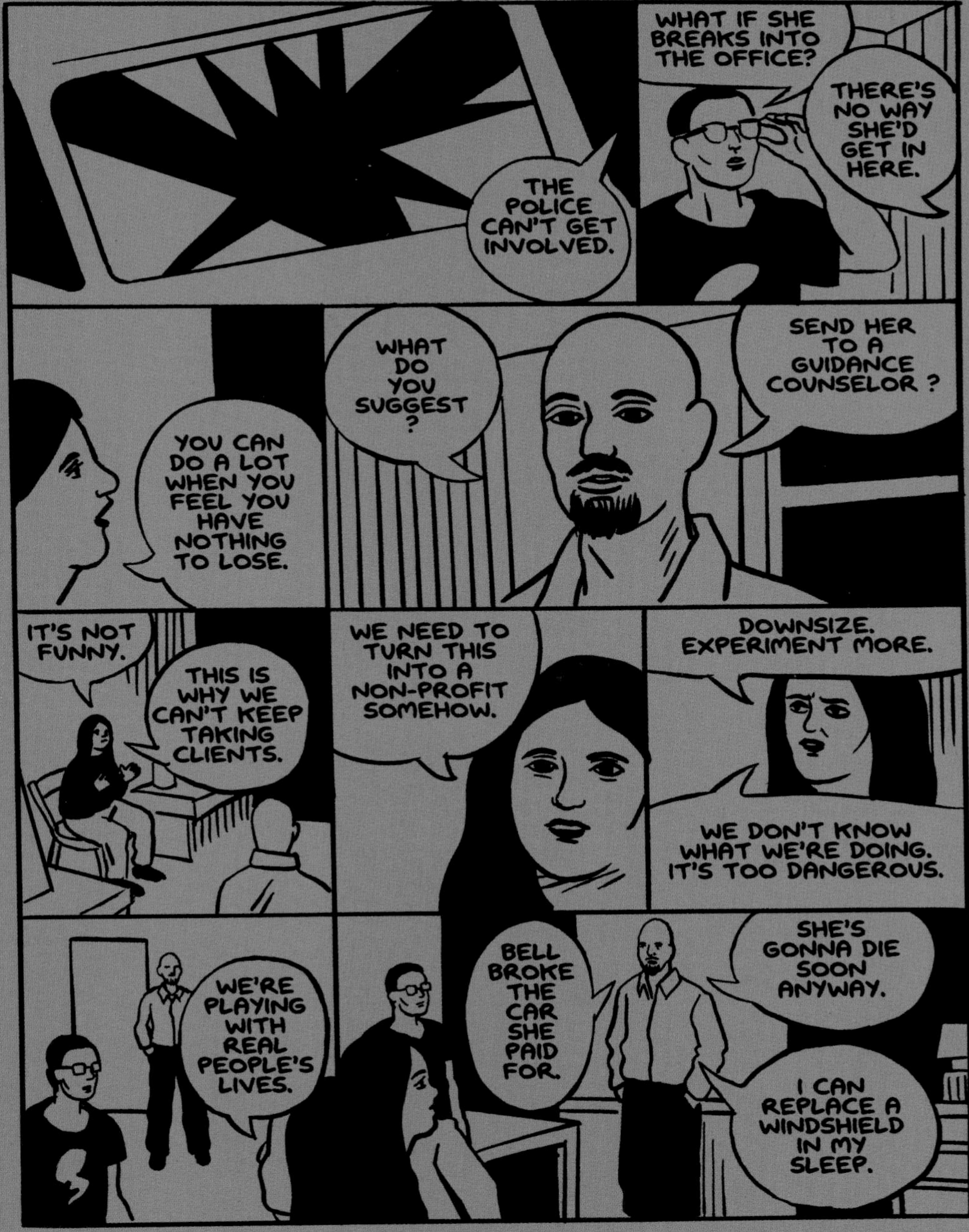

THE POLICE CAN'T GET INVOLVED.
WHAT IF SHE BREAKS INTO THE OFFICE?
THERE'S NO WAY SHE'D GET IN HERE.
YOU CAN DO A LOT WHEN YOU FEEL YOU HAVE NOTHING TO LOSE.
WHAT DO YOU SUGGEST ?
SEND HER TO A GUIDANCE COUNSELOR ?
IT'S NOT FUNNY.
THIS IS WHY WE CAN'T KEEP TAKING CLIENTS.
WE NEED TO TURN THIS INTO A NON-PROFIT SOMEHOW.
DOWNSIZE. EXPERIMENT MORE.
WE DON'T KNOW WHAT WE'RE DOING. IT'S TOO DANGEROUS.
WE'RE PLAYING WITH REAL PEOPLE'S LIVES.
BELL BROKE THE CAR SHE PAID FOR.
SHE'S GONNA DIE SOON ANYWAY.
I CAN REPLACE A WINDSHIELD IN MY SLEEP.

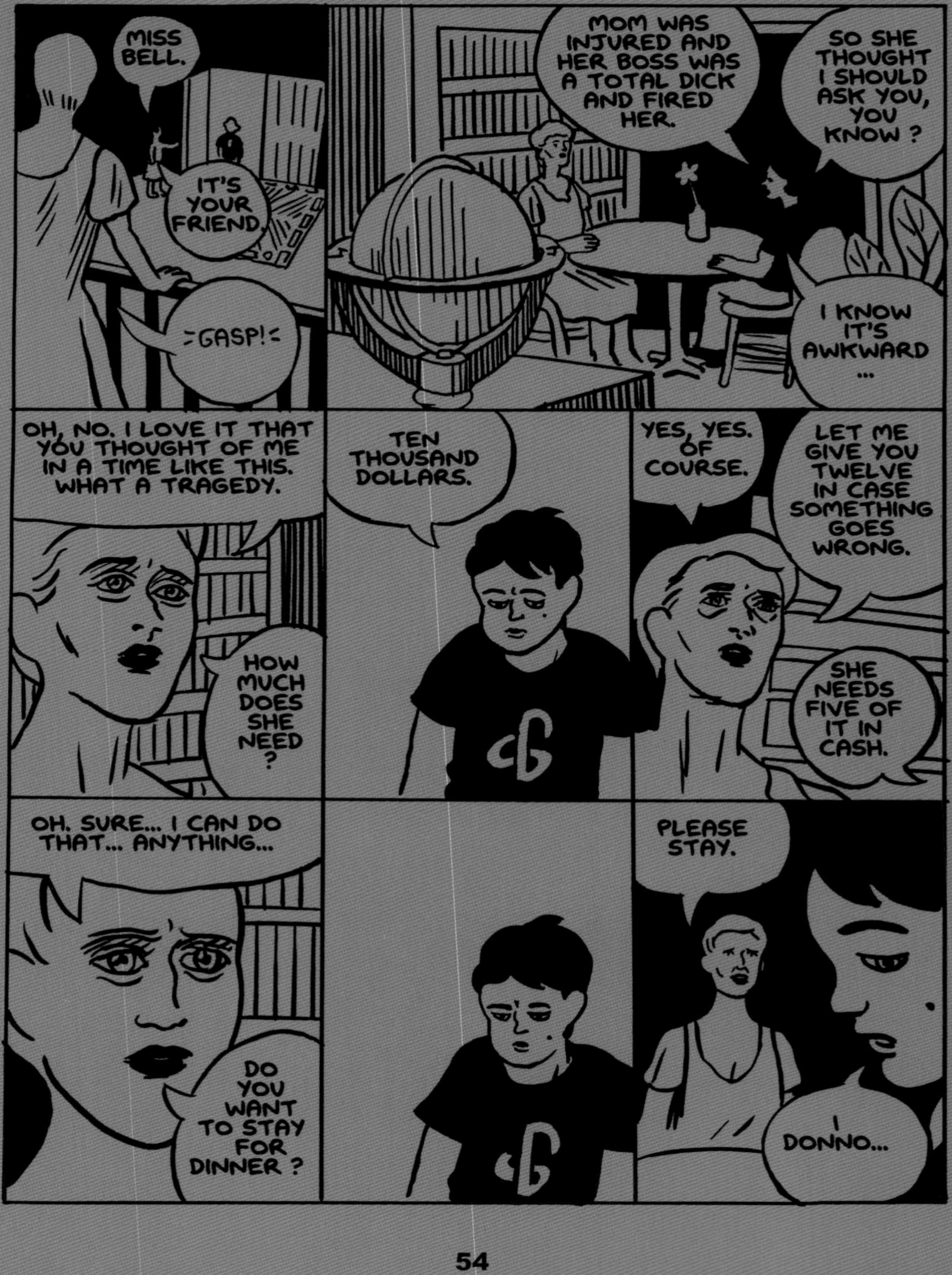

MISS BELL.
IT'S YOUR FRIEND.
=GASP!=
MOM WAS INJURED AND HER BOSS WAS A TOTAL DICK AND FIRED HER.
SO SHE THOUGHT I SHOULD ASK YOU, YOU KNOW ?
I KNOW IT'S AWKWARD ...
OH, NO. I LOVE IT THAT YOU THOUGHT OF ME IN A TIME LIKE THIS. WHAT A TRAGEDY.
HOW MUCH DOES SHE NEED ?
TEN THOUSAND DOLLARS.
YES, YES. OF COURSE.
LET ME GIVE YOU TWELVE IN CASE SOMETHING GOES WRONG.
SHE NEEDS FIVE OF IT IN CASH.
OH. SURE... I CAN DO THAT... ANYTHING...
DO YOU WANT TO STAY FOR DINNER ?
PLEASE STAY.
I DONNO...

THE ELONGATED PENNIES AT THE "BODY WORLDS" EXHIBITION

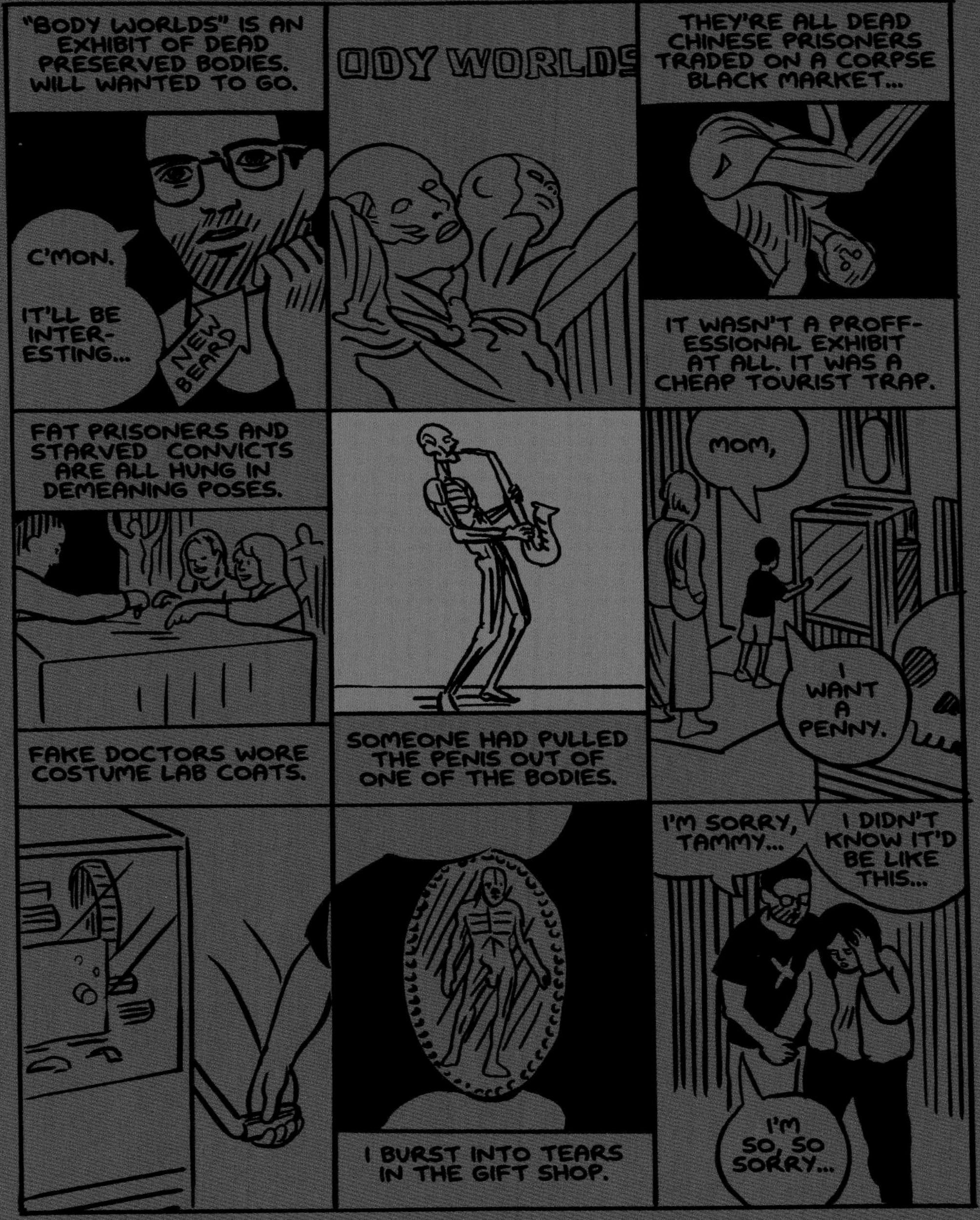

"BODY WORLDS" IS AN EXHIBIT OF DEAD PRESERVED BODIES. WILL WANTED TO GO.
C'MON.
IT'LL BE INTER-ESTING...
NEW BEARD
ODY WORLDS
THEY'RE ALL DEAD CHINESE PRISONERS TRADED ON A CORPSE BLACK MARKET...
IT WASN'T A PROFF-ESSIONAL EXHIBIT AT ALL. IT WAS A CHEAP TOURIST TRAP.
FAT PRISONERS AND STARVED CONVICTS ARE ALL HUNG IN DEMEANING POSES.
FAKE DOCTORS WORE COSTUME LAB COATS.
SOMEONE HAD PULLED THE PENIS OUT OF ONE OF THE BODIES.
MOM,
I WANT A PENNY.
I BURST INTO TEARS IN THE GIFT SHOP.
I'M SORRY, TAMMY...
I DIDN'T KNOW IT'D BE LIKE THIS...
I'M SO, SO SORRY...

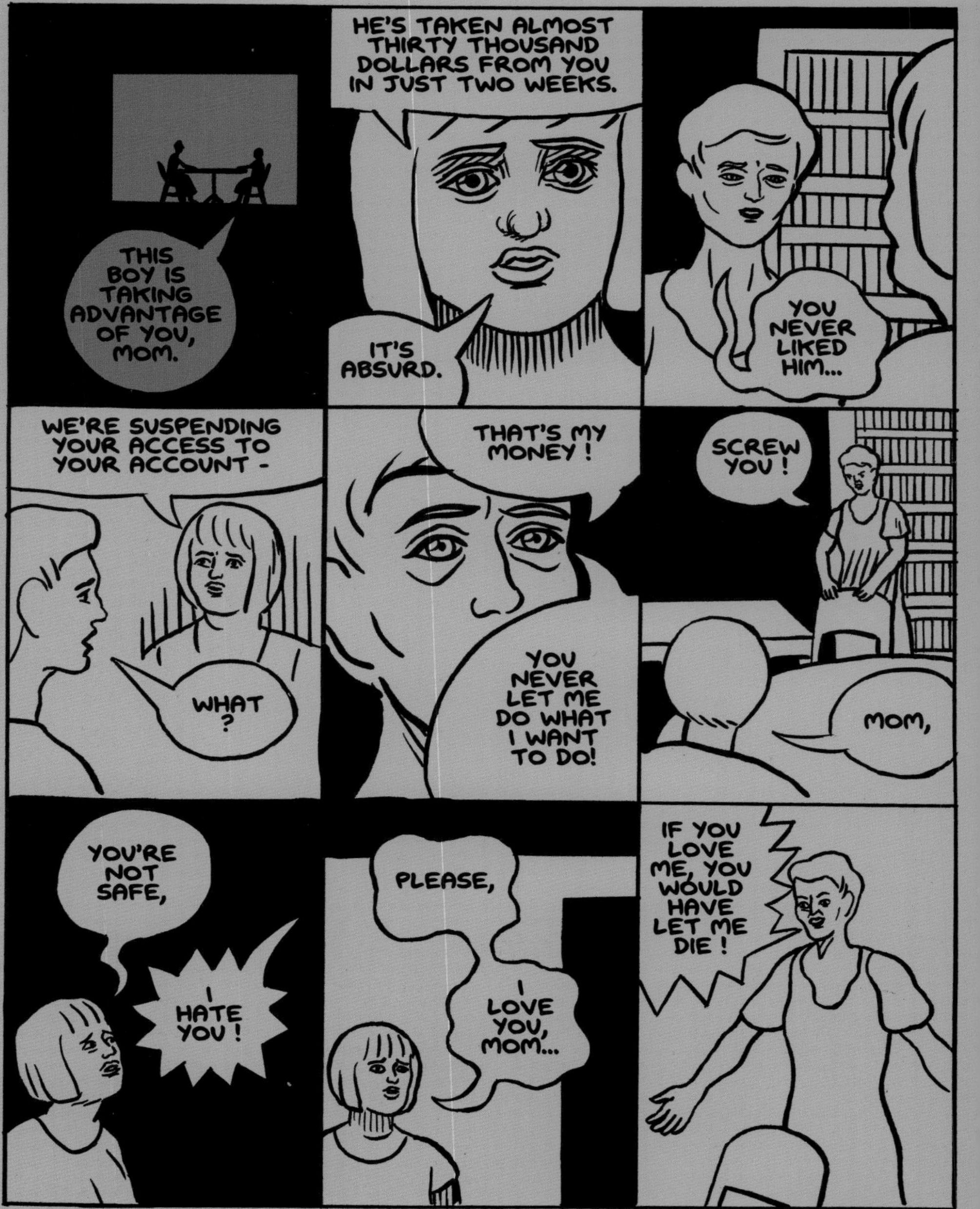
THIS BOY IS TAKING ADVANTAGE OF YOU, MOM.
HE'S TAKEN ALMOST THIRTY THOUSAND DOLLARS FROM YOU IN JUST TWO WEEKS.
IT'S ABSURD.
YOU NEVER LIKED HIM...
WE'RE SUSPENDING YOUR ACCESS TO YOUR ACCOUNT -
WHAT ?
THAT'S MY MONEY !
YOU NEVER LET ME DO WHAT I WANT TO DO!
SCREW YOU !
MOM,
YOU'RE NOT SAFE,
I HATE YOU !
PLEASE,
I LOVE YOU, MOM...
IF YOU LOVE ME, YOU WOULD HAVE LET ME DIE !

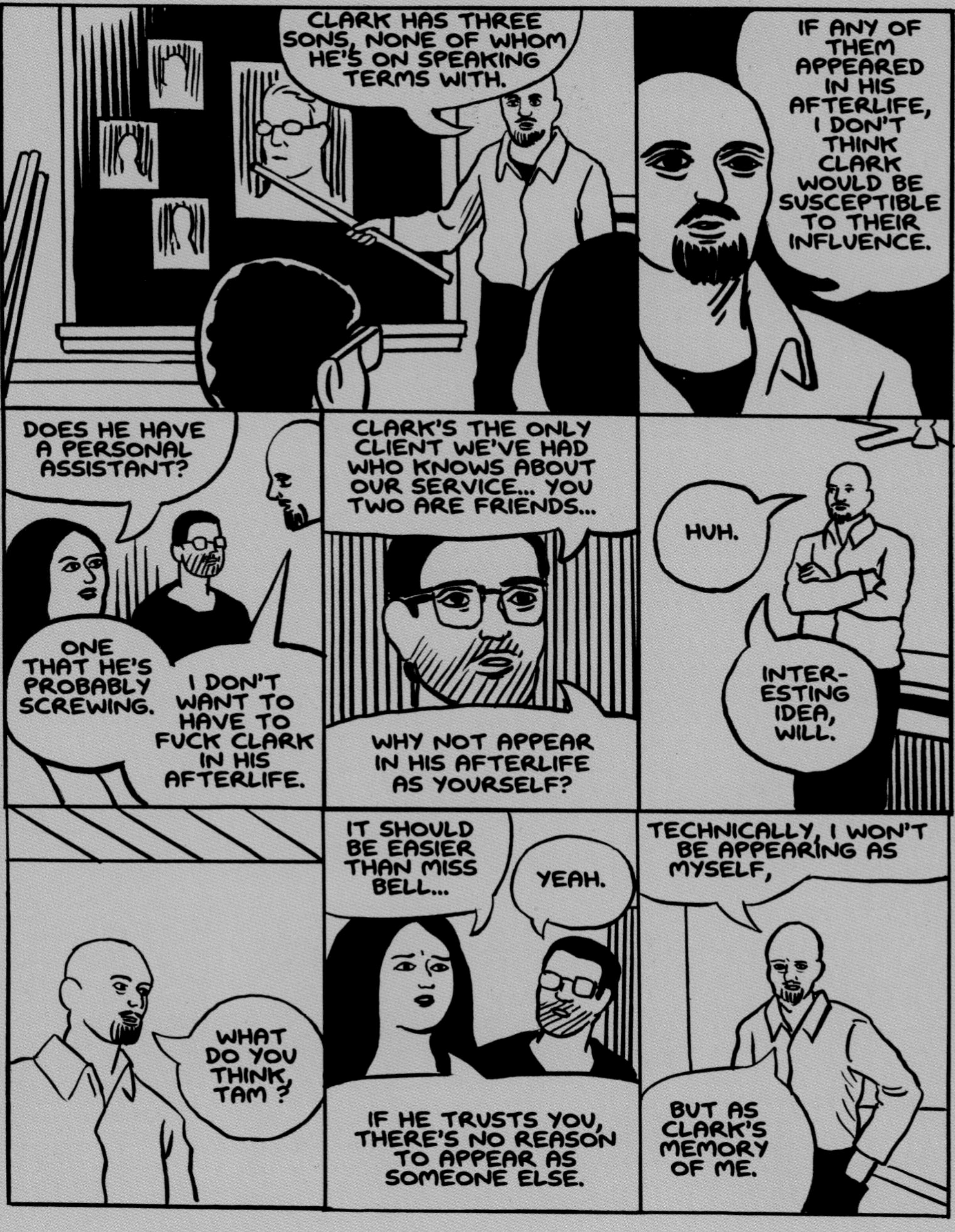
CLARK HAS THREE SONS, NONE OF WHOM HE'S ON SPEAKING TERMS WITH.
IF ANY OF THEM APPEARED IN HIS AFTERLIFE, I DON'T THINK CLARK WOULD BE SUSCEPTIBLE TO THEIR INFLUENCE.
DOES HE HAVE A PERSONAL ASSISTANT?
ONE THAT HE'S PROBABLY SCREWING.
I DON'T WANT TO HAVE TO FUCK CLARK IN HIS AFTERLIFE.
CLARK'S THE ONLY CLIENT WE'VE HAD WHO KNOWS ABOUT OUR SERVICE... YOU TWO ARE FRIENDS...
WHY NOT APPEAR IN HIS AFTERLIFE AS YOURSELF?
HUH.
INTER-ESTING IDEA, WILL.
WHAT DO YOU THINK, TAM ?
IT SHOULD BE EASIER THAN MISS BELL...
YEAH.
IF HE TRUSTS YOU, THERE'S NO REASON TO APPEAR AS SOMEONE ELSE.
TECHNICALLY, I WON'T BE APPEARING AS MYSELF,
BUT AS CLARK'S MEMORY OF ME.

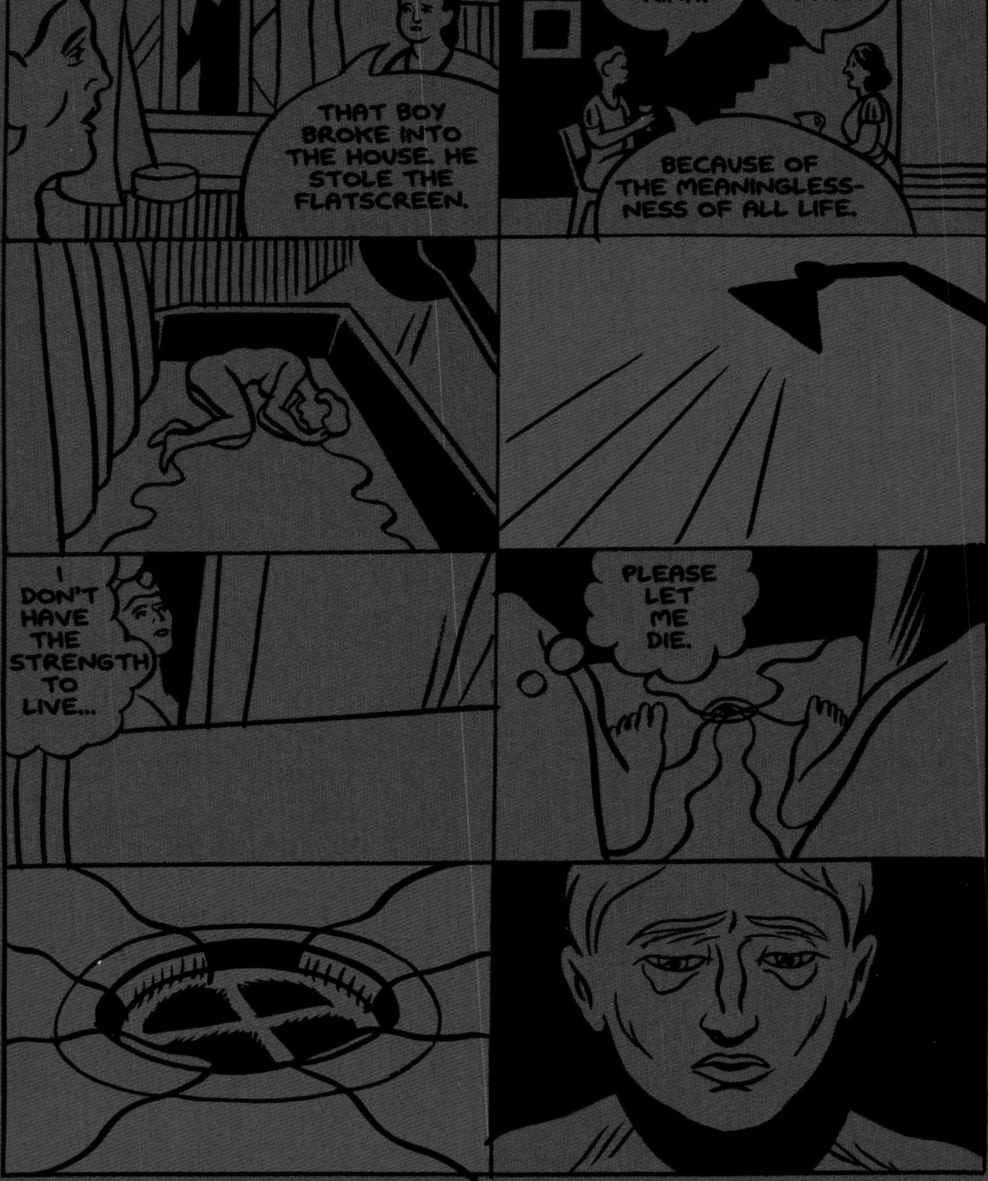
THAT BOY BROKE INTO THE HOUSE. HE STOLE THE FLATSCREEN.
BECAUSE OF THE MEANINGLESS-NESS OF ALL LIFE.
I DON'T HAVE THE STRENGTH TO LIVE...
PLEASE LET ME DIE.

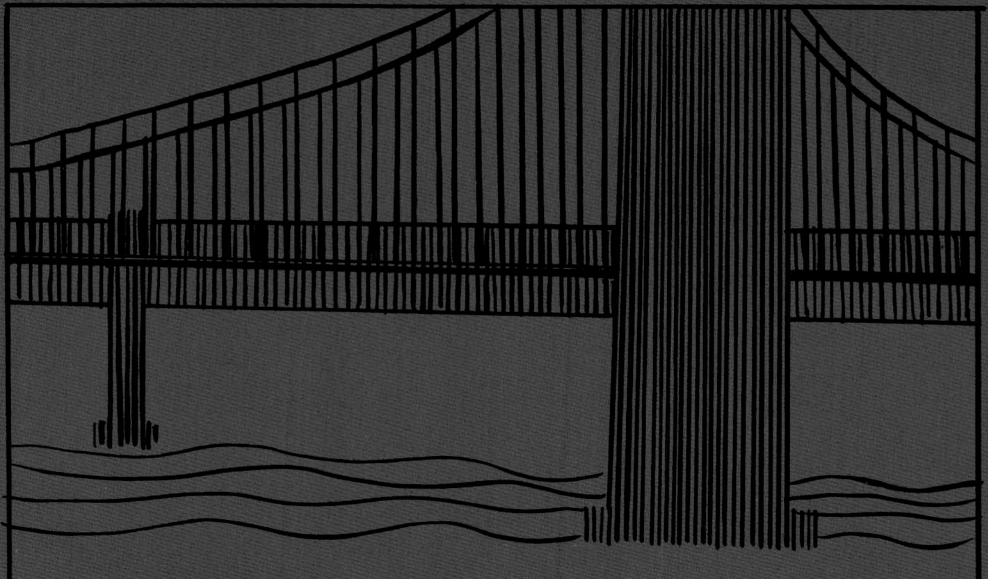
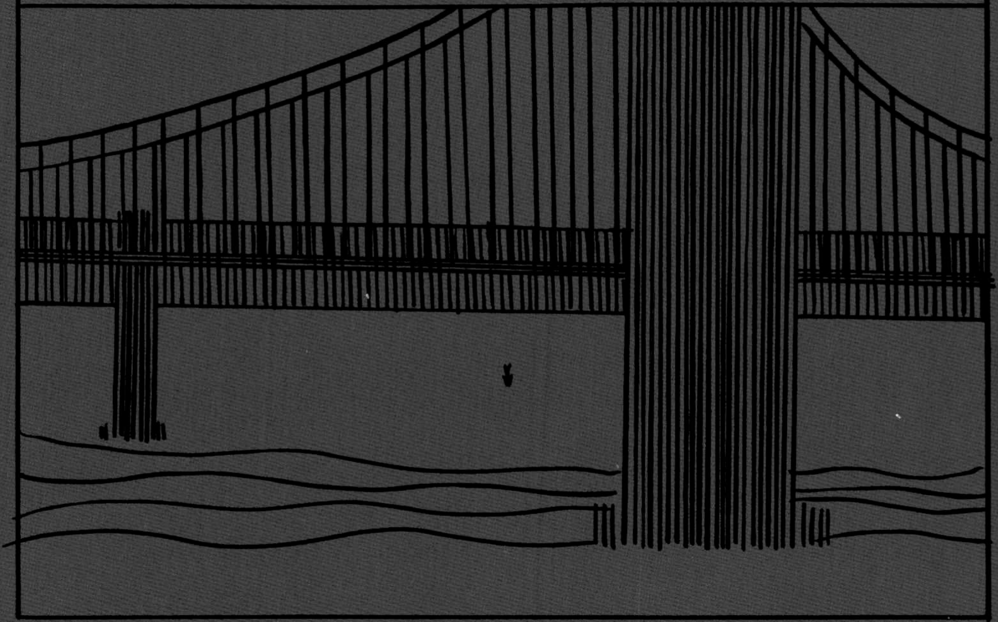

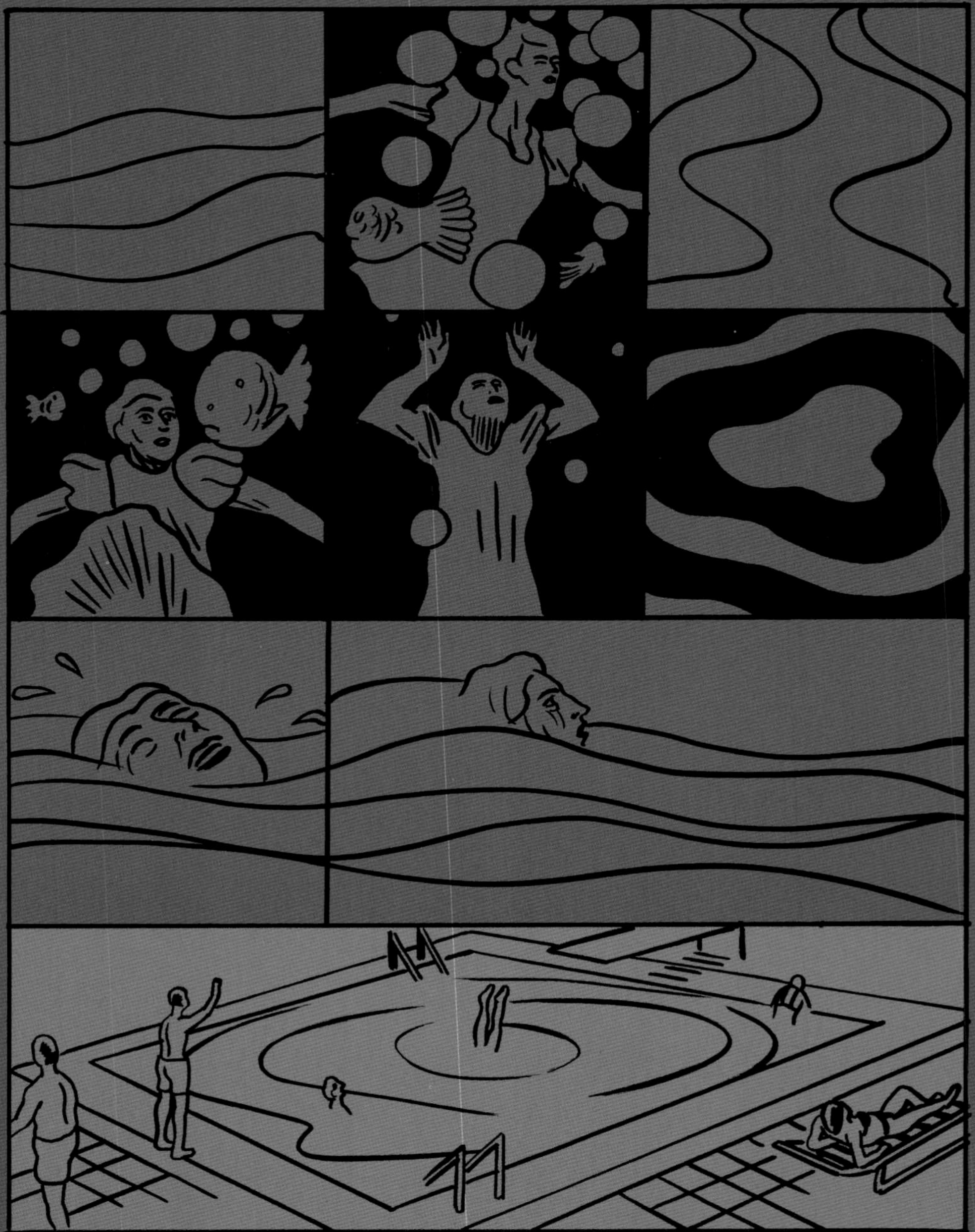

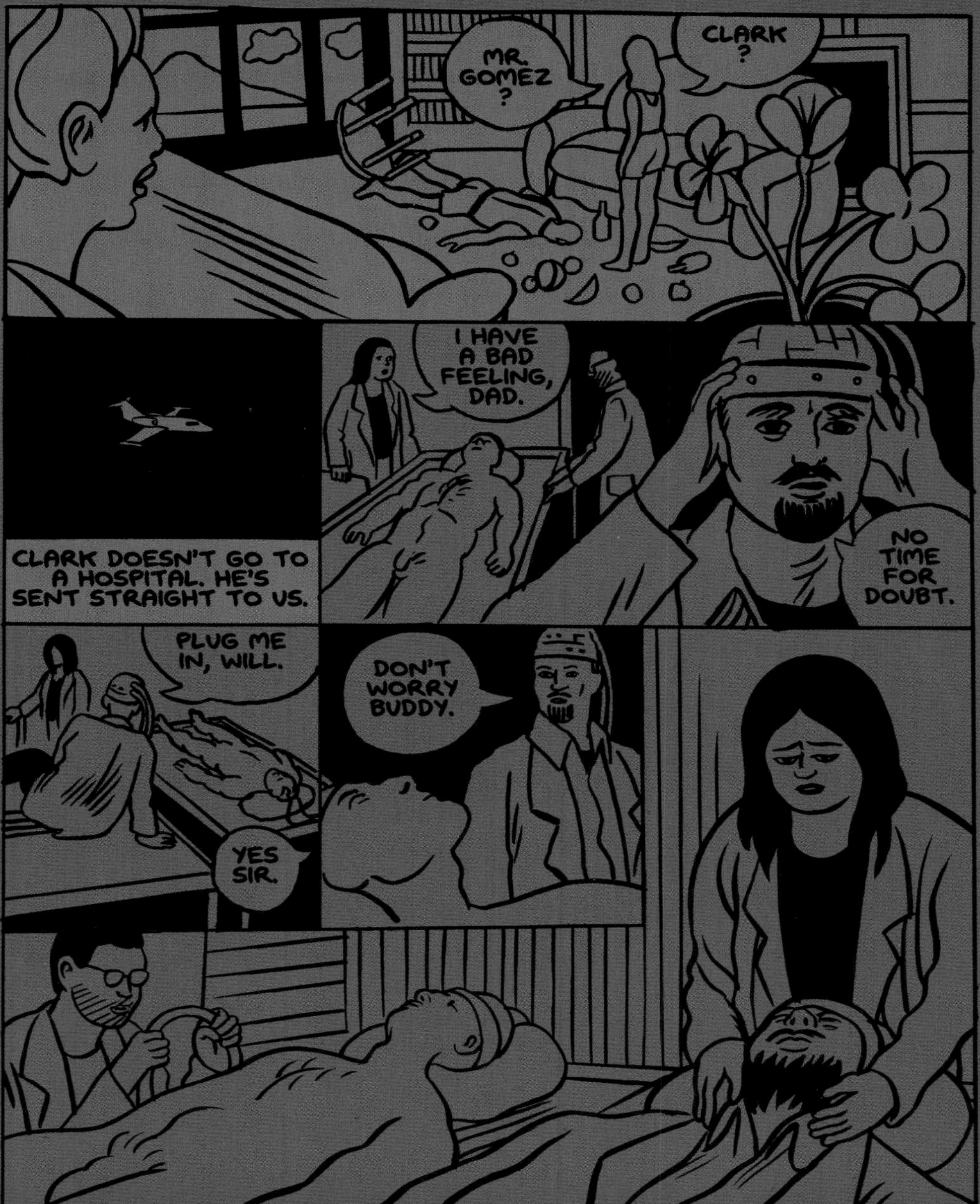
MR. GOMEZ ?
CLARK ?
CLARK DOESN'T GO TO A HOSPITAL. HE'S SENT STRAIGHT TO US.
I HAVE A BAD FEELING, DAD.
NO TIME FOR DOUBT.
PLUG ME IN, WILL.
YES SIR.
DON'T WORRY BUDDY.

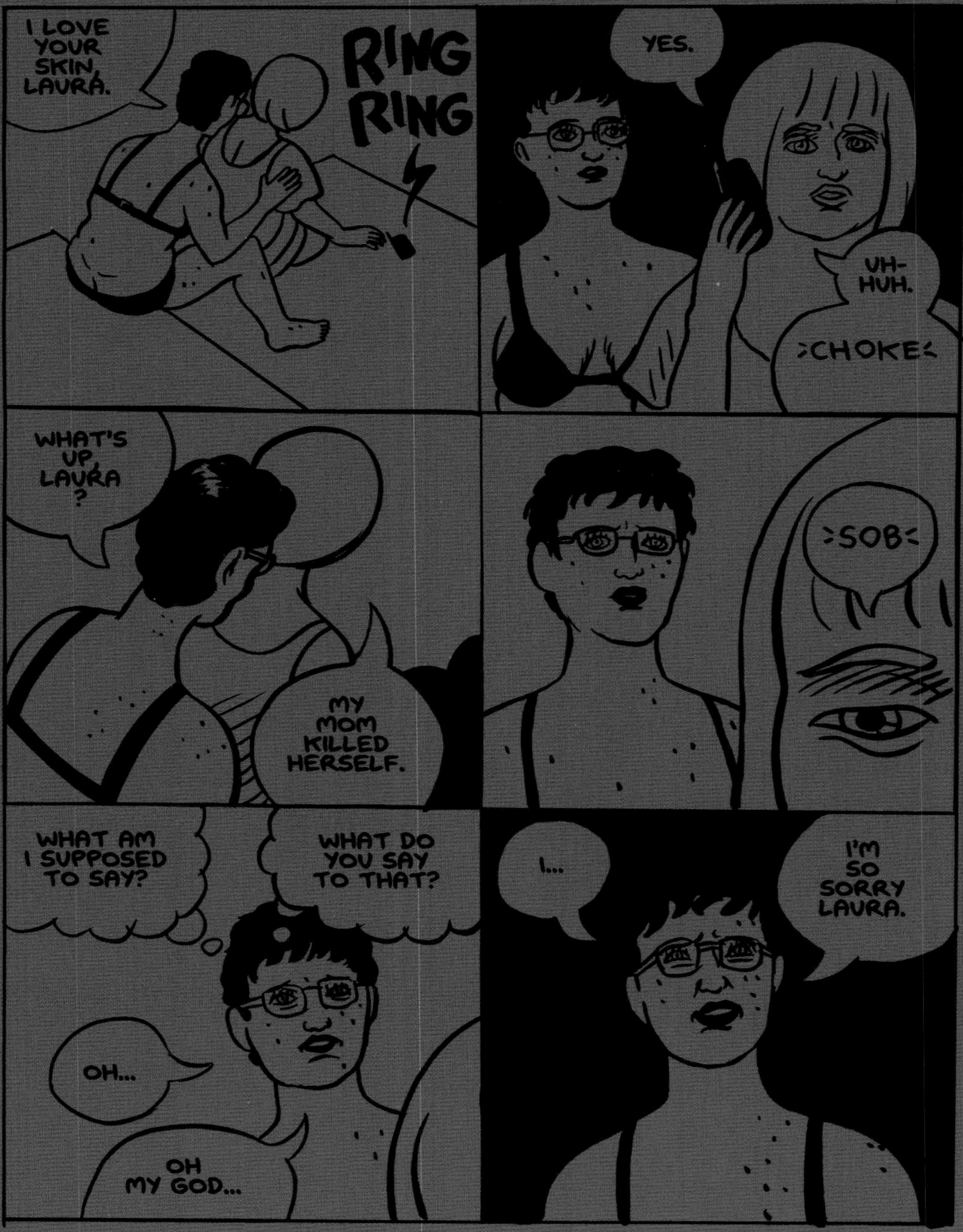
I LOVE YOUR SKIN, LAURA.
RING RING
YES.
UH-HUH.
>CHOKE<
WHAT'S UP, LAURA?
MY MOM KILLED HERSELF.
>SOB<
WHAT AM I SUPPOSED TO SAY?
WHAT DO YOU SAY TO THAT?
OH...
OH MY GOD...
I...
I'M SO SORRY LAURA.

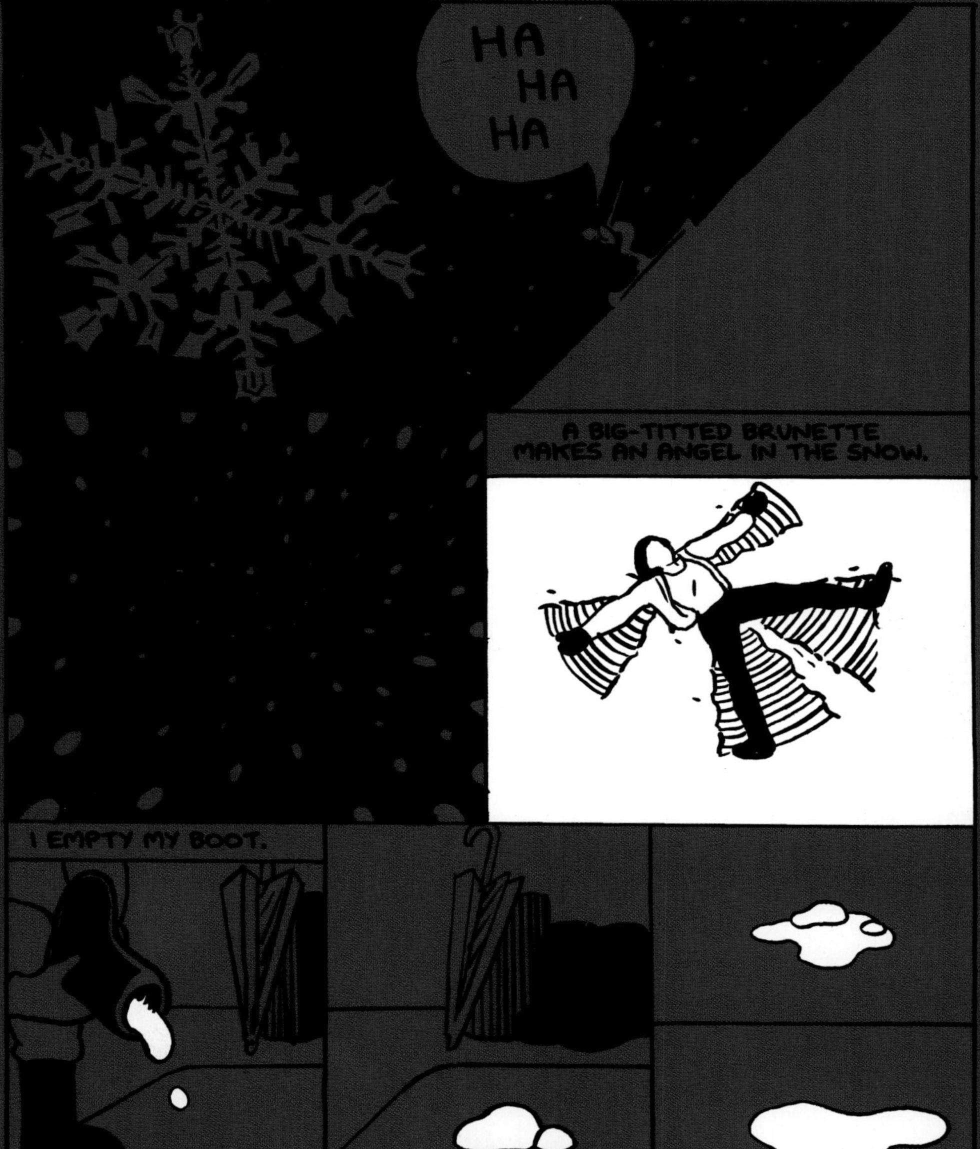
HA
HA
HA
A BIG-TITTED BRUNETTE MAKES AN ANGEL IN THE SNOW.
I EMPTY MY BOOT.

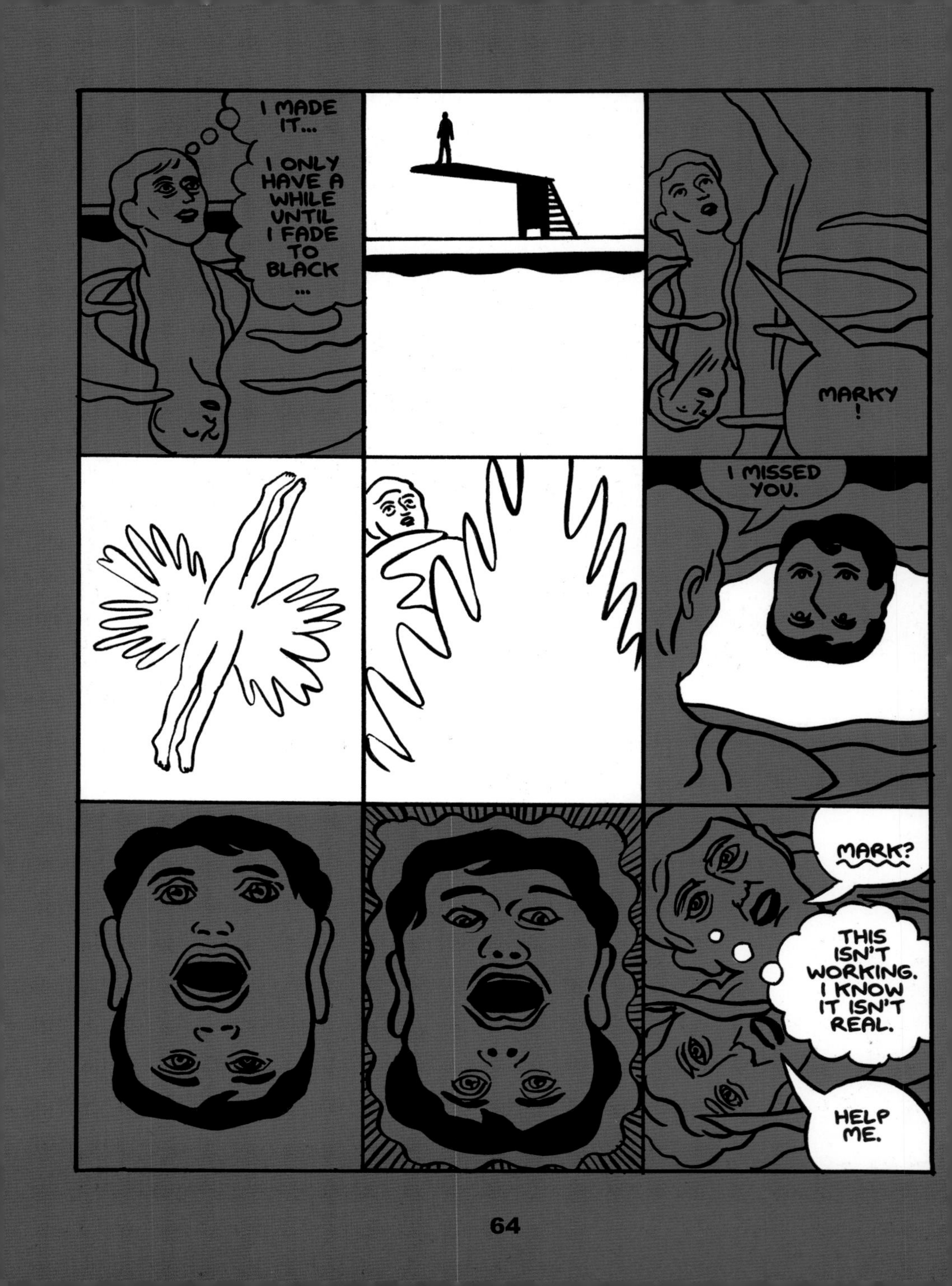
I MADE IT...
I ONLY HAVE A WHILE UNTIL I FADE TO BLACK ...
MARKY !
I MISSED YOU.
MARK?
THIS ISN'T WORKING. I KNOW IT ISN'T REAL.
HELP ME.

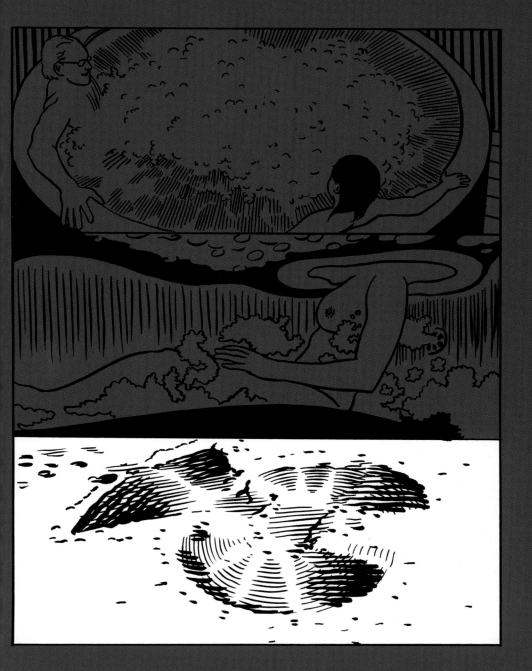

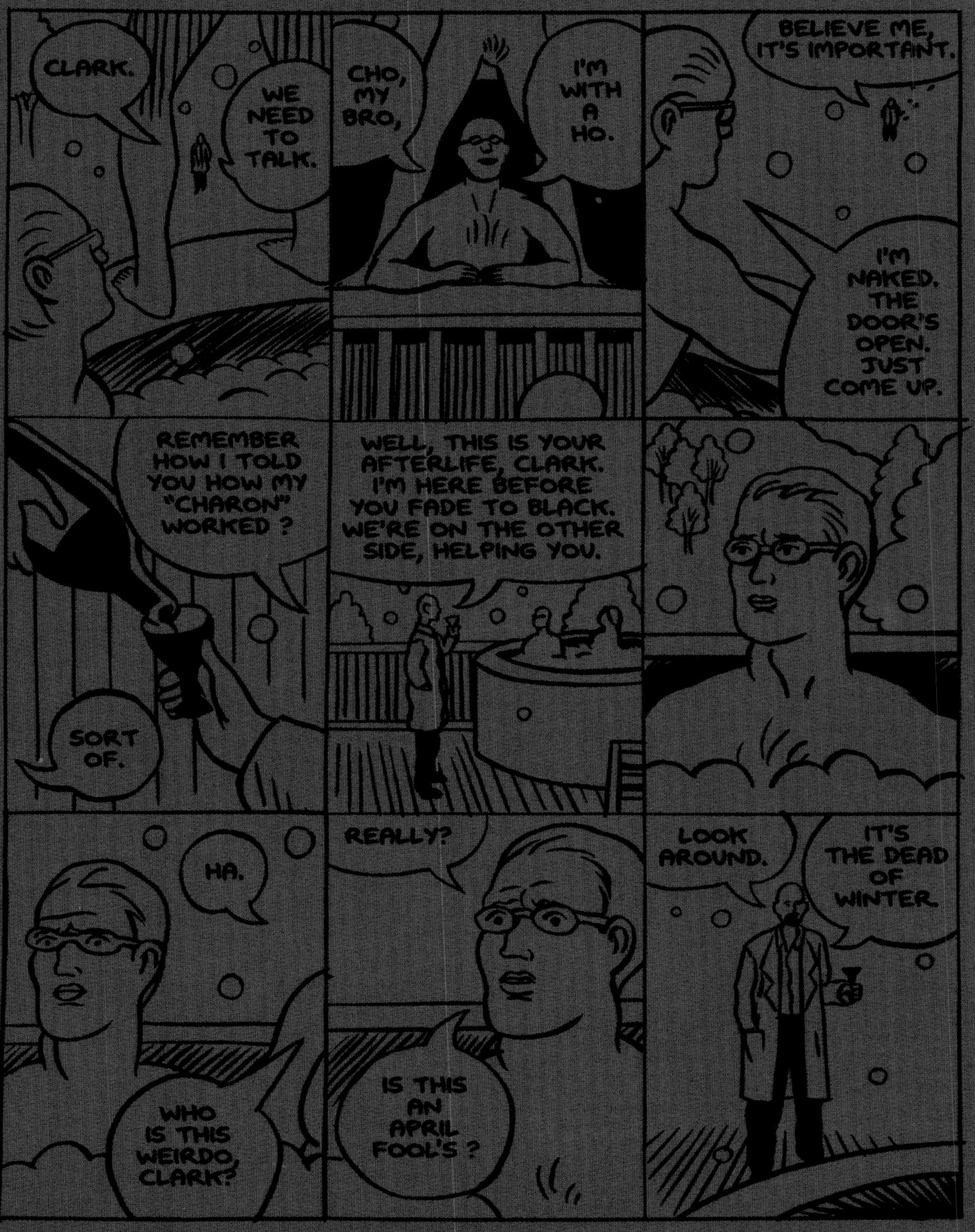
CLARK.
WE NEED TO TALK.
CHO, MY BRO,
I'M WITH A HO.
BELIEVE ME, IT'S IMPORTANT.
I'M NAKED. THE DOOR'S OPEN. JUST COME UP.
REMEMBER HOW I TOLD YOU HOW MY "CHARON" WORKED ?
SORT OF.
WELL, THIS IS YOUR AFTERLIFE, CLARK. I'M HERE BEFORE YOU FADE TO BLACK. WE'RE ON THE OTHER SIDE, HELPING YOU.
HA.
WHO IS THIS WEIRDO, CLARK?
REALLY?
IS THIS AN APRIL FOOL'S ?
LOOK AROUND.
IT'S THE DEAD OF WINTER.

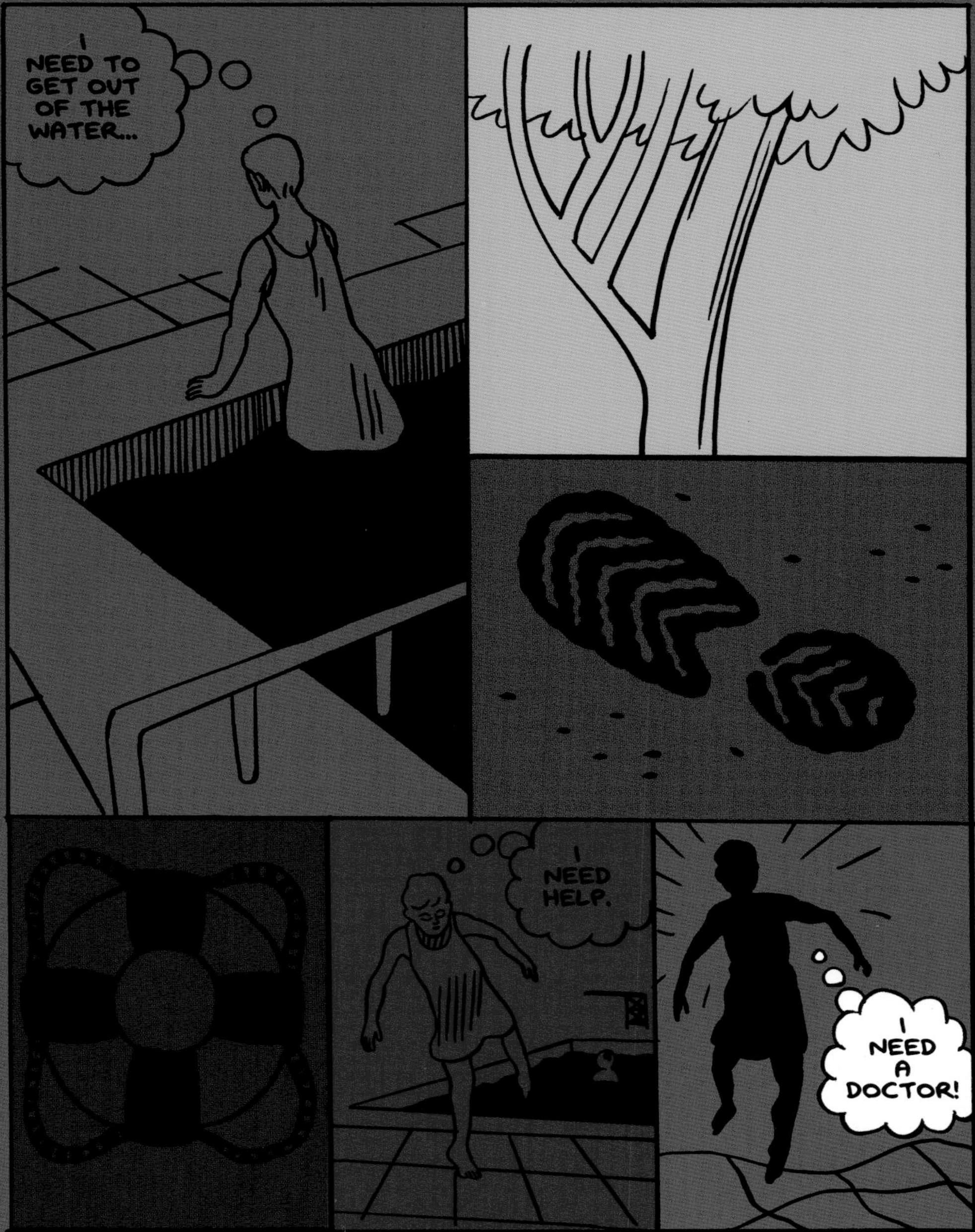
I NEED TO GET OUT OF THE WATER...
I NEED HELP.
I NEED A DOCTOR!

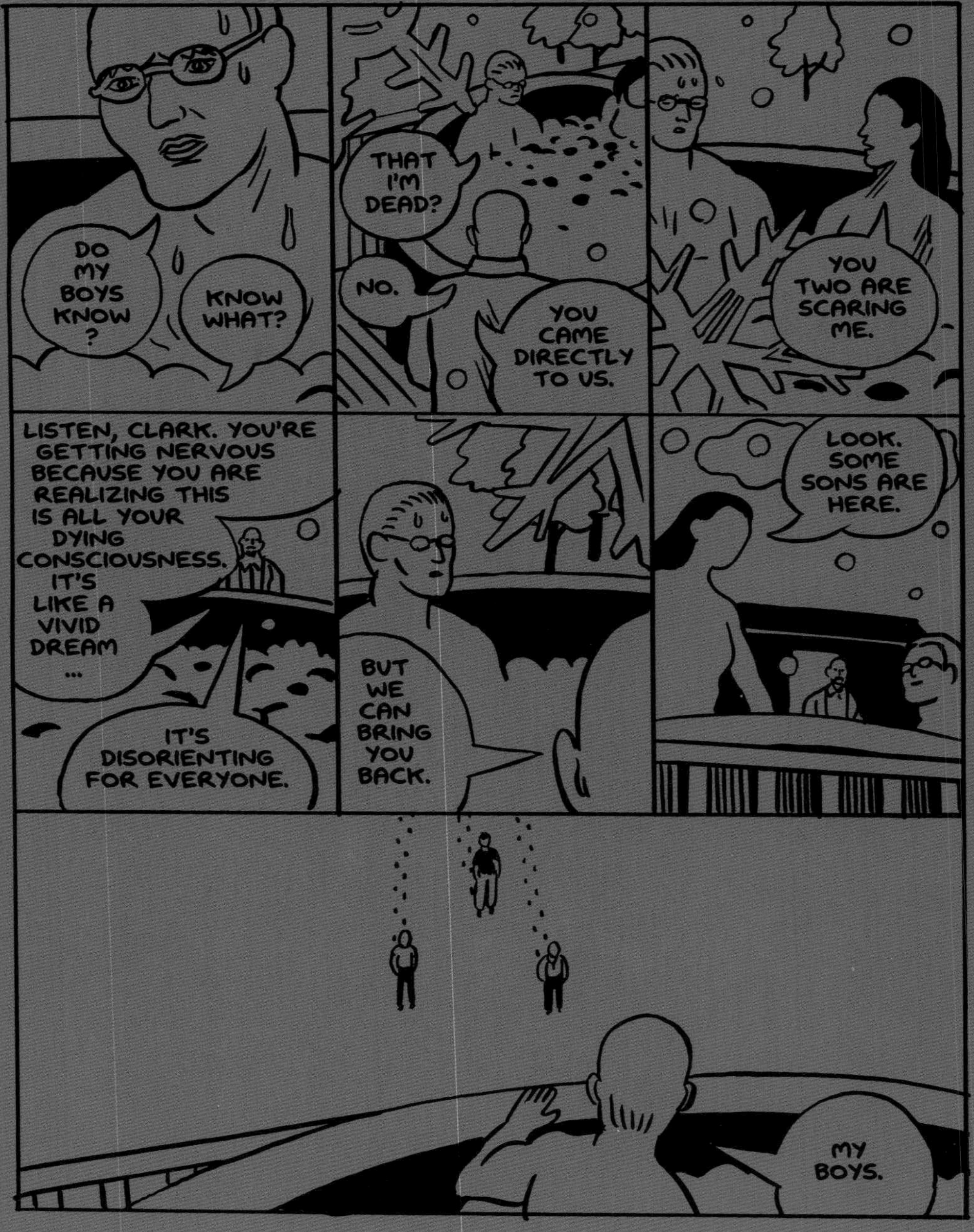
DO MY BOYS KNOW ?
KNOW WHAT?
THAT I'M DEAD?
NO.
YOU CAME DIRECTLY TO US.
YOU TWO ARE SCARING ME.
LISTEN, CLARK. YOU'RE GETTING NERVOUS BECAUSE YOU ARE REALIZING THIS IS ALL YOUR DYING CONSCIOUSNESS. IT'S LIKE A VIVID DREAM ...
IT'S DISORIENTING FOR EVERYONE.
BUT WE CAN BRING YOU BACK.
LOOK. SOME SONS ARE HERE.
MY BOYS.

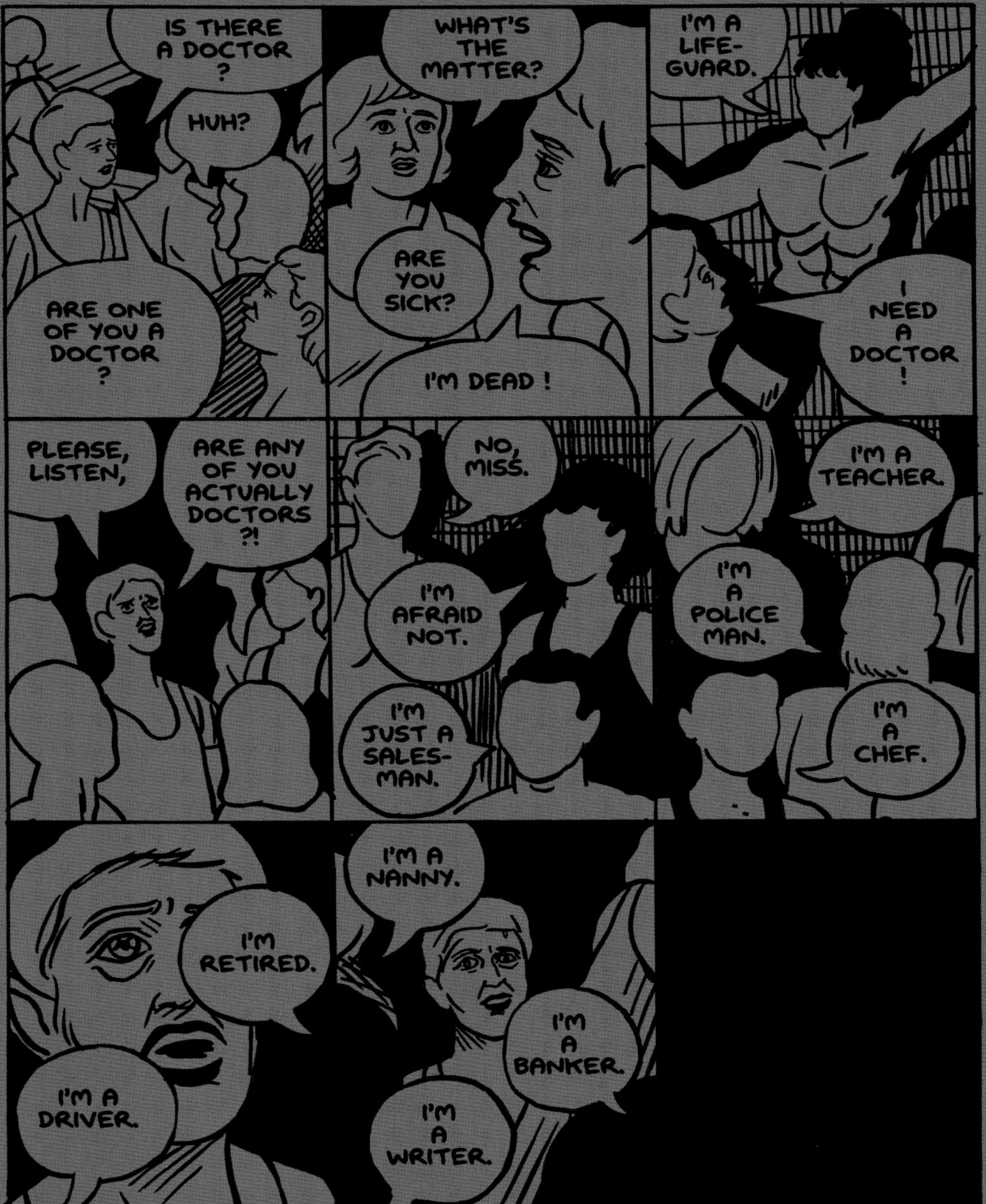
IS THERE A DOCTOR ?
HUH?
ARE ONE OF YOU A DOCTOR ?
WHAT'S THE MATTER?
ARE YOU SICK?
I'M DEAD !
I'M A LIFE-GUARD.
I NEED A DOCTOR !
PLEASE, LISTEN,
ARE ANY OF YOU ACTUALLY DOCTORS ?!
NO, MISS.
I'M AFRAID NOT.
I'M JUST A SALES-MAN.
I'M A TEACHER.
I'M A POLICE MAN.
I'M A CHEF.
I'M RETIRED.
I'M A DRIVER.
I'M A NANNY.
I'M A BANKER.
I'M A WRITER.

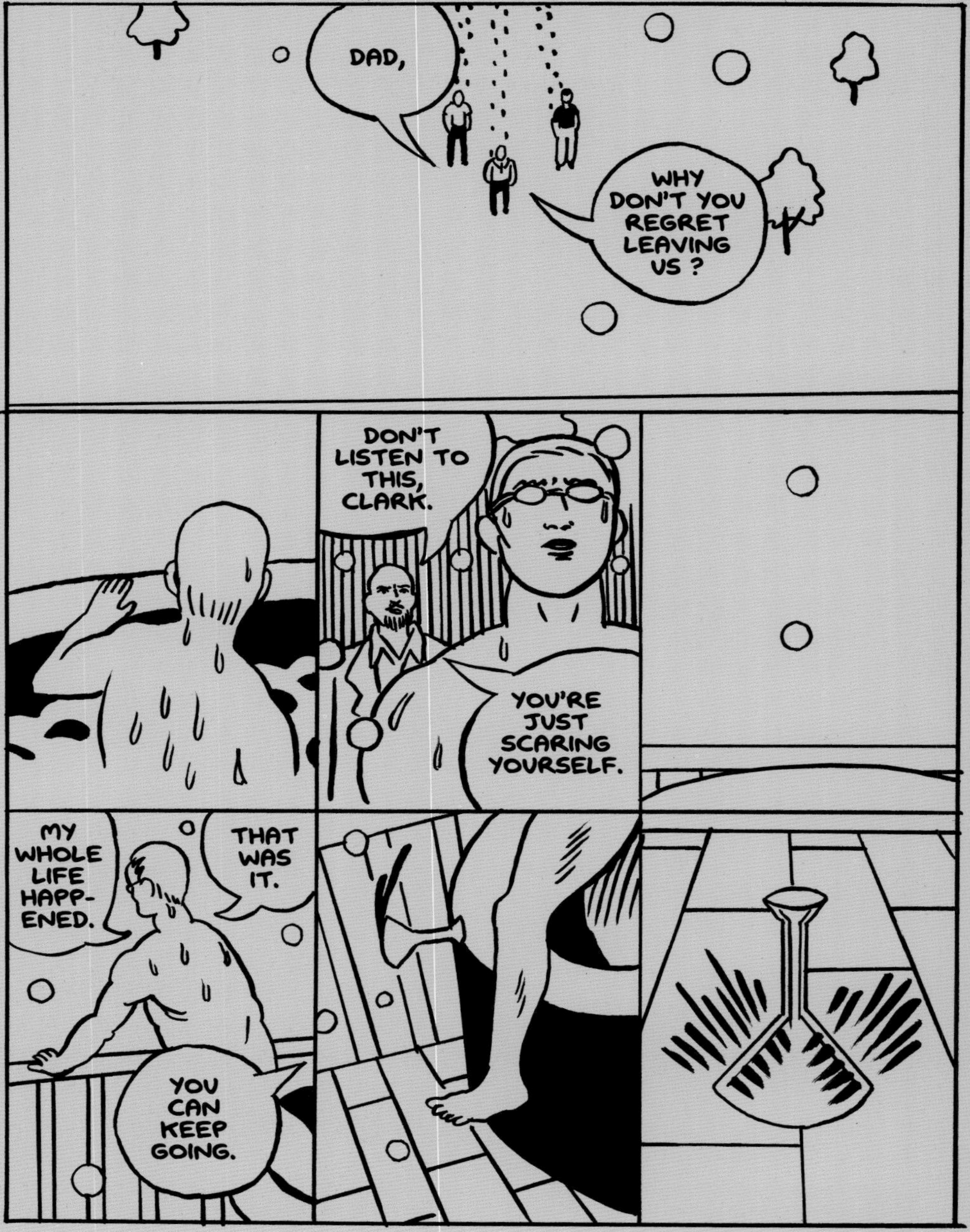
DAD,
WHY DON'T YOU REGRET LEAVING US ?
DON'T LISTEN TO THIS, CLARK.
YOU'RE JUST SCARING YOURSELF.
MY WHOLE LIFE HAPP-ENED.
THAT WAS IT.
YOU CAN KEEP GOING.

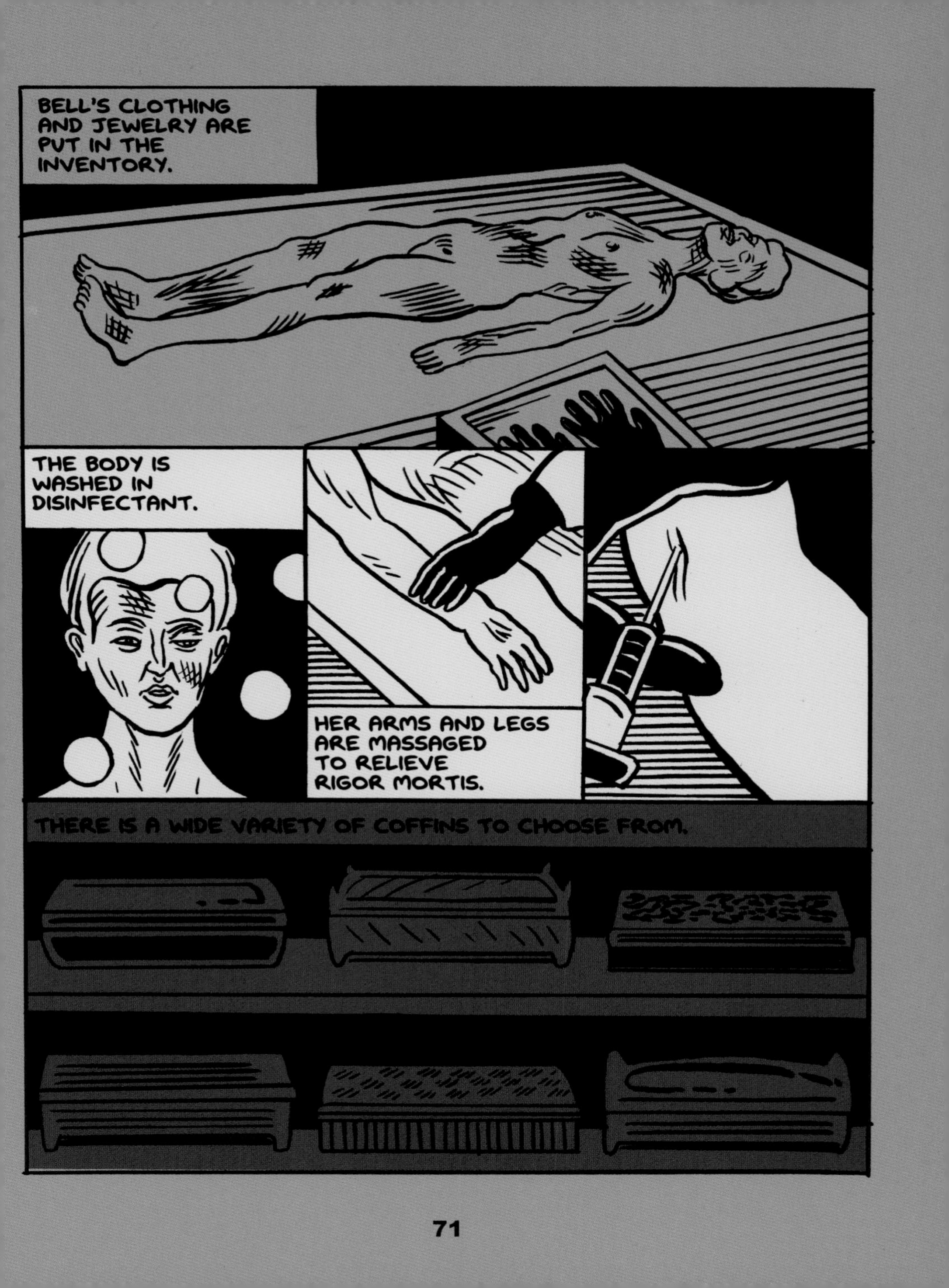
BELL'S CLOTHING AND JEWELRY ARE PUT IN THE INVENTORY.
THE BODY IS WASHED IN DISINFECTANT.
HER ARMS AND LEGS ARE MASSAGED TO RELIEVE RIGOR MORTIS.
THERE IS A WIDE VARIETY OF COFFINS TO CHOOSE FROM.

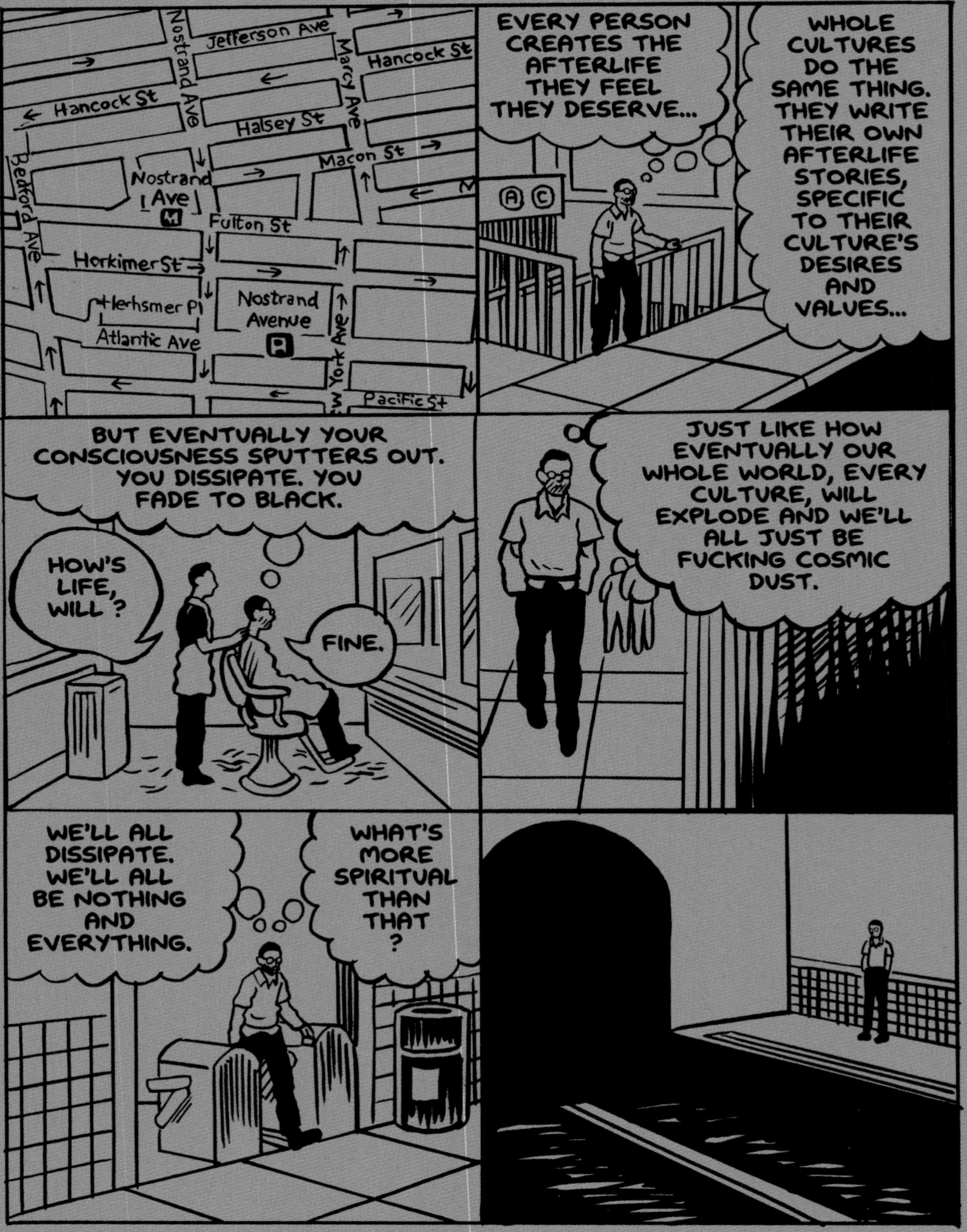
Jefferson Ave
Nostrand Ave
Marcy Ave
Hancock St
Hancock St
Halsey St
Macon St
Bedford Ave
Nostrand Ave
Fulton St
Herkimer St
Herkimer Pl
Nostrand Avenue
Atlantic Ave
New York Ave
Pacific St
EVERY PERSON CREATES THE AFTERLIFE THEY FEEL THEY DESERVE...
WHOLE CULTURES DO THE SAME THING. THEY WRITE THEIR OWN AFTERLIFE STORIES, SPECIFIC TO THEIR CULTURE'S DESIRES AND VALUES...
BUT EVENTUALLY YOUR CONSCIOUSNESS SPUTTERS OUT. YOU DISSIPATE. YOU FADE TO BLACK.
HOW'S LIFE, WILL ?
FINE.
JUST LIKE HOW EVENTUALLY OUR WHOLE WORLD, EVERY CULTURE, WILL EXPLODE AND WE'LL ALL JUST BE FUCKING COSMIC DUST.
WE'LL ALL DISSIPATE. WE'LL ALL BE NOTHING AND EVERYTHING.
WHAT'S MORE SPIRITUAL THAN THAT ?

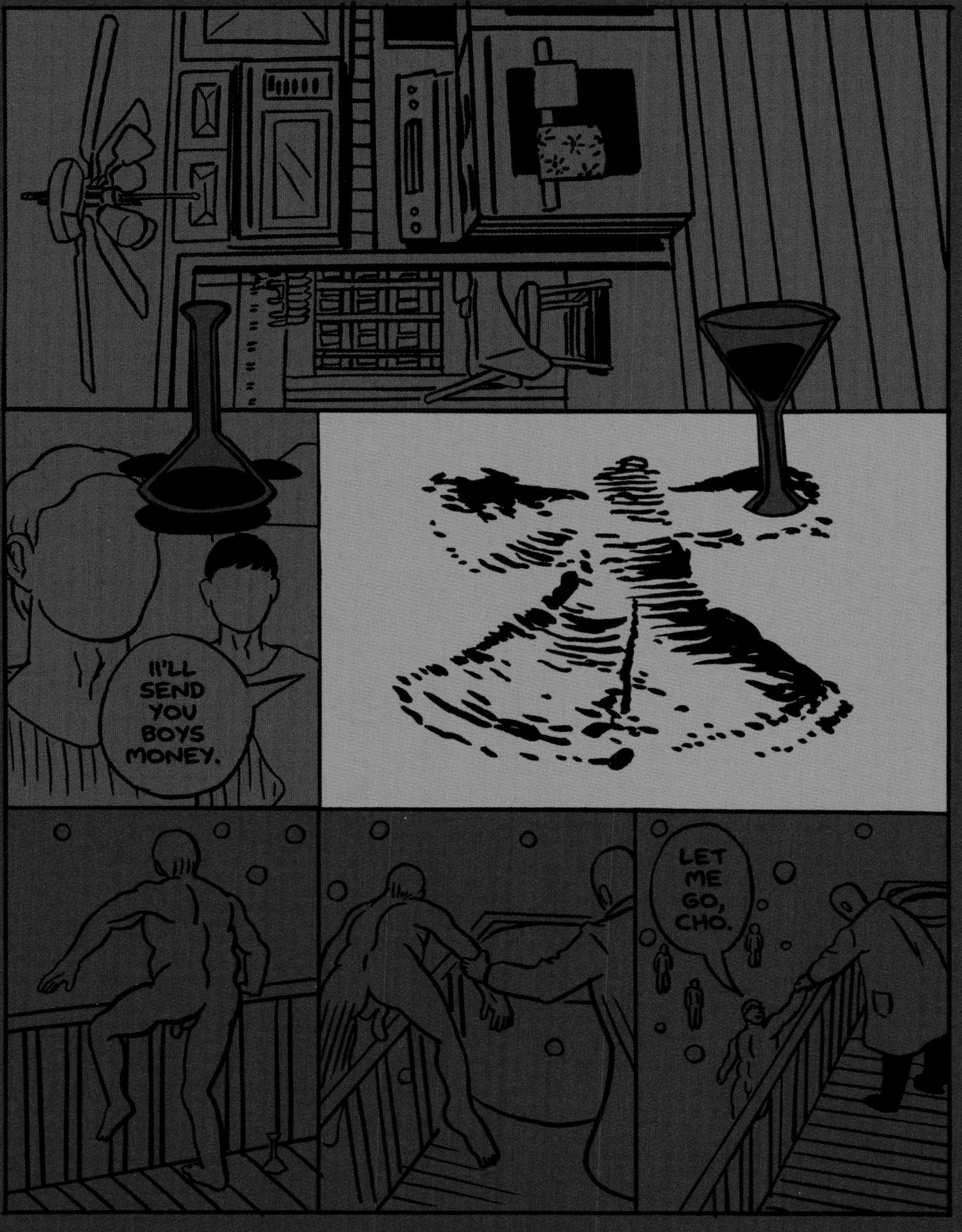
I'LL SEND YOU BOYS MONEY.
LET ME GO, CHO.

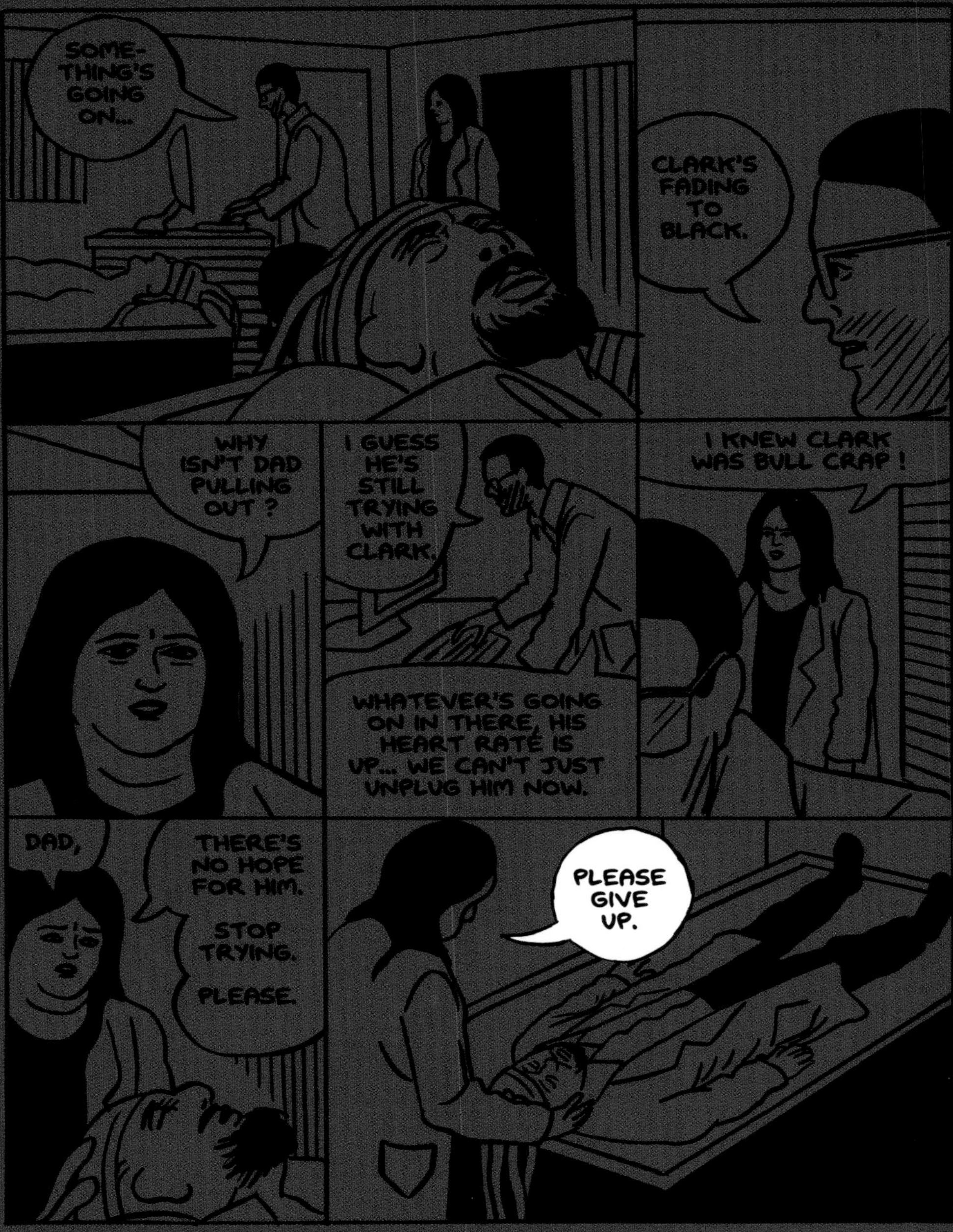
SOME-THING'S GOING ON...
CLARK'S FADING TO BLACK.
WHY ISN'T DAD PULLING OUT ?
I GUESS HE'S STILL TRYING WITH CLARK.
WHATEVER'S GOING ON IN THERE, HIS HEART RATE IS UP... WE CAN'T JUST UNPLUG HIM NOW.
I KNEW CLARK WAS BULL CRAP !
DAD,
THERE'S NO HOPE FOR HIM.
STOP TRYING.
PLEASE.
PLEASE GIVE UP.

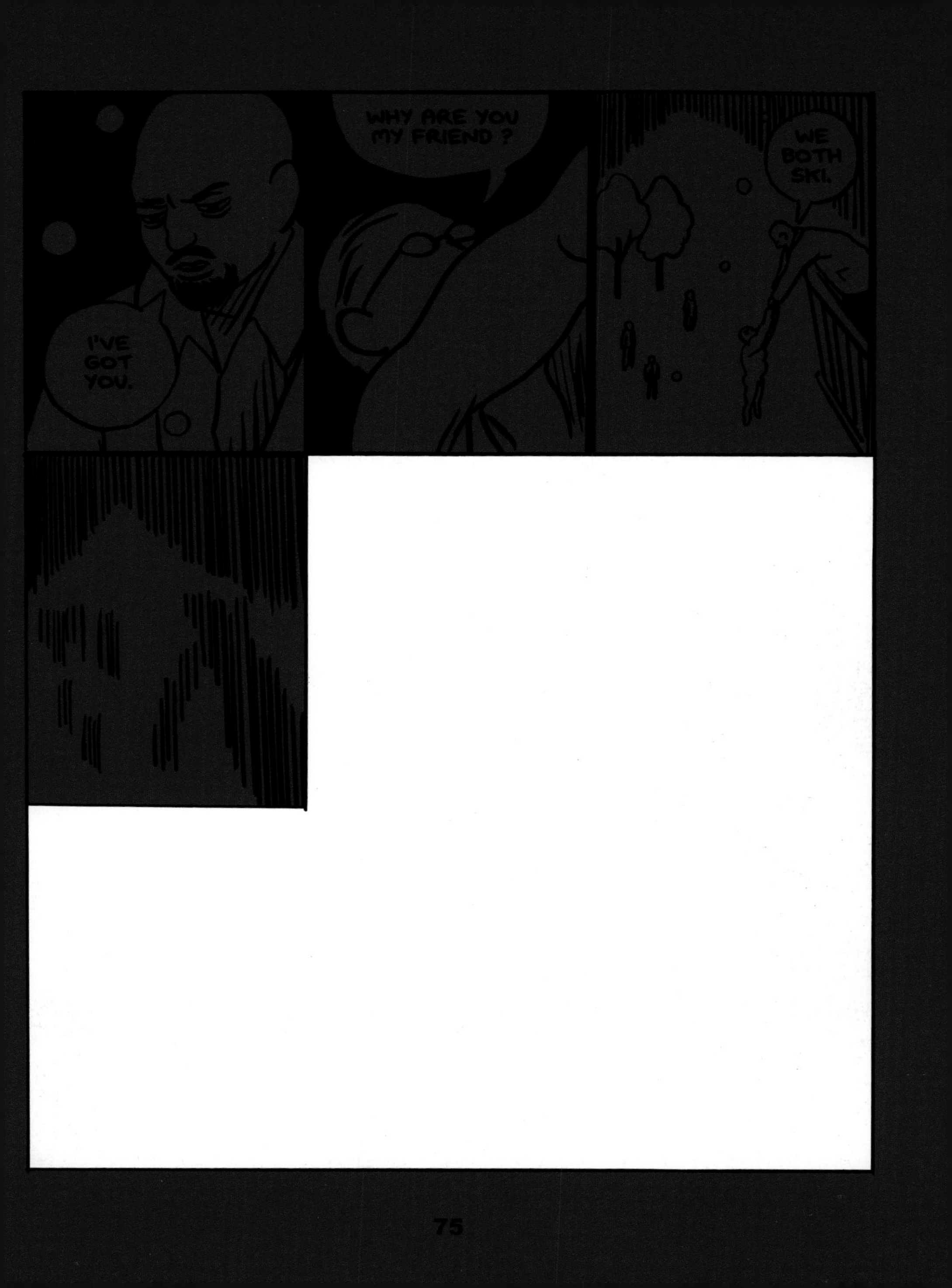
I'VE GOT YOU.
WHY ARE YOU MY FRIEND ?
WE BOTH SKI.

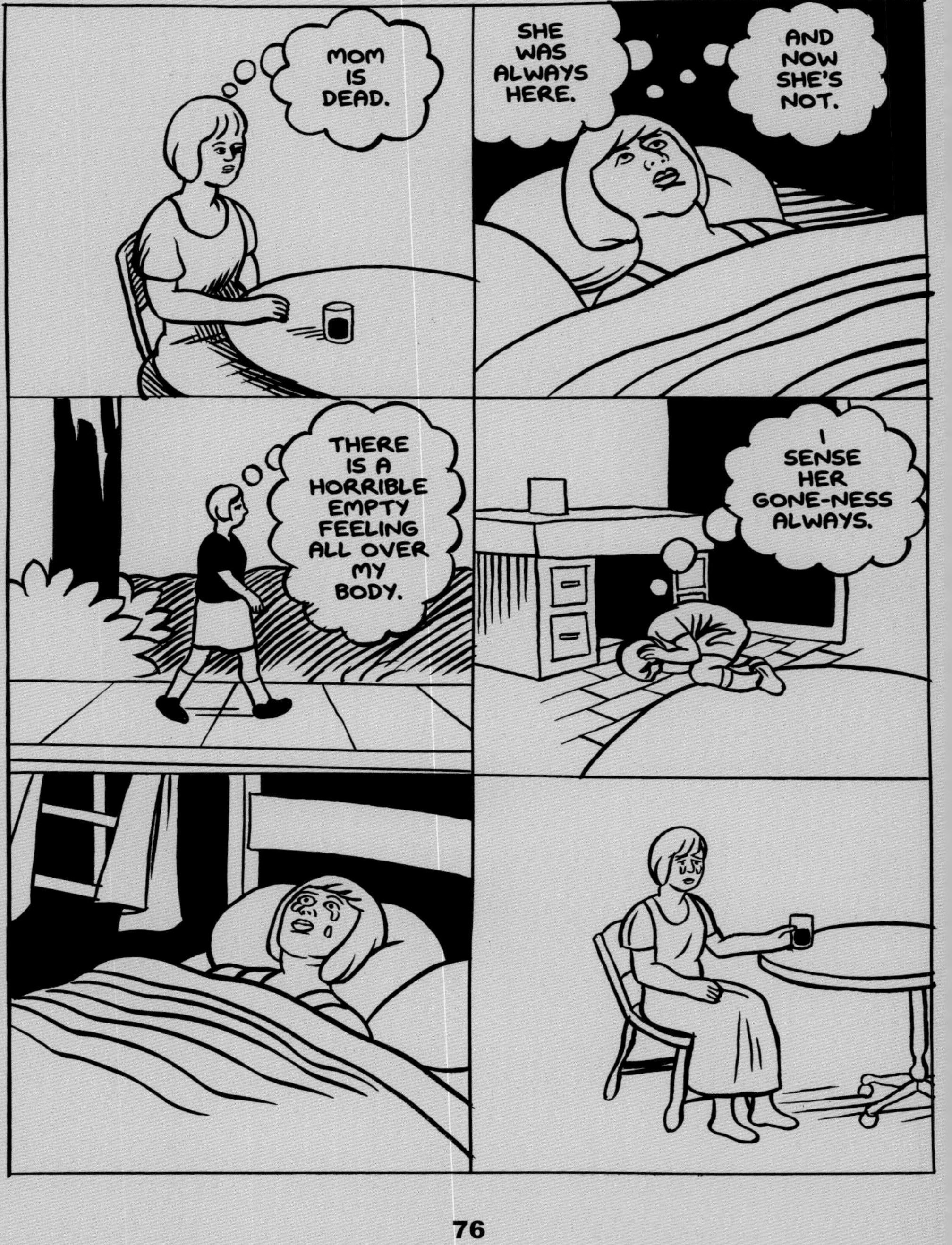
MOM IS DEAD.
SHE WAS ALWAYS HERE.
AND NOW SHE'S NOT.
THERE IS A HORRIBLE EMPTY FEELING ALL OVER MY BODY.
I SENSE HER GONE-NESS ALWAYS.

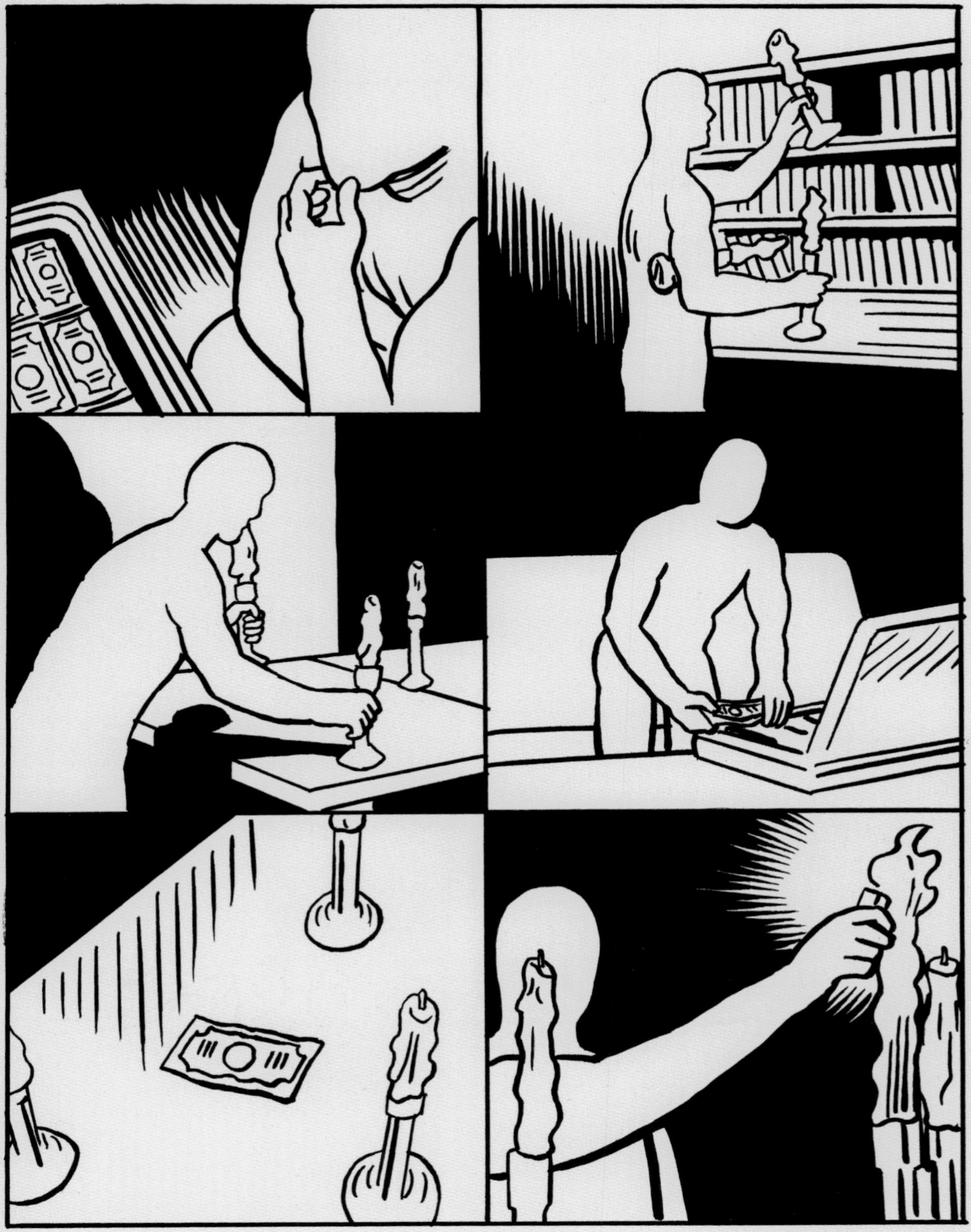

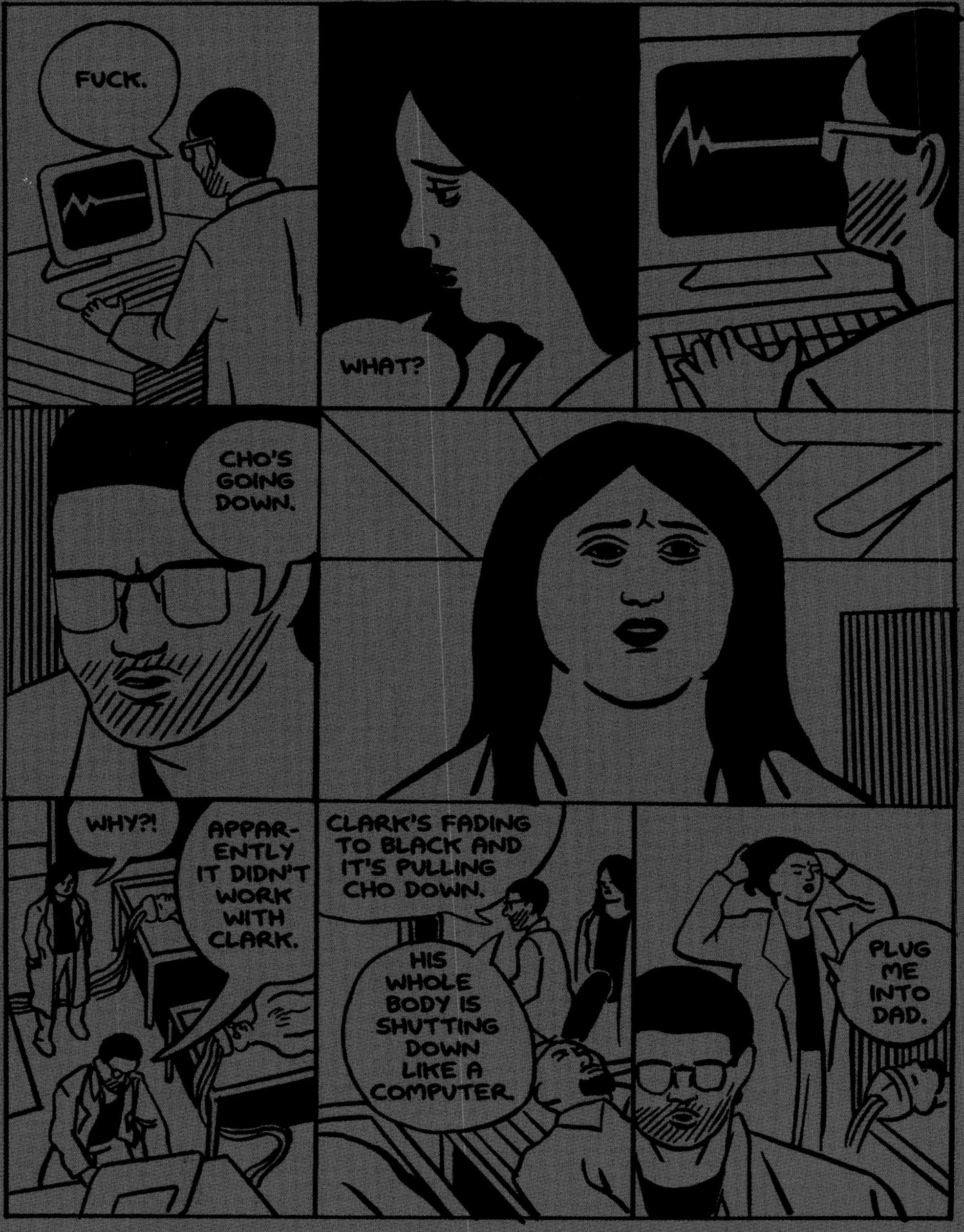
FUCK.
WHAT?
CHO'S GOING DOWN.
WHY?!
APPAR-ENTLY IT DIDN'T WORK WITH CLARK.
CLARK'S FADING TO BLACK AND IT'S PULLING CHO DOWN.
HIS WHOLE BODY IS SHUTTING DOWN LIKE A COMPUTER.
PLUG ME INTO DAD.

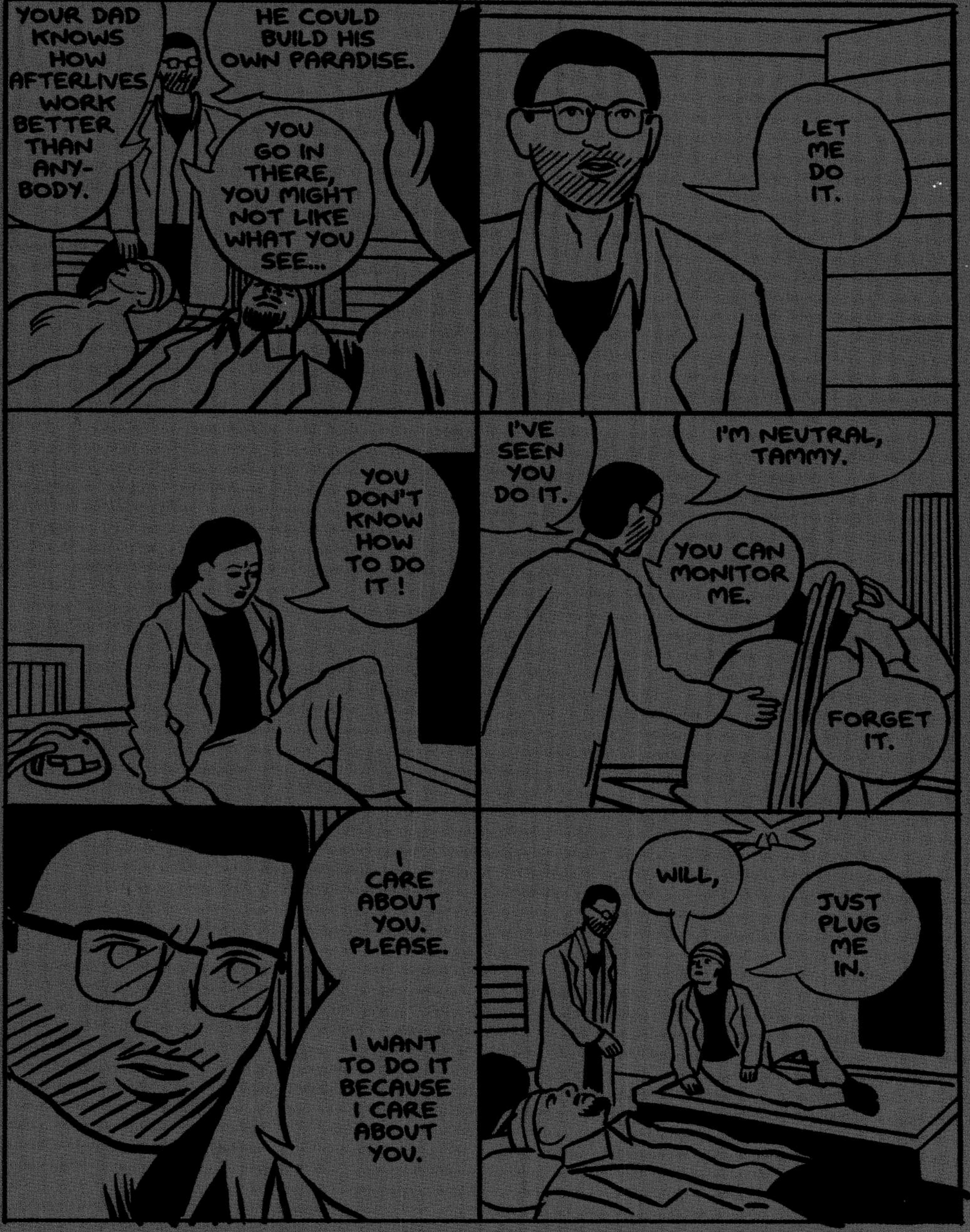
YOUR DAD KNOWS HOW AFTERLIVES WORK BETTER THAN ANY-BODY.
HE COULD BUILD HIS OWN PARADISE.
YOU GO IN THERE, YOU MIGHT NOT LIKE WHAT YOU SEE...
LET ME DO IT.
YOU DON'T KNOW HOW TO DO IT!
I'VE SEEN YOU DO IT.
I'M NEUTRAL, TAMMY.
YOU CAN MONITOR ME.
FORGET IT.
I CARE ABOUT YOU. PLEASE.
I WANT TO DO IT BECAUSE I CARE ABOUT YOU.
WILL,
JUST PLUG ME IN.

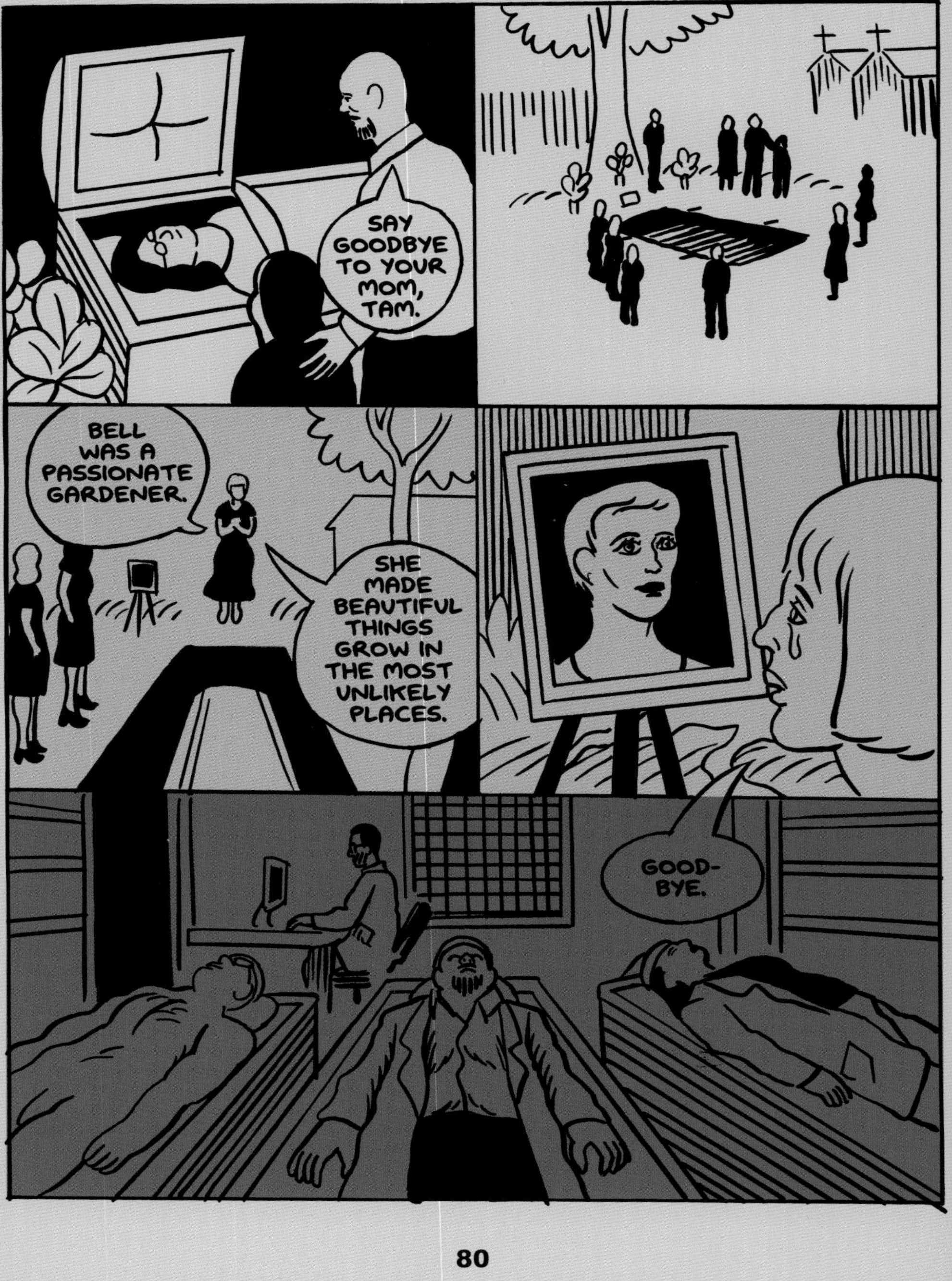
SAY GOODBYE TO YOUR MOM, TAM.
BELL WAS A PASSIONATE GARDENER.
SHE MADE BEAUTIFUL THINGS GROW IN THE MOST UNLIKELY PLACES.
GOOD-BYE.

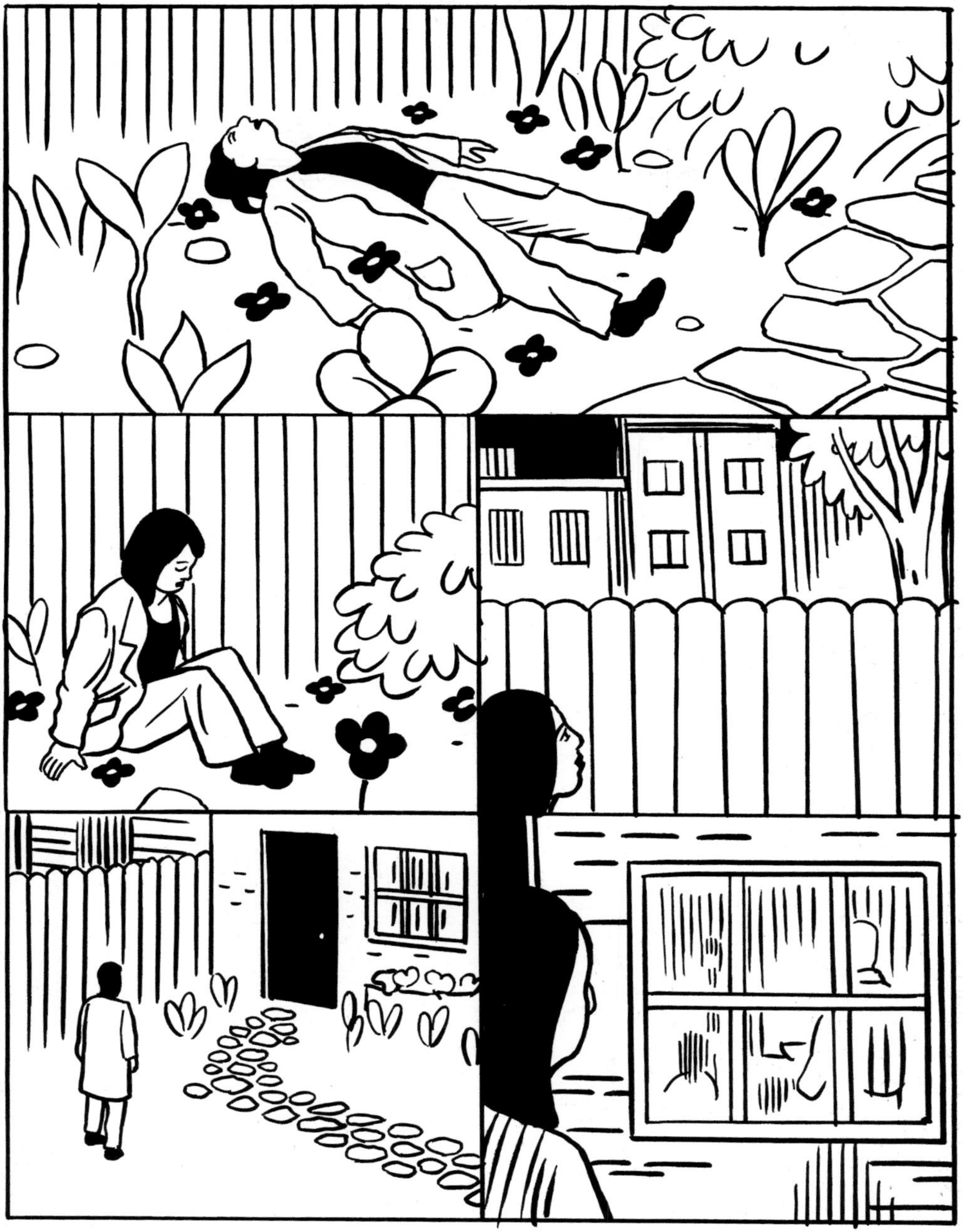

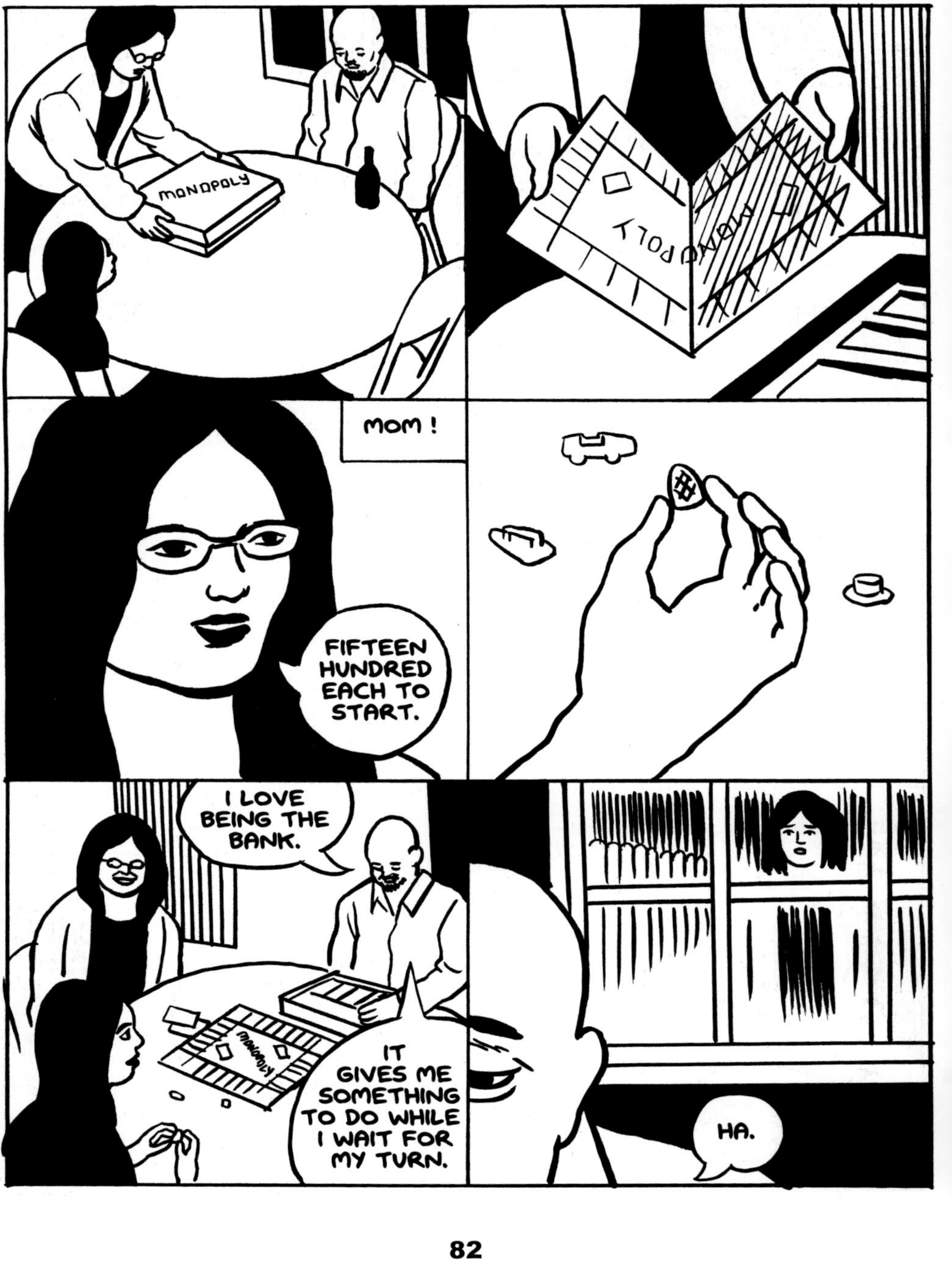
MONOPOLY
MONOPOLY
MOM!
FIFTEEN HUNDRED EACH TO START.
I LOVE BEING THE BANK.
MONOPOLY
IT GIVES ME SOMETHING TO DO WHILE I WAIT FOR MY TURN.
HA.

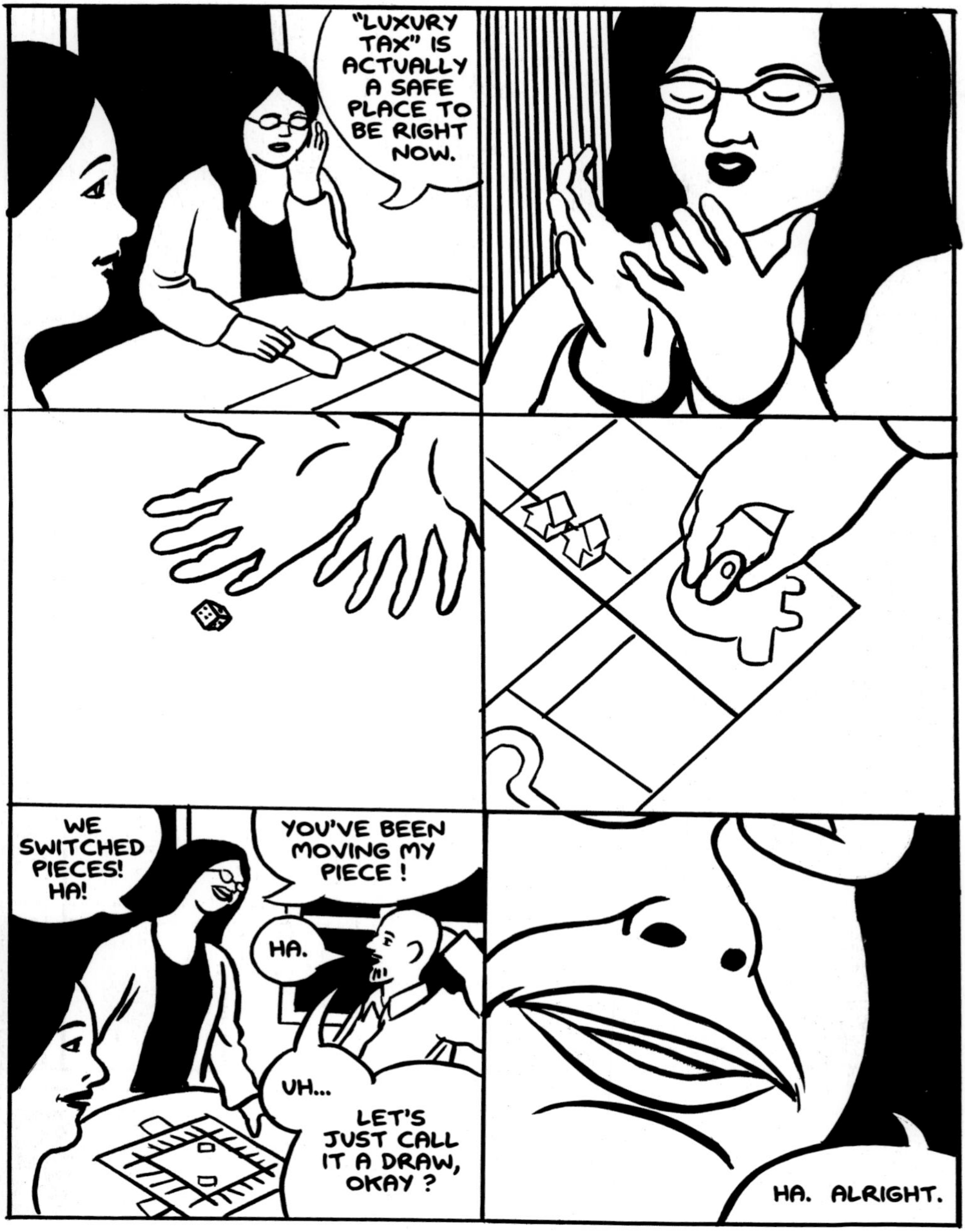
"LUXURY TAX" IS ACTUALLY A SAFE PLACE TO BE RIGHT NOW.
WE SWITCHED PIECES! HA!
YOU'VE BEEN MOVING MY PIECE!
HA.
UH...
LET'S JUST CALL IT A DRAW, OKAY?
HA. ALRIGHT.

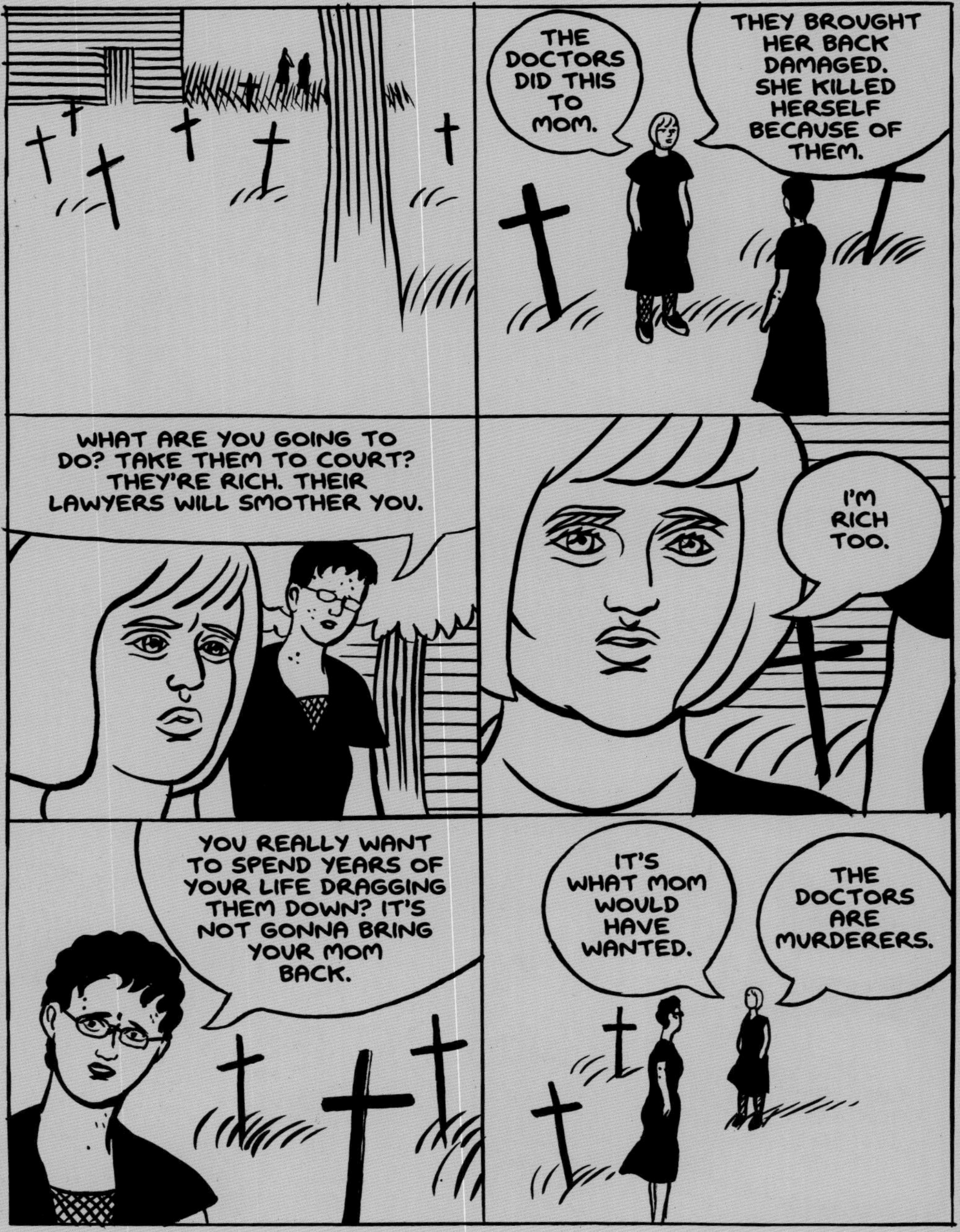
THE DOCTORS DID THIS TO MOM.
THEY BROUGHT HER BACK DAMAGED. SHE KILLED HERSELF BECAUSE OF THEM.
WHAT ARE YOU GOING TO DO? TAKE THEM TO COURT? THEY'RE RICH. THEIR LAWYERS WILL SMOTHER YOU.
I'M RICH TOO.
YOU REALLY WANT TO SPEND YEARS OF YOUR LIFE DRAGGING THEM DOWN? IT'S NOT GONNA BRING YOUR MOM BACK.
IT'S WHAT MOM WOULD HAVE WANTED.
THE DOCTORS ARE MURDERERS.

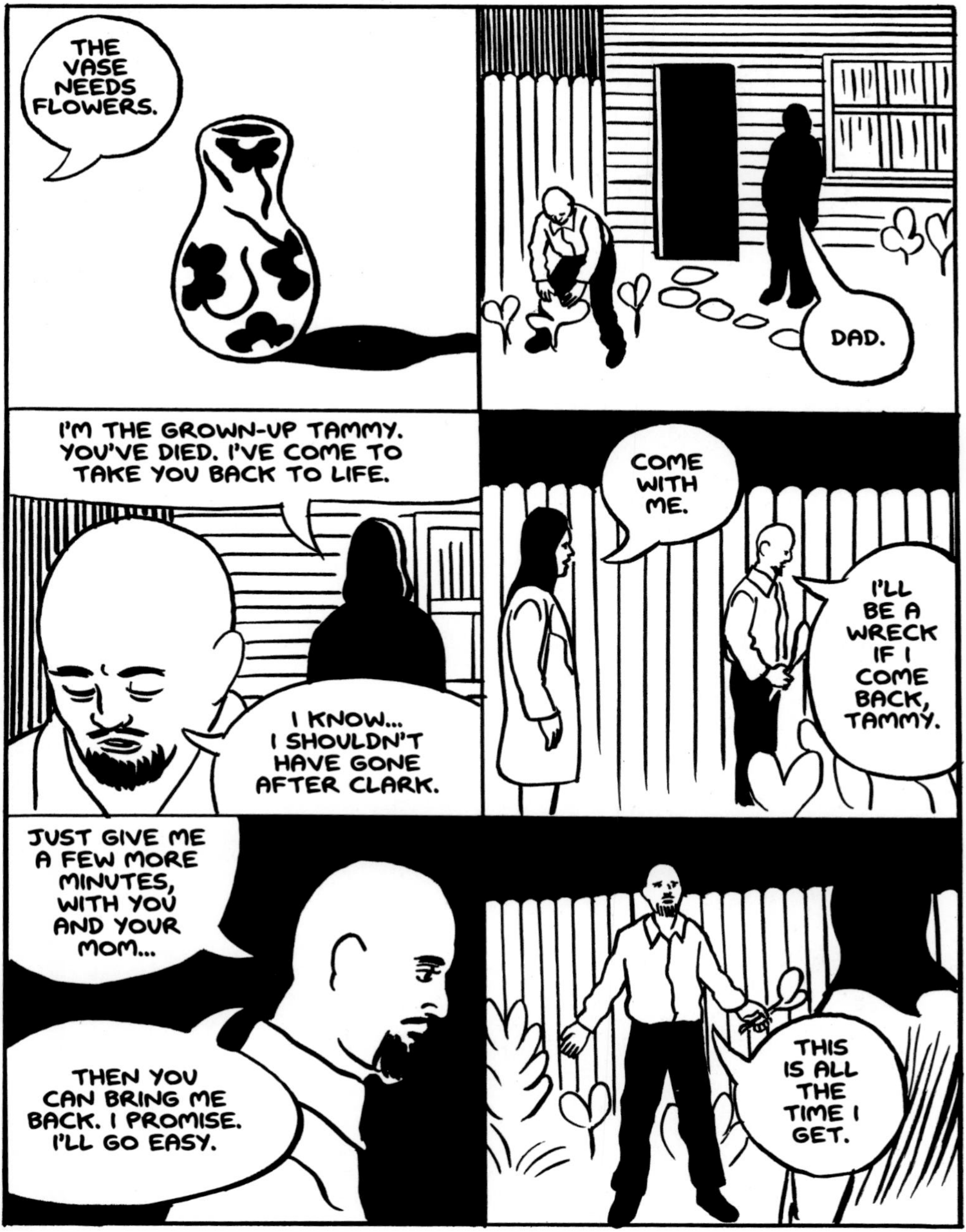
THE VASE NEEDS FLOWERS.
DAD.
I'M THE GROWN-UP TAMMY. YOU'VE DIED. I'VE COME TO TAKE YOU BACK TO LIFE.
I KNOW... I SHOULDN'T HAVE GONE AFTER CLARK.
COME WITH ME.
I'LL BE A WRECK IF I COME BACK, TAMMY.
JUST GIVE ME A FEW MORE MINUTES, WITH YOU AND YOUR MOM...
THEN YOU CAN BRING ME BACK. I PROMISE. I'LL GO EASY.
THIS IS ALL THE TIME I GET.

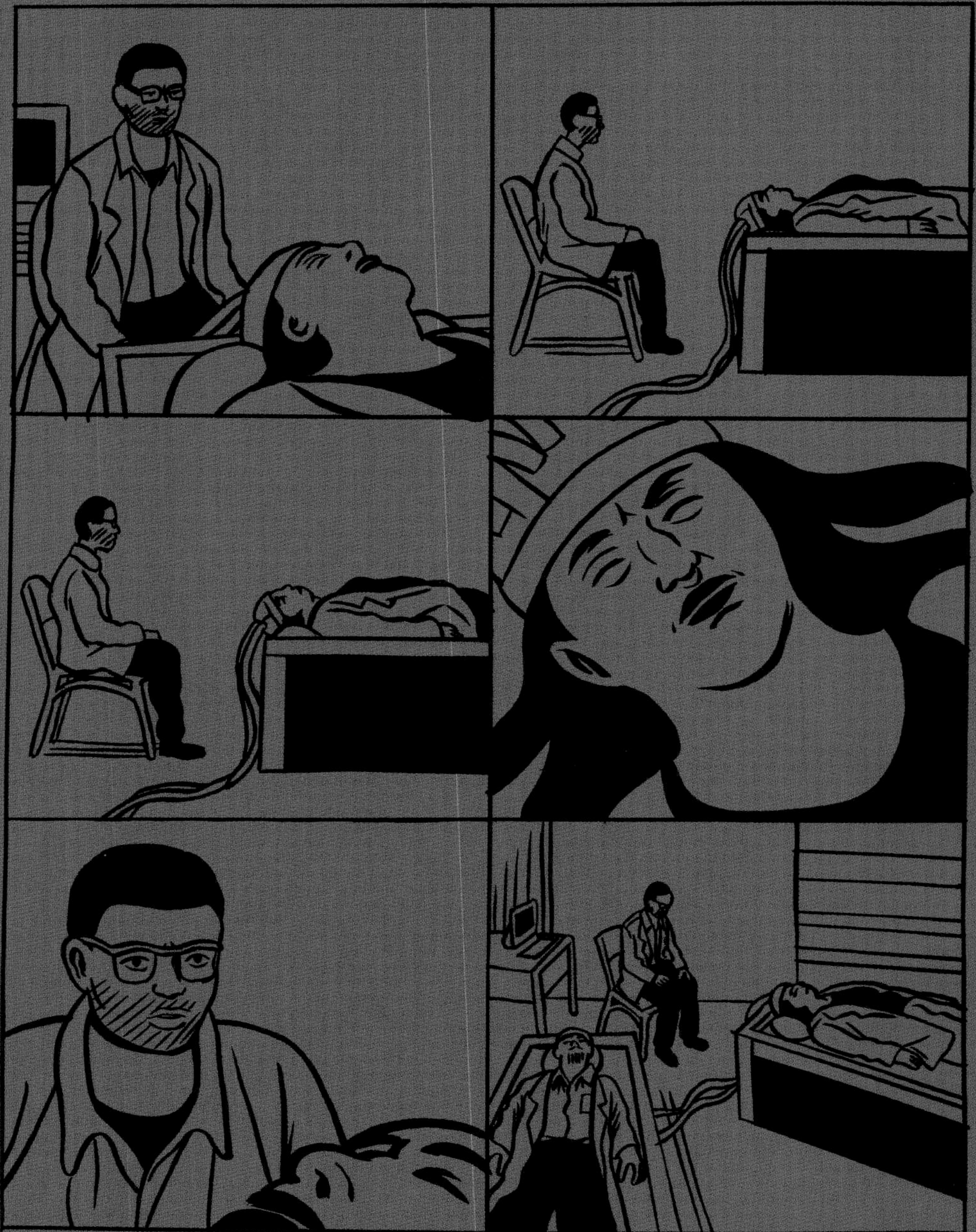

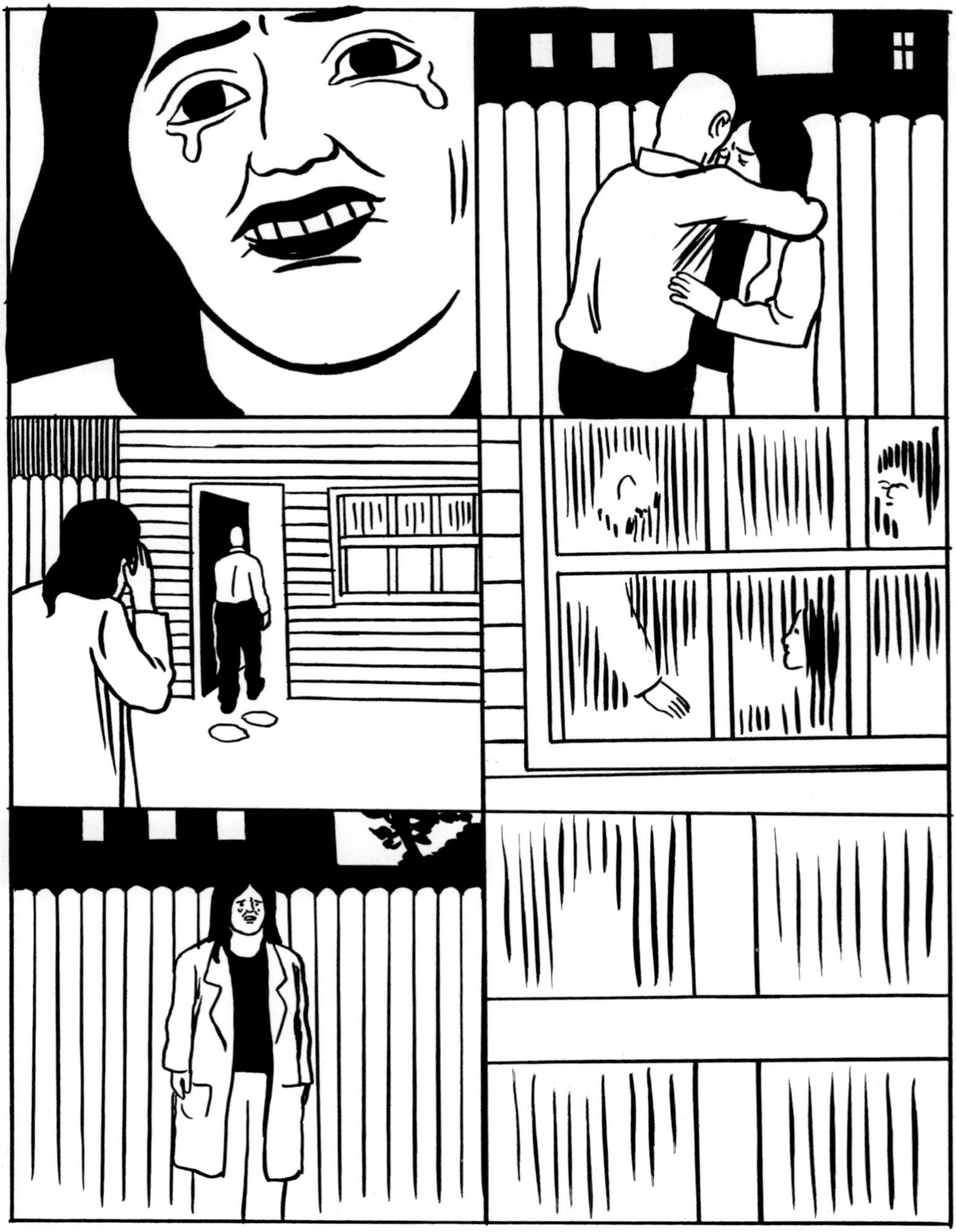

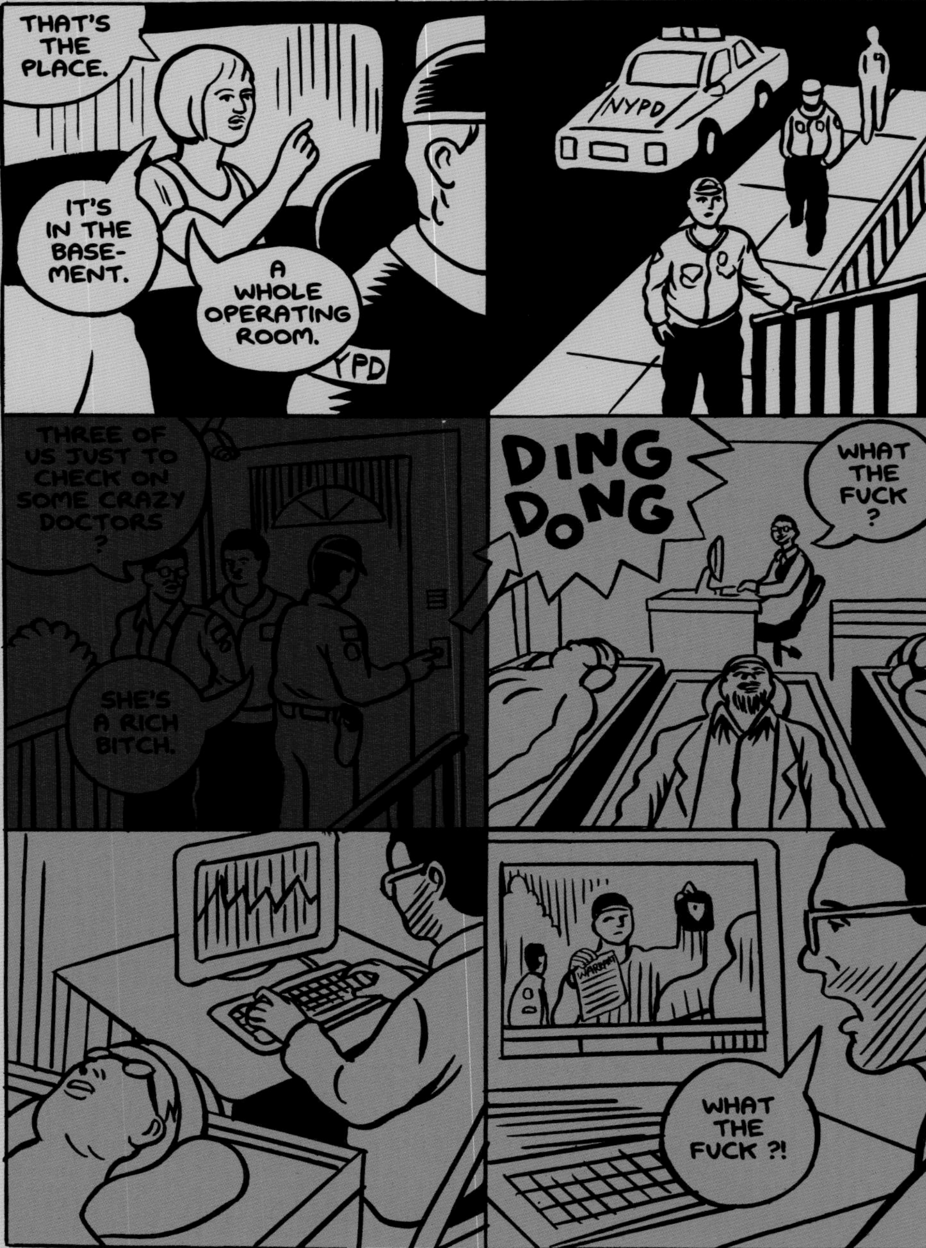
THAT'S THE PLACE.
IT'S IN THE BASE-MENT.
A WHOLE OPERATING ROOM.
YPD
NYPD
THREE OF US JUST TO CHECK ON SOME CRAZY DOCTORS ?
SHE'S A RICH BITCH.
DING DONG
WHAT THE FUCK ?
WARRANT
WHAT THE FUCK ?!

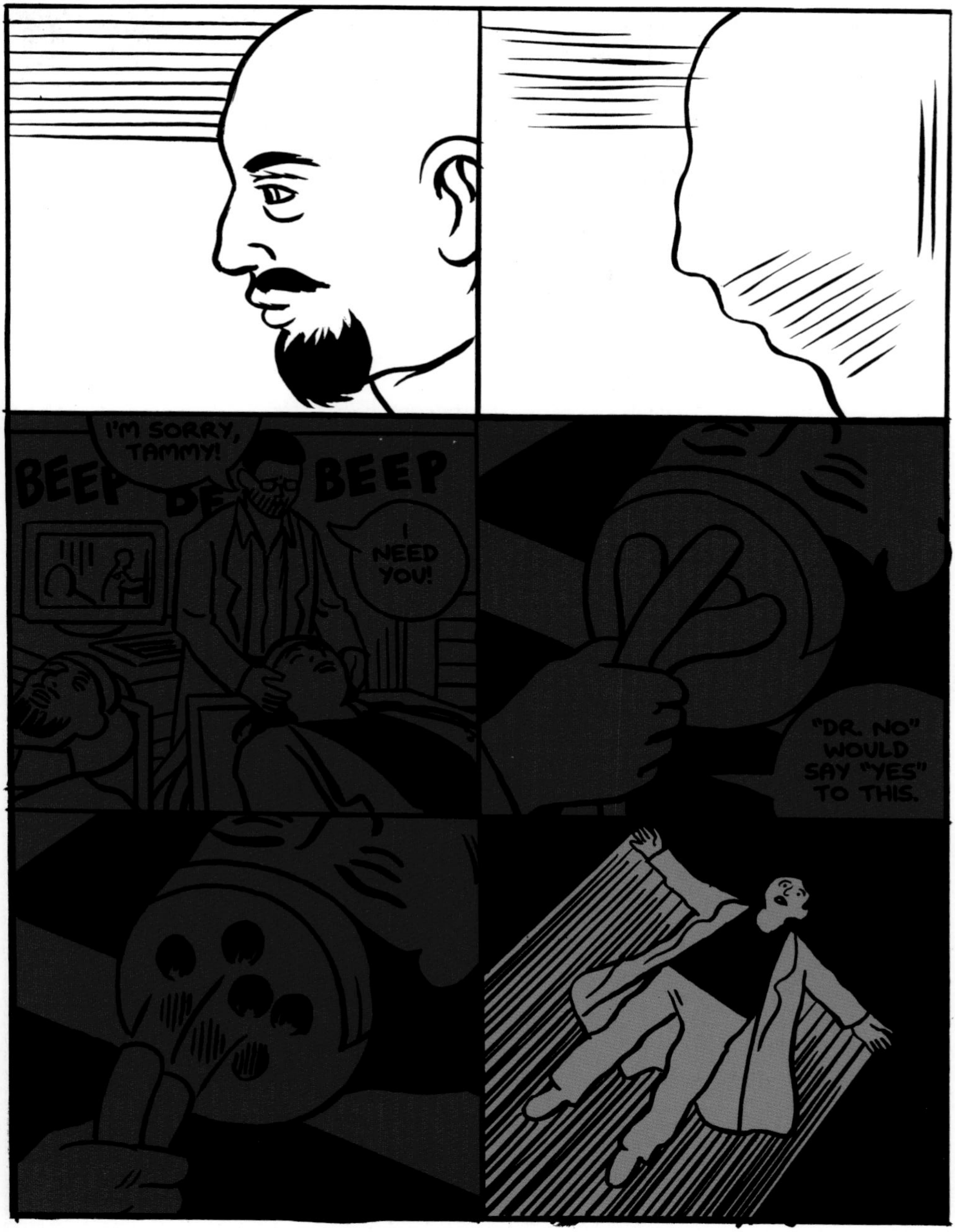
I'M SORRY, TAMMY!
BEEP
BEEP
I NEED YOU!
"DR. NO" WOULD SAY "YES" TO THIS.

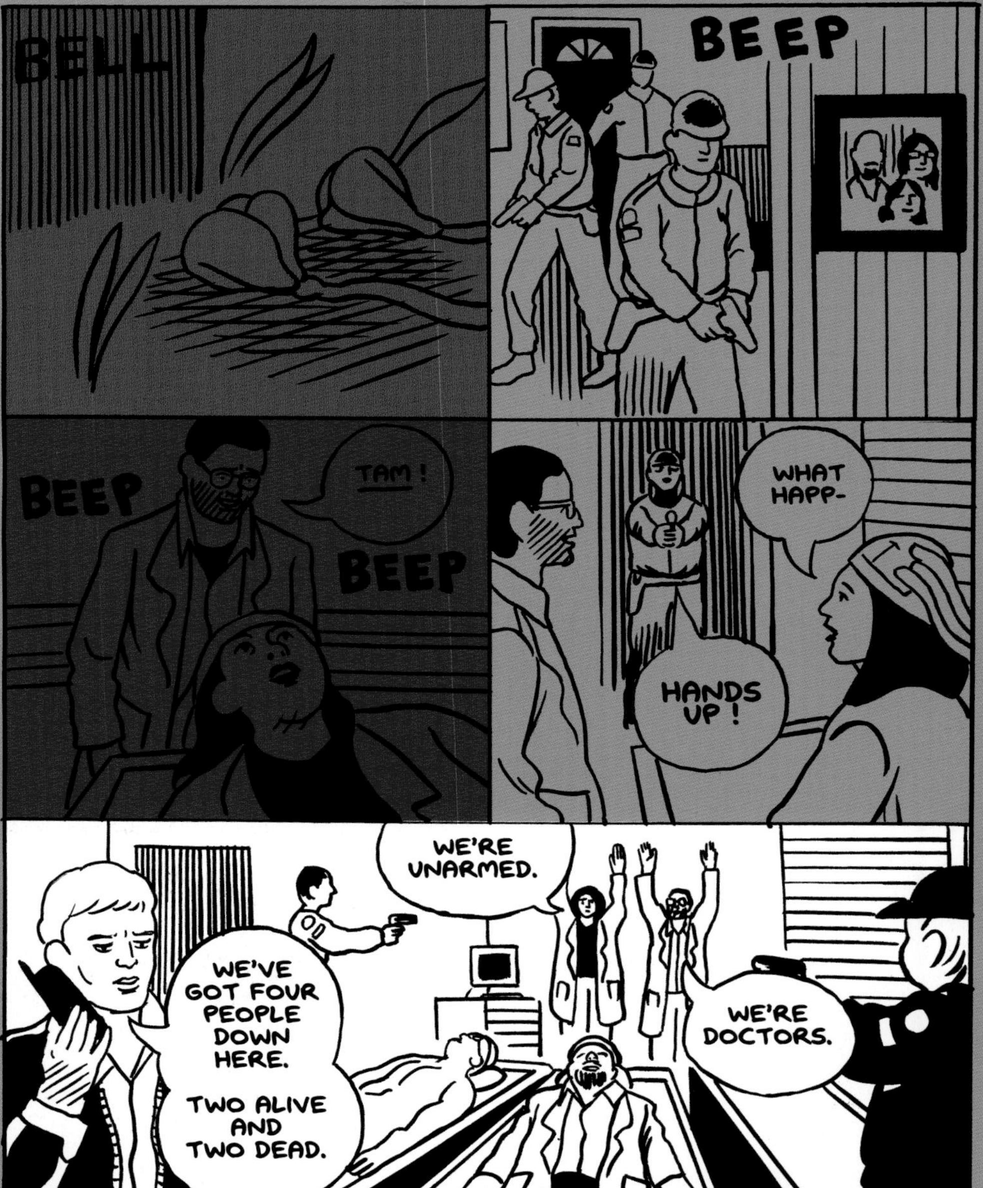
BELL
BEEP
BEEP
TAM!
BEEP
WHAT HAPP-
HANDS UP!
WE'RE UNARMED.
WE'VE GOT FOUR PEOPLE DOWN HERE.
TWO ALIVE AND TWO DEAD.
WE'RE DOCTORS.

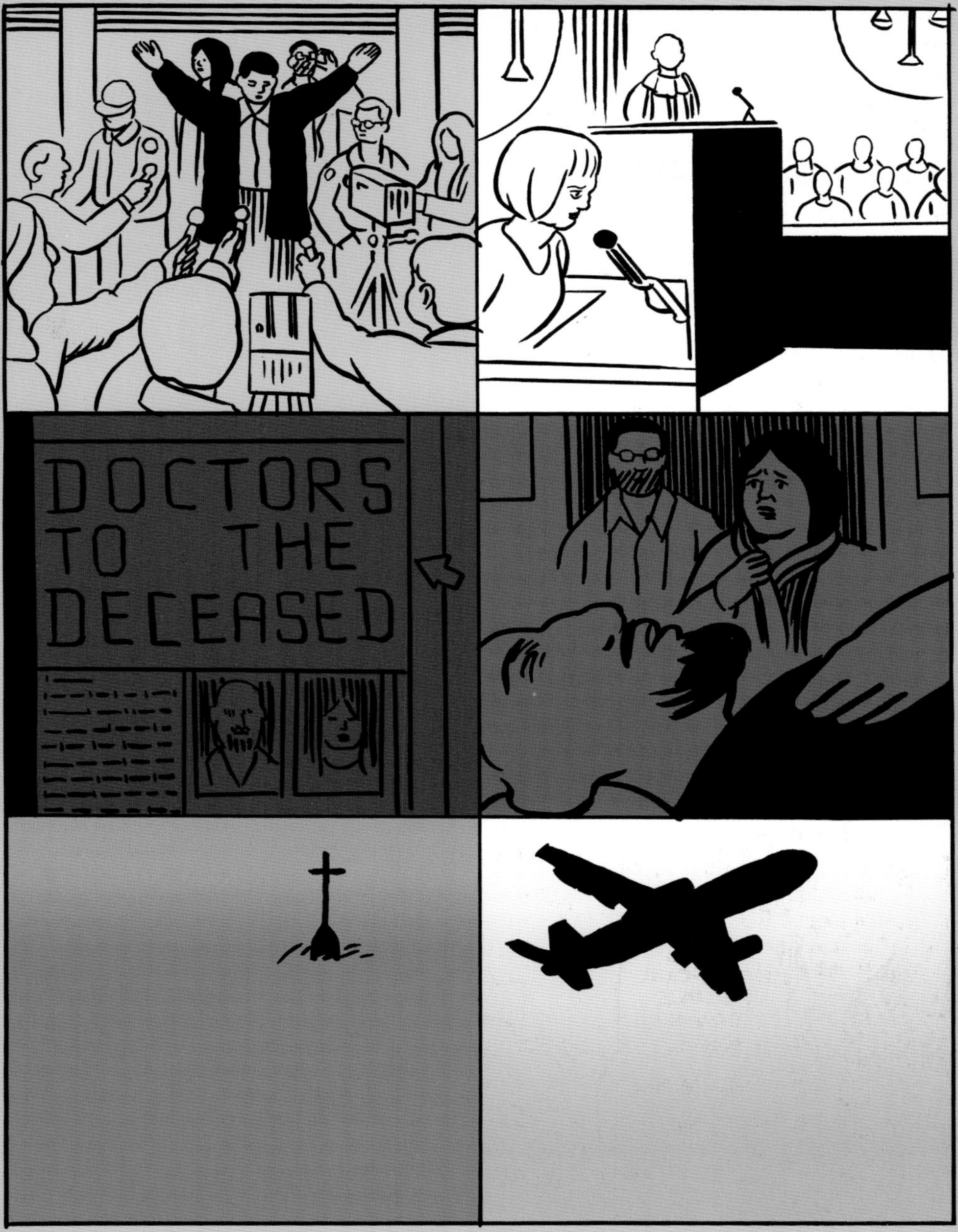
DOCTORS
TO THE
DECEASED

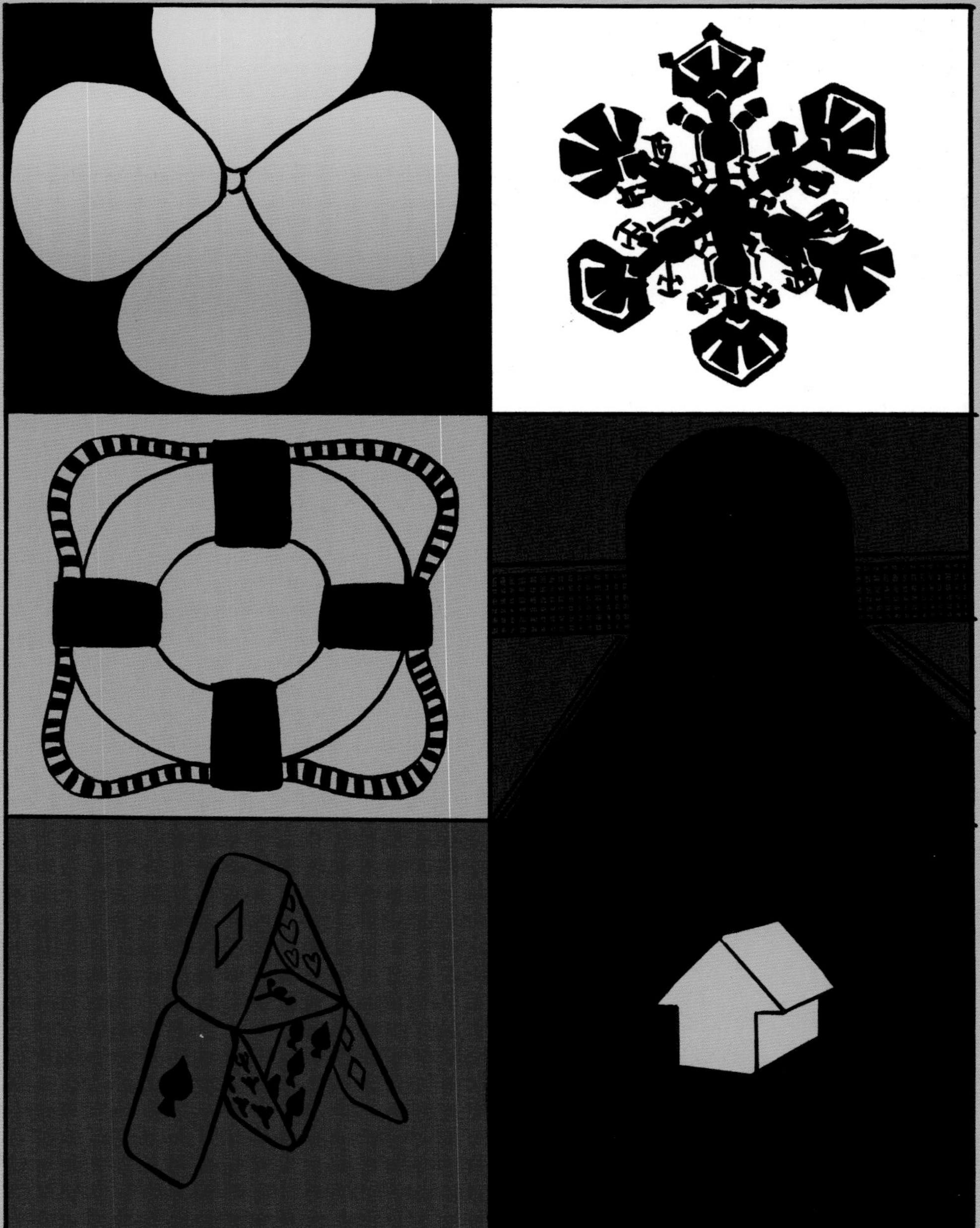

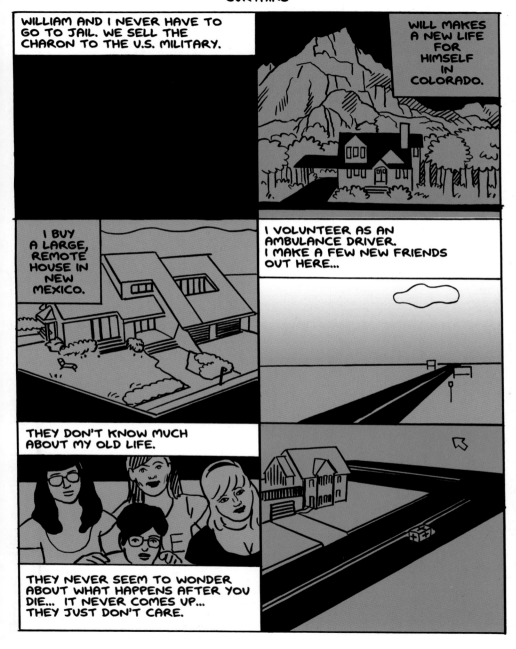

WILLIAM AND I NEVER HAVE TO GO TO JAIL. WE SELL THE CHARON TO THE U.S. MILITARY.

WILL MAKES A NEW LIFE FOR HIMSELF IN COLORADO.

I BUY A LARGE, REMOTE HOUSE IN NEW MEXICO.

I VOLUNTEER AS AN AMBULANCE DRIVER. I MAKE A FEW NEW FRIENDS OUT HERE...

THEY DON'T KNOW MUCH ABOUT MY OLD LIFE.

THEY NEVER SEEM TO WONDER ABOUT WHAT HAPPENS AFTER YOU DIE... IT NEVER COMES UP... THEY JUST DON'T CARE.

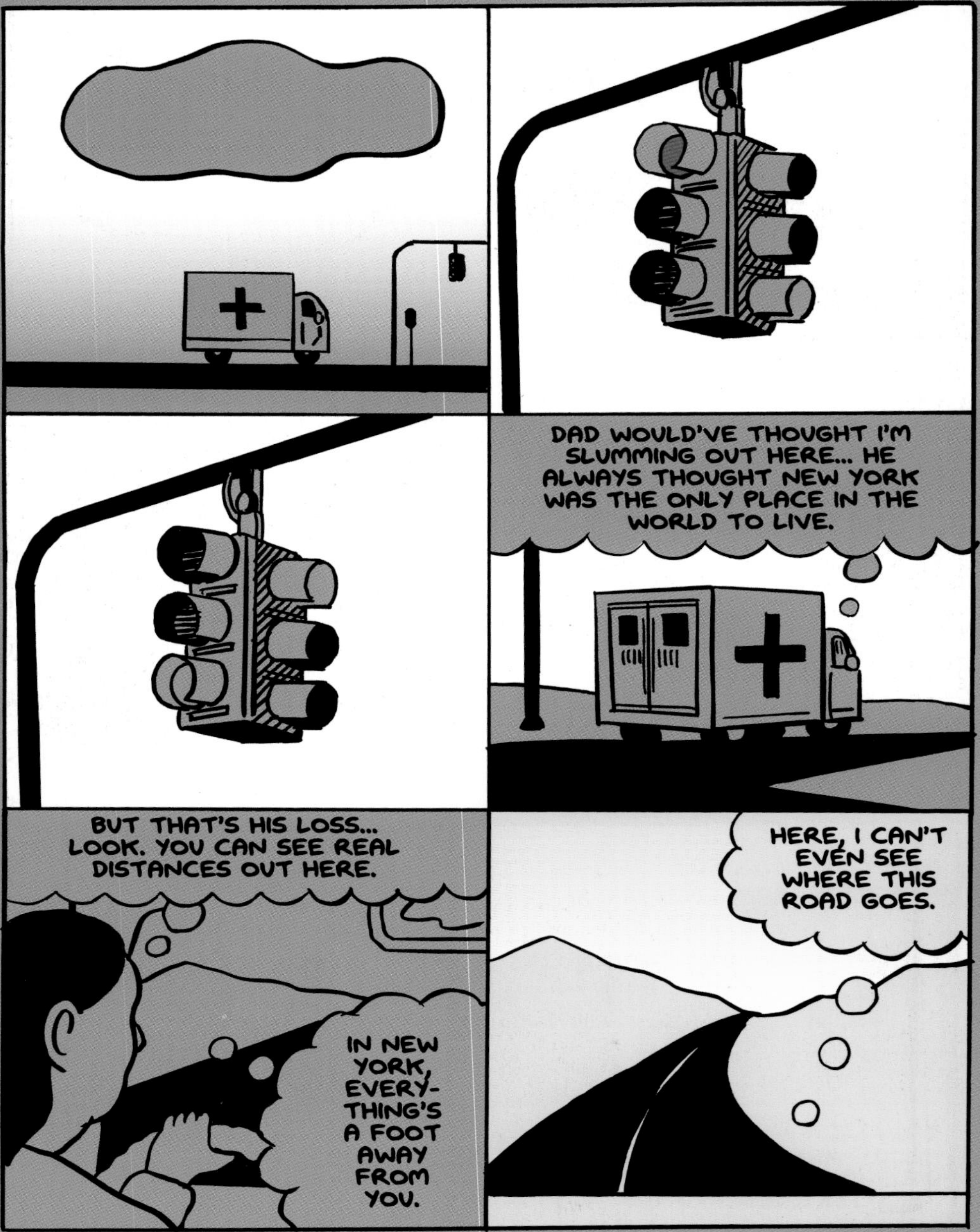
DAD WOULD'VE THOUGHT I'M SLUMMING OUT HERE... HE ALWAYS THOUGHT NEW YORK WAS THE ONLY PLACE IN THE WORLD TO LIVE.
BUT THAT'S HIS LOSS... LOOK. YOU CAN SEE REAL DISTANCES OUT HERE.
IN NEW YORK, EVERY-THING'S A FOOT AWAY FROM YOU.
HERE, I CAN'T EVEN SEE WHERE THIS ROAD GOES.

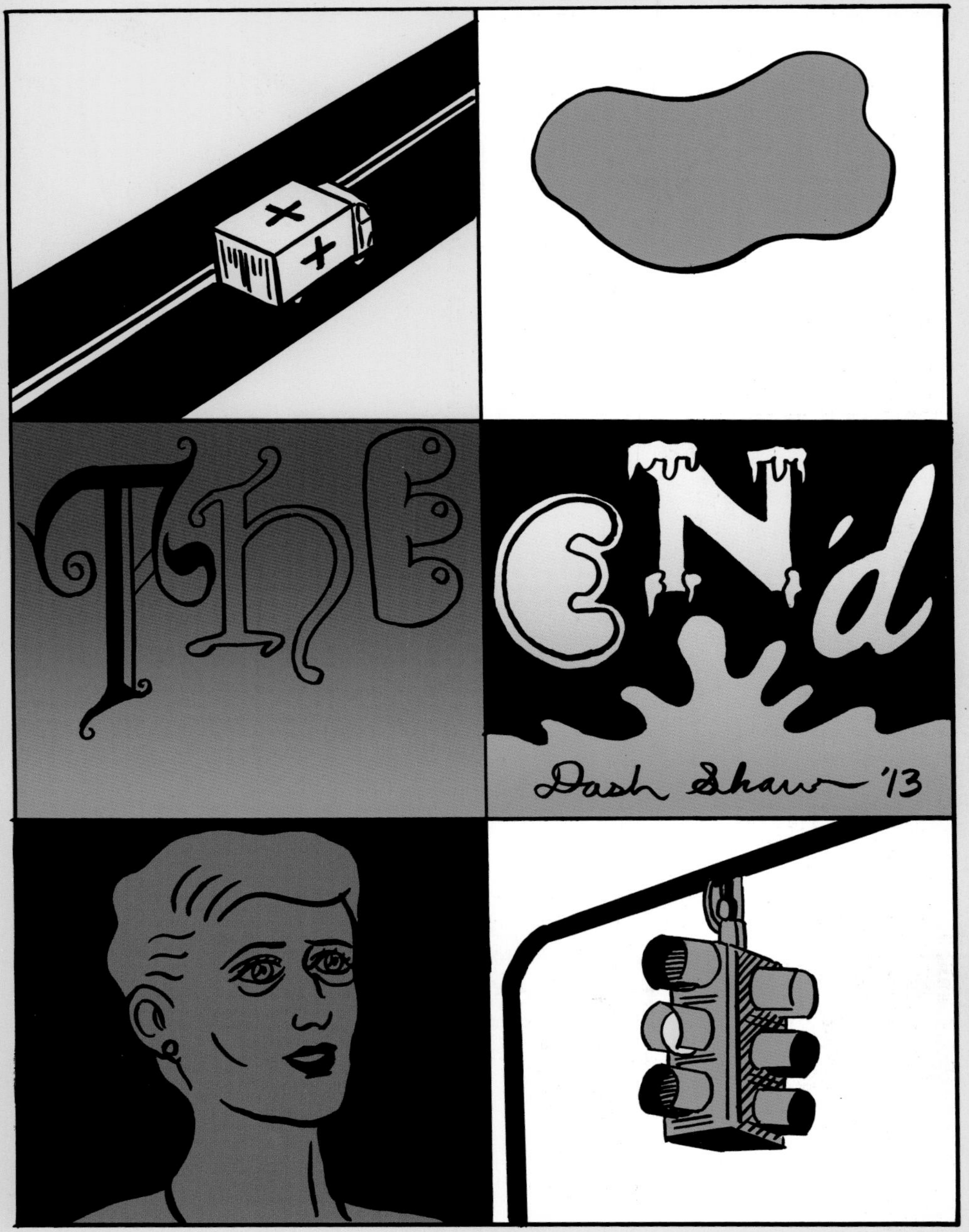
THE END
Dash Shaw '13

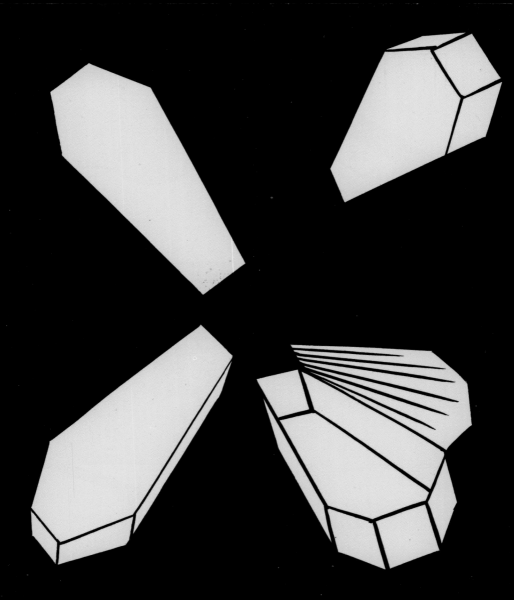

Thanks for reading.

Also by Dash Shaw:
Cosplayers, New School, 3 New Stories,
New Jobs, BodyWorld, The Unclothed Man
in the 35th Century AD, Bottomless Belly Button

dashshaw.tumblr.com